Praise for
Building High-Performance Local Governments

"The HPO Model has helped the City of Brooklyn Park evolve the nature of our work and how we serve our co-workers, community members, and council. The expectation by residents that local government initiate more authentic community engagement and continuously improve service delivery means that we have to internally change how we do business to be more collaborative, innovative, and mission driven."

—*Jamie Verbrugge, City Manager, Brooklyn Park, MN*

"Voters will consistently support high-functioning government with additional investment. Low-performing government initiates a downward spiral with voters refusing to raise taxes to pay for bad service. This methodology can bring your organization into the 21st Century by creating an engaged workforce that does the right work efficiently at the right time."

—*John Marchione, Mayor, Redmond, WA*

"This is a practical book that shows how true, excellent action can be achieved in the local public sector. It is based on the broad, deep engagement of workers and community that authentically energizes people at all levels to think, innovate, and measure success."

—*Jim Oliver, former City Manager*

"The HPO Model concepts outlined in this book have been embraced in our organization. Since putting these concepts into practice, we have seen improvements in our operations as well as our community and organization survey results."

—*Brad Miyake, City Manager, Bellevue, WA*

"Implementing the HPO Model as outlined in this book has put Johnson County Government on the path to creating a REAL culture of constant improvement. These strategies provide liberating and positive culture change outcomes to help make our community become better and smarter. It has been the best organizational change model I have seen in my thirty years in City/County Management and this book captures, in text and case studies, practical ways for its implementation."

—*Hannes Zacharias, County Manager, Johnson County, KS*

"Since we put together the HPO Model thirty years ago, it has been enhanced by what has been learned from the leaders who have employed it at every organizational level in the public sector. And yet, three critical things remain essential. There must be an inspired, enlivened, and productive workforce. They have to understand the work of leadership and be engaged to undertake it. And they must organize themselves and their colleagues to accomplish it together. The case studies in this book demonstrate how these come together to achieve high-performance."

—*Robert Matson, former Director, Federal Executive Institute;*
former Director, Senior Executive Institute and LEAD programs,
University of Virginia

BUILDING HIGH-PERFORMANCE LOCAL GOVERNMENTS
CASE STUDIES IN LEADERSHIP AT ALL LEVELS

JOHN PICKERING · GERALD BROKAW · PHILIP HARNDEN · ANTON GARDNER

WITH

KAY HUDSON · A. TYLER ST.CLAIR · THOMAS WARD

RIVER GROVE
BOOKS

Published by River Grove Books
Austin, TX
www.rivergrovebooks.com

Distributed by River Grove Books

For ordering information or special discounts for bulk purchases, please contact River Grove Books at PO Box 91869, Austin, TX 78709, 512.891.6100.

Design and composition by Greenleaf Book Group
Cover design by Greenleaf Book Group and Anton Khodakovsky

Publisher's Cataloging-In-Publication Data
Pickering, John W.
   Building high-performance local governments : case studies in leadership at all levels / John Pickering [and 3 others].—First edition.

   pages : illustrations ; cm

   Issued also as an ebook.
   Includes bibliographical references and index.

   1. Local government—United States—Case studies. 2. Leadership—United States—Case studies. 3. Government productivity—United States—Case studies. 4. Local government—United States—Personnel management—Case studies. I. Title. II. Title: Building high performance local governments

JS331 .P53 2014
352.140973   2014940109

Print ISBN: 978-1-938416-99-6
eBook ISBN: 978-1-63299-000-6

First Edition

CONTENTS

INTRODUCTION

Our nation is emerging from the most devastating recession most of us have ever encountered. Faced with dramatic revenue reductions, staggering levels of unemployment, foreclosures, and outcries for service reductions, local governments have responded out of necessity. They have looked afresh at what they do and how they do it, stopped providing many things that are either no longer needed or are of marginal importance, developed new ways of delivering the services that remain priorities, and changed processes to become more efficient. Quoted in the *Wall Street Journal*,[1] then New York City Mayor Michael Bloomberg put a positive spin on what many have learned:

> *". . . the silver lining in any economic crisis is that it can force government to take necessary steps that, in more comfortable times, would fall victim to inertia."*

Oregon Governor John Kitzhaber said:

> *"The way we responded to recessions in the past was to do less of the same, with the hope of having more money later so we could do more of the same. There's a once-in-a-generation opportunity to do some things we should have done a long time ago but couldn't make the politics work."*[2]

Rampant change is still occurring. School systems are closing underutilized schools. Local governments have revamped snow removal operations. Daytime support programs for the frail elderly are being replaced with non-profit, higher-capacity services providing comparable care levels. Permitting, inspections, and regulatory systems are being streamlined for more accessible and faster customer service.

It is common to hear people refer to this Great Recession as a "game changer," and many in local government have suggested that if only things would settle down, "we'd be all right." For those with this view, the changes and improvements made possible by forced belt tightening have set them on the right path—forever vigilant to avoid the excesses of the past. There seems to be a new resolve not to return to program expansion, bureaucratic layering, and staff buildups, and to keep systems and processes streamlined and efficient.

Sadly, those harboring such beliefs are often just kidding themselves. Remember that annual New Year's resolution about losing weight? After eating our way through the holidays, we join a fitness club or buy an elliptical machine and actually lose some weight in a crash diet. We are convinced that, this time, we'll be dedicated to working hard to keep that weight off for the long term. When you think about it, this is a very optimistic sentiment: We have learned our lesson, will remember it, and will remain ever-vigilant against the inertia that in previous times crept into our organizational lives. This book explains how our collective past has demonstrated over and over again that most of us don't learn such lessons. Rather, we gradually accommodate to new conditions, become complacent, and quit examining carefully what we do and how we do it. So while the games may change some, how our organizations are set up to operate, the values on which they are based, and the levels of engagement of people throughout them tend to remain the same.

Does all of this sound familiar? In the past, local governments have faced similar challenges and other crises—perhaps not quite so deep as this one, but hauntingly familiar still. Each time, they emerged with a new resolve to avoid becoming complacent again. And each time, of course, some version of it did grow back. Why did our systems again grow unwieldy, our schools become half-empty, our snow removal systems remain static, our money-losing underutilized programs continue to operate, and our bureaucratic regulatory systems remain on separate, unfriendly turfs? Let's look at this cycle.

This pattern has local governments rising to the occasion in crisis and reverting to complacency when the crisis retreats. There's no getting around it: We do crises very well. We handle emergencies, we fill the gaps, and we make the tough decisions when we have to. Some of us even thrive on chaos! These extraordinarily hard recessionary years have challenged localities to confront some bedrock decisions impacting every facet of service delivery: portfolio composition, benefit systems costs, more efficient organizations, and so on. Some solutions, though, have been short-term emergency responses. Vacancies were held, less pressing duties were left to build up a backlog, work was added to some employees who pitched in during the crisis, dead wood was removed, early retirement reduced current costs by replacing current staff with lower-wage new hires, etc.

As we go through a crisis, energy is high, we are challenged, and our senses are sharpened. The public eye is on us, resources remain tight, and the political demand for responsiveness is huge. The workforce often exerts higher levels of discretionary effort in such times because the seriousness of the emergency calls for them to contribute for a range of reasons, from attaining a higher moral purpose to saving their jobs in the midst of financial crisis. Once the emergency subsides, however, the tendency is to settle back into old ways. As things stabilize, we gradually tend to relax, our current state becomes the new normal, embedded in how we operate, and we become less attentive to the things we focused on during the crisis. Levels of discretionary effort tend to return to the way they were before the crisis.

So what can make *this* time different from all the failed resolutions of the past? What will really keep us from becoming complacent again? First, recognizing that retaining the success achieved during this Great Recession requires disciplined attention to strategic thinking throughout the organization and then committing to follow through with it. It requires a continuous, clear, and widespread understanding of where our organization is going and why, and how we build well-defined systems and structures that keep everyone on track effectively and efficiently. This can only flourish in a work culture that is developed to engage the discretionary effort of the talented people throughout the organization. **Discretionary effort** refers to the amount of effort a person chooses to put into any work or challenge. One can give a lot of energy and apply all her talents, skills, and abilities, or she can hold back some or a lot of it. In most cases, it is up to the individual to decide the amount of effort to contribute. The level of commitment to assure that these things occur is hard to maintain—just like going back to the gym the next week or regularly jumping on the new elliptical machine. Yet this commitment is required for an organization to avoid the inertia that overtakes many. These are the ideas that this book is based on. Here is a breakdown of what will be discussed in the following five chapters:

CHAPTER 1: THE NEED FOR LEADERSHIP AT ALL LEVELS

There *are* some very successful organizations that anticipated the recession, weathered it reasonably well, made judicious choices about their range of products and services, and focused on additional ways to reinvent or redesign their processes. They recognize that to be truly high performing, an organization must take a systematic approach to the work of leadership. They also understand that older definitions of leadership leave an organization reliant on a few people at the top to do all the heavy lifting. Successful organizations, however, redefine leadership as an organizational—rather than an individual or positional—set of responsibilities that must be undertaken throughout the organization. Thus the concept of **leadership at all levels** emerges, in which all individuals are leaders as they accomplish their leadership responsibilities, no matter their technical functions or level in the organization. Leadership work must be done widely for the local government to meet its purpose over the long term. We'll examine a different way of operating, called the **Networked Talent Model**, which challenges many of our inherited assumptions by arguing for leadership at all levels of the organization.

As we will see in Chapter 1, many local government organizations use traditional hierarchical structures that assign most non-technical decision-making authority to the managerial ranks. The more important the decision is, the higher the level that decides it. Furthermore, the values and cultures of these organizations reinforce the notion that "leadership and management" are primarily the responsibility of managers. The primary role of line workers is to follow what they are directed to do, leaving them generally disengaged from the organization outside their own technical work. Managers become inundated with operational and policy decisions, technical matters, and solving pressing near-term production problems that leave little time to attend to the longer-term aspects of leadership and learning. (Do you know *any* manager who complains about not being busy enough?) Thus, they rely on what they already know, fail to examine the relationship between what the organization does and what the citizen/customer wants, and continue to do more or less what they have always done. Managers become the bottleneck for problem solving, decision making, and innovation. Front-line workers can become disengaged and legitimately say, "It's not my job."

Employee engagement has been measured by several organizations with surprising but consistent results.[3] The majority of workers in the United States, as well as around the world, tend not to be engaged in their workplace. They come in, do what they are told to do, and then go home. They are not passionate about what they do, do not "own" their responsibilities, and do not feel the need to manage, improve, or be accountable for their effectiveness. They certainly don't feel a sense of stewardship for the success of the organization as a whole. In many cases, this is not an issue of the individual workers' personal attitudes, but rather a problem with the assumptions, beliefs, values, and resulting business processes of the organizations themselves. If the organization does not create an expectation and ways for the workforce to be engaged, then it is hardly surprising that it will not be engaged.

While these leadership responsibilities could reasonably be shared with lower-level managers and people on the front line, the positioning of authority at higher levels doesn't allow leadership to flourish at all levels. Thus, most workers remain disengaged; they rarely seek out citizen/customer feedback or undertake reviews of how they do things. They distance themselves from managerial concerns like business processes, financial management, and integration with other units. In many localities, managers are satisfied as long as their employees do the tasks they are expected to do, as they have been laid out. The consequences of such disengagement, though, are substantial.

In one example within the Sanitation Department of New York City,[4] a new deputy commissioner discovered early in his tenure that in the fleet maintenance facility half of the vehicles were out of service and the ones that were sent out had a one in three chance of breaking down each day. He found a workforce that was miserable and disengaged. Yet, as he later learned, these employees knew many ways to improve the performance of the Sanitation Department. Their disengagement kept them from contributing their knowledge, ideas, and skills to fix the problems in the shop until the new deputy commissioner found a way to invite them in and engage them in having a stake in getting the place to run well. Only when they felt that they had an important role that was valued, their abilities were respected, and they were enlisted in solving problems did their discretionary effort increase substantially. Once this occurred, the Sanitation Department's vehicle maintenance workers transformed the organization from mediocre into an award-winning high-performing service.

This echoes the Gallup survey organization's findings that world-class organizations have a far greater number of engaged employees. Relatively consistent data over several decades show that about one in every four workers is "engaged" in his work, more than half are "not engaged," and close to one in five is "actively disengaged." Several studies point to the connection between such low levels of engagement and only average organizational performance. Further, their findings show that average-performing organizations have just below two engaged workers for each actively disengaged worker, while world-class organizations have almost ten engaged workers for every actively disengaged worker.[5] The concept of entropy teaches us that any organization that does not develop additional energy over time will wither away. Engaged workers help organizations flourish and can continue to supply their energy for higher performance if they remain well engaged in their work.

In Chapters 1 and 4, we'll explore why some organizational styles have produced disengaged employees while others are more likely to support workforce engagement, plus what organizations can do to design engagement into their DNA.

CHAPTER 2: THE HIGH-PERFORMANCE ORGANIZATION DIAGNOSTIC/CHANGE MODEL™

Local government senior managers are often so busy making key decisions, dealing with councils and boards, and running political interference that they often neglect the longer range investment in strategic thinking, research, and planning needed to shape the organization's future. They set in motion few disciplined, systemic, beyond flavor-of-the-month efforts to critically examine the programs and services they offer and the efficiency and effectiveness with which they are delivered. Such leadership work in the traditional hierarchy is seen as the sole purview of top management. In Chapter 2 we will suggest that leadership work is instead an assertive, disciplined approach exercised at all levels to address the key questions that expose the organization's current state in relation to its potential and then to utilize major change levers to improve performance.

This chapter introduces the **High-Performance Organization Diagnostic/ Change Model** (HPO Model), which is just such a disciplined approach. The HPO Model has been the core material at the University of Virginia's (UVA) Senior Executive Institute (SEI) and the U.S. Office of Personnel Management's Federal Executive Institute. It was developed to assist those who want to be part of a positive change process, continually driving their organizations toward becoming higher performing. Through its use of **key diagnostic questions (KDQs)** and **change levers (CLs)**, coupled with the establishment of **change mechanisms** throughout the organization, it provides a handy road map leading to higher performance.

The HPO Model identifies two main bodies of work necessary to improve an organization's success: moving from a common vision to successful outcomes and creating an engaging work culture based upon fundamental values and aligned behaviors. With its redefinition of what constitutes *organizational leadership* and where it must be accomplished in the organization, the model provides an ongoing antidote to falling back into old habits. It focuses attention on clearly understanding the purpose, vision, and outcomes that the locality seeks, identifying the strategies that will achieve them, implementing them effectively and efficiently, and measuring the results. It makes sense of the variety of tools that organizations use (like Lean and Six Sigma quality improvement programs) and highlights the need for integration of these approaches through a set of fundamental principles. The HPO Model provides a framework to make these tools more effective.

One key leadership function included in this model is the development of a work culture that unleashes the discretionary effort of an engaged workforce. Organizations often begin improvement efforts by layering new tools and processes on top of control-oriented, centralized, overly hierarchical, autocratic management systems. Most improvement tools and concepts, however, are based upon mind-sets and philosophical underpinnings of employee engagement that differ dramatically from such autocratic management systems. When these tools and concepts are deployed without first redefining the values of the work culture, organizations—at best—achieve no long-term gain and may even find they have significantly increased the cynicism and hostility of their workforces. The HPO Model encourages that the work of performance improvement coincides with an examination and appropriate redefinition of the fundamental assumptions and values that guide managerial and business process behavior. This way, the techniques, tools, and processes have significantly greater potential to improve performance.

CHAPTER 3: FROM VISION TO PERFORMANCE

This chapter follows with a series of explanations and case studies of the work required to move from a vision of what an organization *wants* to accomplish to the actual achievement of that outcome. It identifies the continuous strategic thinking necessary to connect such a vision to the strategy, structures, and systems of the organization. Asking key diagnostic questions helps focus leadership teams at all levels on the motivating purpose of the organization, its major outcomes, its key products and services, and how well it delivers them. These leadership teams then evaluate how well the strategy, structure, and systems currently support their efforts. Engagement of citizens/customers/stakeholders in this process ensures that what emerges is relevant and reflects an appropriate level of satisfaction.

From visioning and strategic thinking emerges a deliberate multiyear plan with substantive goals and performance measures that sets the organization's direction and identifies any gaps in its capacity to achieve them. These, in turn, lead to tactics and resource allocations to implement the plan, with appropriate monitoring and correction.

CHAPTER 4: ENGAGEMENT THROUGH VALUES TO WORK CULTURE

So which comes first: an engaged workforce or engaging the workforce? Can employees suddenly become engaged after an organization has inhibited their engagement in the past? Unlikely! Employees do not become engaged unless the culture of the organization is developed and reinforced to support it. This requires developing a shared set of organizational values that lead to a positive work culture and the creation of disciplined ways to continuously involve employees in the decisions that affect their units and business areas.

An organization's values work consists of addressing three key sets of values: leadership philosophy, individual behavioral values, and operating systems values. **Leadership philosophy** permeates the organization. It states beliefs about the nature of the people in the organization and their attitudes toward work, what makes people choose to be motivated, the distribution of knowledge and creativity (and therefore how we choose to make decisions), and how work is defined. The systems of the organization have to be connected with the leadership philosophy so that expected behaviors are clear. Implementation of the leadership philosophy requires appropriate evaluation, feedback, and coaching. **Individual behavioral values** need to be identified to guide personal actions; these have to be enhanced with examples so that the valued behaviors are relevant in real-life situations and can be measured. Similarly, **operating systems values** are necessary to guide the work processes and administrative systems of the organization to support a positive work culture. These three values sets are explored with case studies in Chapter 4.

CHAPTER 5: CREATING CHANGE MECHANISMS TO ACCOMPLISH THE WORK OF LEADERSHIP

Getting organized to accomplish this work is no small task. Just knowing about a model for improving performance, applying it at the top of the organization, working on parts of the model, or applying flavor-of-the-month programs alone will not make significant lasting improvement in any organization. Rather, such improvement requires a long-term disciplined effort. People throughout the organization must see themselves as responsible for the collective success of their unit and of the organization as a whole.

This means that change mechanisms have to be established throughout the organization. It requires that groups of people doing this work form leadership teams at every level of the organization. Managers must see the vision and values work as "real work," just as important as technical and task work.

They must support team members with appropriate resources, training, and information. This concept is explored with case studies in Chapter 5.

The crux of this book is to help organizations improve their performance. This means we must *simultaneously* (1) create efficient business systems and production processes to deliver products and services of appropriate quality, (2) deliver outstanding citizen/stakeholder/customer value, and (3) achieve sound financial performance. This is not solo work; few can do it alone in any organization. It will require committed people and dedicated time across your organization to ensure that your community receives the best it can get from its government.

A few words about our case studies and use of language

When the authors work with our local government clients, the most frequent request we get is for examples of how local governments have actually put into practice the concepts described in this book. Therefore, we include numerous case studies of such experiences. Some are relatively short and focused on only a few of the concepts. Others are extended examples bringing together a number of the actions a government might implement to improve its performance. Thus a case study in one chapter may also address points in other chapters in the book. The cases are sometimes written by the individuals who experienced them. In other cases the book authors or our colleagues have described how the situation progressed. When appropriate, we have identified the individual authors at the beginning of the case study.

Regarding our use of language, we try to alternate the use of pronouns and adjectives to refer to genders equally in this book rather than saying his/her or s/he and the like.

---

1   Dougherty, Conor and Merrick, Amy, *Wall Street Journal*, February 7, 2011.
2   Ibid.
3   Among others, Gallup Inc. and Blessing White publish important research in this area.
4   NYC Sanitation Department featured on video *Work Worth Doing*.
5   Gallup, Inc. *State of the Global Workforce: Employee Engagement Insights for Business Leaders Worldwide*, 2013.

Leadership at All Levels

Our constrained resources and continuing, even growing, demands for community services and the changing expectations of the workforce require us to examine how we view the roles that we play in serving the public. Especially as younger people enter the workforce, we witness their expectations for meaningful roles in accomplishing purposes that are important, for steering and managing their activities to achieve them, and for collaborating with others who share the same goals. The same desire dwells within the existing workforce, perhaps smothered by years of routine job requirements that have lulled them into accepting less fulfillment and satisfaction in favor of job security and less hassle from their supervisors.

Yet we see emerging in both the public and private sectors a new understanding of how workers at all levels can be galvanized to take roles in broadening their responsibilities and achieve far beyond what used to be simply their jobs. Let's look at an example.

CASE STUDY

Reducing Traffic Accidents in Montgomery, Ohio[1]

A team of fire, medic, and police emergency responders in Montgomery, Ohio, had just arrived at the scene of an auto accident involving two vehicles. Multiple injuries were involved; a fire truck and two ambulances were deployed. The scene was a moving collage of emergency vehicles and scurrying emergency personnel. Police at the scene were controlling and re-routing traffic, moving the mass of curiosity seekers and frustrated commuters through the clogged highway, and completing the accident investigation. All the emergency responders at the scene were able to perform their roles with precision, efficiency, and skill, as was commonly the case in Montgomery; eventually, as the cleanup and pack-up phase began, the men and women talked about less urgent things.

In the conversation that morning, fire, medic, and police personnel on the scene concurred that they needed no accident scatter diagrams to understand that the spot was a magnet for dangerous accidents. A large parking lot; a narrow, no-merge shoulder; and fast-moving traffic made for a dangerous, problematic intersection that had recently been causing an average of about sixteen accidents per month. Three times a month, serious injuries resulted from frequent side-impact accidents. After recognizing the trend, several front-line responders at the scene came up with an idea that could lead to preventing such accidents.

These police, fire, and medic front-line personnel quickly formed a team to flesh out their idea, then took their problem assessment and its proposed solution to the Montgomery director of public works. He listened to their analysis and suggestion to place flexible plastic pylons to funnel the traffic exiting the lot and alert drivers on the highway of the merging traffic. They knew that the Ohio Department of Transportation and county officials also had some responsibilities in this area, so they met with those partners, too. There, the police, fire, and medic employees laid out their ideas and worked through some technical issues, and it was agreed to implement their solution. This all took place over the course of a few meetings, totaling approximately thirty-two staff hours.

The result: In the years that followed, not a single accident occurred in the problem area. Lives were saved, serious injuries were prevented, hundreds of emergency calls were eliminated, and thousands of staff hours and equipment deployments were reprogrammed.

This case about Montgomery gives us a look into the future. What is exciting here is that these front-line police, fire, and medic responders took ownership of a problem that was outside their traditional narrow job descriptions. They looked beyond their own departments and even beyond the boundaries of their own municipality. They then solved a major problem, even though they were not working for the department of public works, which has primary responsibility for roads and street signage, transportation maintenance, and traffic flow. The city of Montgomery had been using the HPO Model to broaden the perspective and responsibilities of its workforce to create a sense of stewardship for the entire city's performance. The city expanded front-line worker roles beyond the traditional task and technical work to include leadership, management, and working collaboratively. New job descriptions made explicit that broader view (these can be seen in the Appendix). Envision the functional description of a front-line worker in a typical traffic department, a police department, and a fire department. They are different!

This is the way all local governments should operate in the future, because it is the way higher-performing organizations operate now. At the time the Montgomery story took place, the city already held a common vision and mission for the future and was working to implement them across the city. Many police, fire, and emergency responders had assumed responsibility for stewardship of the success of the entire city government and the community. In short, they had been doing the broad **work of leadership** that we will be describing in this book—work that the best local governments of the future will do.

Imagine how the Montgomery traffic story would unfold in a typical local government operation using a traditional hierarchy and only task-based job descriptions. In this scenario, police, fire, and medic responders would cooperate only to the extent that task coordination would be required to get the accident cleared. Figuring out the cause of the accident would be someone else's job, either in traffic engineering or public works, and the remedy would not even be considered by the first responders. In this structure, if a solution were to be envisioned by the police, fire, and medic responders on the scene, they would immediately dismiss it as too hard to get done and not within their responsibilities or authority. After all, there's a chain of command: All ideas go up through the supervisor, who, if she doesn't arbitrarily shoot it down, will give it to *her* boss, who will perhaps take credit for it and pass it on to *his* boss, who then represents the department in discussions some months later with other departments, all of whom jockey for credit, ownership, control, and their piece of the action. Ultimately, after a consultant study, a feasibility analysis, a traffic survey, and maybe a solicitation for proposals, some remedy may actually be implemented. But even this extraordinarily bureaucratic process is usually not what happens when a front-line person has a good idea. Usually, we know, nothing at all happens because the organization's culture and systems don't expect these individuals to work across organizational lines, ideas don't float freely to the top, and the players generally find it safer and more expedient to stick to their own knitting, so nothing happens.

This mind-set held by both management and the front-line workforce determines the way many organizations operate. People inherited this way of thinking when scientific management in the Industrial Revolution introduced a regimented approach to run our factories. But it wasn't always this way. The Industrial Revolution started in earnest only about two hundred years ago. Before that, most people in small businesses, craft production, and on farms acted the way these front-line police, fire, and medic responders did: They would see a problem, take responsibility, and fix it. This mind-set was bred into us over the thousands of years that preceded the Industrial Revolution. One reason employees are often so alienated and disengaged today is that many organizations discourage them from taking such broad responsibility and instead force them to work in dysfunctional environments. So, from a longer historical perspective, acting in this dysfunctional *industrial* way is what is foreign, not the other way around.

When employees are engaged, enabled, and empowered, however, good things happen. Here's another case, also from Montgomery, Ohio, that shows how powerfully engagement can work. By this time, a few years after the traffic solution, cross-functional group problem solving had become the norm.

CASE STUDY

Street Deicing in Montgomery, Ohio[2]

As this story opens, Montgomery has been working to simultaneously provide outstanding customer value, appropriate product and service quality, and sound financial results to its residents, businesses, and visitors. Its mission statement, "Taking responsibility together to provide superior services," was now tagged with supporting phrases showing employee intent to carry out this mission with responsiveness, leadership at all levels, and decision making based on creative problem solving, collaboration, continuous improvement, and stewardship of the entire organization with the budget of the enterprise in mind.

In late fall of 2008, Montgomery's values were put to the test. The November deicing rock salt bids showed a near tripling over the previous winter's cost. Another disconcerting announcement rubbed salt in the financial wound: A severe shortage of deicing rock salt was expected to affect the midwestern and northeastern United States, where snow removal and roadway deicing rely on a readily available supply. A significant price increase coupled with uncertainty in the supply chain for rock salt raised significant concerns. The business and service of snow removal would require change from prior years to ensure that snow removal services met the challenge. The risk of negative impact to the city's snow removal operations was now quite high.

Montgomery residents and businesses had grown accustomed to fast, thorough snow removal. The news about deicing rock salt prices and inventories would fuel dire predictions by local media of poor and unsafe road conditions. The city faced a public relations and public safety nightmare with three challenges: to keep roadway conditions safe, to cope with rock salt prices rising from $46 to $125 per ton, and to put residents and business owners at ease. To address these challenges, the city engaged front-line and other staff in creative problem solving to take advantage of their varied perspectives. Members were provided information about the facts surrounding the salt shortage, expected service levels, and tools available to meet this challenge. They were asked to present the most innovative way to solve the problem in the short timeframe—just one month—until snow removal operations would be implemented, typically in early to mid-December.

The department team, from front-line staff to the department head, reviewed the existing policy to determine which standards and performance measures could be met within the possible changes to snow removal operations now facing them. This policy established an agreement among city staff, city council, and residents and businesses on how snow removal would be completed during winter storms. It included utilizing a roadway priority system, staffing of trucks and equipment, how deicing chemicals and plowing of snow would be used, environmental stewardship in operations, and completing final cleanup of the trucks and supply yards. It also outlined performance measures for specific completion times for clearing roads after accumulating snow ended, which was perhaps the most important concern for residents and businesses.

The department team examined all aspects of its snow removal operations. They coordinated with the local school district to ensure that prioritization of school bus routes was incorporated into the snow removal triage plans. They tested and evaluated the use of other methods, such as the use of salt brine and removal of snow from roadways through plowing at lower accumulation thresholds. They developed plans to reduce the amount of rock salt used and identified alternative methods of snow removal to compensate for consequent reduction of snow and ice meltage. Further, they outfitted light-duty trucks that had not been used during snow removal with plows for use on less traveled and narrower side streets so that larger snow removal trucks could spend more time on major thoroughfares.

This review also concluded that work was necessary throughout the organization to think strategically about how well their operations actually met external customers' and stakeholders' needs. Internal partners were also identified, including the public works department, communications director, customer service department staff, and police and fire departments. Each department held meetings at the unit level where front-line staff considered possible scenarios while developing ideas and action steps for individual and department operations. These sessions resulted in innovative strategies, such as enhanced and improved communications with external customers and stakeholders and revisions to snow removal route assignments. The public works team assumed the responsibility for outlining a continuous, multifaceted process designed to reassure residents that despite media reports to the contrary, city staff would be prepared and equipped for snow removal operations and work would be done in a manner in which other city services would not be compromised

Preparations for the winter included a communication plan for the snow season to keep residents informed using newsletters, postcards, call-in numbers for roadway condition information via pre-recorded messages, the city website, and local TV stations. For instance, the community was informed through the monthly Montgomery newsletter and city website, which identified steps being taken to address the rock salt shortage, carried the message that safety was of paramount concern to the city, and provided community roadway condition reports. Message templates were developed for the city's reverse 911 system, Code RED, to follow whenever pre-recorded messages went to residents and businesses in snow emergencies.

Their analysis produced several revisions to the snow policy, including a modest increase in the length of time required to complete snow removal. This became a performance standard that would serve as a common scoreboard for the entire city. When ratified and approved, the standards were posted prominently on the city's website.

Throughout the winter, city staff met within the department following winter storms to discuss the successes and failures during snow removal. Operations and services adhered to a model of "Plan, Do, Check, Act" to monitor performance effectiveness. These discussions were not to establish blame but instead to capitalize on successful actions and outcomes. They also included reviews of actions and procedures which seemed to be of limited value, and consensus was reached on whether changes in these activities were necessary to meet the needs of internal partners and external customers.

Anecdotal reports from Montgomery's residents and businesses indicated the season's snow removal was effective in meeting expectations. Common metrics such as tallies of complaints, complimentary calls, cards, and email comments showed positive results compared to the previous year. At winter's end, the city asked all residents and businesses for feedback to assess the winter operations using Web-based and print media, including anonymous remark options. The city's reaction was over 70 percent positive. Narrative comment analysis revealed that most of the roughly 30 percent negative responses referred to roads close to Montgomery but maintained by another public agency.

At the same time the city was getting these favorable customer reactions, it also used 300 fewer tons of rock salt than the 1,200 tons previously required for comparable snowfalls, thus saving $38,000 in operating costs alone.

Unfortunately, similar actions were not taken by a number of other area communities that ran out of rock salt and reacted to the crisis in ways that negatively affected service delivery. The Montgomery approach—which included engaging the entire workforce when the potential for a crisis was first identified—allowed city staff at all levels in the organization to explore options and share equally in creative problem solving. This served to stabilize city finances and resources while developing and improving lines of communication among staff, residents, and businesses.

While it is sometimes difficult to place a value on credibility, the city's response during the rock salt crisis reflected that its mission statement,

"Taking responsibility together to provide superior services," is not simply a motto but the way it conducts business and delivers services. Sustained high performance, the subject of this collection of case studies, is determined by many critical factors, fueled largely by personal engagement and motivation. In local government, opinions vary on how best to harness this potential energy. Human experience suggests that we have been hardwired for engagement for thousands of years and that no amount of extrinsic or external motivation (like carrots and sticks) can cause most staff to be more engaged and motivated. So, if being engaged and solving problems across departmental "silos" is so natural, then what happened to make these stories so exceptional?

HOW THE NATURE OF WORK HAS EVOLVED

To understand this, we need to explore, briefly, how we got to where we are today including how the nature of work evolved over time. Where in this evolution did we lose this natural engagement mind-set and create the "traditional hierarchies" we find in many organizations today?[1]

Imagine the first human job, as a hunter-gatherer. Here, job success is survival. The work is complicated by the dual challenge to simultaneously *acquire* food while avoiding *being* food. It is a nomadic existence with a short life span and a retirement plan short on benefits. Get sick, break a leg, or grind your teeth down too far to maintain sufficient nutrition for strength, and you're *in* the food chain. Much of our development as a species took place during this period. Survival causes intense engagement and intrinsic motivation. So, being engaged is more natural than being disengaged. Gradually, and at different times around the globe, significant climatic, demographic, social, technical, and other changes caused a shift from migrating hunter-gatherers to stationary, agriculture-based subsistence farming and craft work.

Like hunter-gathering before it, job success in this **Farmer/Crafts Phase** is survival. This phase requires the shoemaker, for example, to understand

- who his customers are and what they want, need, and expect now and in the future
- how he is going to treat his customers (with honesty, dependability, etc.) to keep them coming back to him

- what products and services he will focus on
- how he will stay on the cutting edge of his craft
- how he will develop his children/apprentices so he can grow the business

This set of work, more future-focused and less pressing on a daily basis, but critical to his long-term success, is called the **work of leadership**. If the shoemaker doesn't do this work personally, it won't get done and he is likely to fail in his business.

In addition, the shoemaker must also be simultaneously concerned with issues like

- delivering shoes to his customer on schedule, with appropriate quality, and at the price promised
- ensuring that he has the methods, tools, and materials required
- getting every possible piece of leather out of the hide (efficient use of resources)

This set of work, more immediately focused and more pressing on a daily basis, is about efficiency and is critical to his short-term success; it's called the **work of management**. Finally, the shoemaker must actually make the shoes, the **task/technical work**. If the shoemaker doesn't do all this work personally, it won't get done. Figure 1.1 displays all three pieces of the subsistence farmer/craftperson's work. Since the farmers or craftsmen have to do it all or it won't get done and they won't survive, they are engaged.

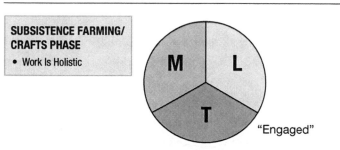

Before 1800

SUBSISTENCE FARMING/
CRAFTS PHASE
- Work Is Holistic

M   L
T
"Engaged"

FIGURE 1.1 The Subsistence Farming/Crafts Phase

Work is **holistic** in this phase; it integrates leadership, management, and task/technical aspects in a single job. It was during the Industrial Revolution that work was split apart, segmented, and dumbed down to fit the demographic and economic forces of the time. Unlike the earlier Farmer/Crafts Phase, where one person was responsible for everything, the Industrial Model of organization divided work vertically, separating leadership and management work from task/technical work. Leadership work generally went to upper-class owners, consultants, and executives whose social class status gave them the right to rule.

Today when you are asked "Who's 'the leadership' in your organization?" what is your typical response? "Top management?" or "Somewhere above me?" Farmers and craftspeople knew the things we now include in the work of leadership were inherent parts of their own personal work; they had to do them or they wouldn't survive. Now, leadership is seen as someone else's job—the top managers who comprise "the leadership." Eliminating the work of leadership as a responsibility of everyone in the organization has muddled the meaning of the term *leadership*. Today, many academics and management practitioners stumble over defining leadership—does it mean the set of people in top management, or is it a set of functions to be distributed throughout the levels of an organization, as it is used in this book?

Management work went to managers of the same social class as the owners. The class association let managers move up to become leaders and helps explain today's confusion over who's a leader and who's "just" a manager.

Task/technical work went to working-class laborers, often immigrants, mostly uneducated, and plentiful. This work was divided horizontally into mind-numbing, repetitive, simple, and straightforward tasks. Figure 1.2 displays this traditional model.

Many of today's administrative systems and task/technical work processes—human resources, finance/budget, purchasing/contracting, information technology, facilities, legal, and technical work processes—date from this industrial era. These systems and processes reflect an Industrial Model of **leadership philosophy** and **values**, the oldest of which can be described as **exploitative autocratic**: "Do what I [the upper-class boss] tell you or I'll fire/ punish you." Leadership philosophy will be discussed in more detail in the section on Values to Work Culture in Chapter 4.

1900

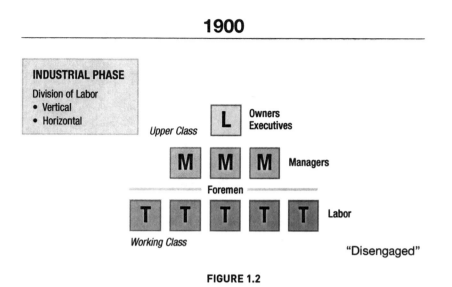

FIGURE 1.2

As the Industrial Era emerged, this prevailing management view held that most workers were untrustworthy and/or inept and therefore had to be closely watched and controlled. Workers, who could not be trusted to think for themselves, needed someone to watch over them, give them task assignments, and hold them accountable. This required foremen and managers with "super vision." Platforms built along assembly lines afforded raised vantage points, allowing somebody from the upper class to sit up high and watch those "jokers" down below who were becoming more actively disengaged over time.

This cumbersome pyramidal structure and belief set made for higher production numbers of low-quality goods compared to earlier production models (e.g., Farmer/Crafts) and allowed the United States to flourish in the early part of the twentieth century. Eventually, though, the level of disengagement among the workforce became too significant for management to ignore. By mid-century, most of the workforce had high school educations and task/technical work was growing increasingly complex, raising the cost of turnover. To reduce such turnover, Industrial Model management generally adopted a new leadership philosophy—**benevolent autocratic**:

> *"We reward loyalty here. You just sign on with us, go the whole thirty years of your career doing just what we ask you to do, and we will take care of you (as long as it in our best interest). I really do care*

*for you (little) people, but I (the parent) need to make the important
decisions (since you kids can't make serious, high-level organizational decisions as well as I can.) Stay with us, and at the end of
thirty years, you will make out well in the retirement system."*

[Note: Words and phrases in parentheses above are thought by management but not said aloud. This leadership philosophy manipulates to prevent
turnover.]

This "parent-child" behavior leads to "organizational silos." The mid-
manager is encouraged to do whatever is necessary to optimize his unit's
success and please his "parent" (immediate boss), regardless of organization-wide priorities. When asked to be more productive, employees are likely
to say, "It's not my job!" or "If you want me to 'think' or 'learn more skills,'
pay me more. Why should I do what you managers get paid to do?" For the
first time in history on such a large scale, people in the Industrial Era could
survive on task work alone and feed the family by "dumbly and loyally" following instructions, with no responsibility for organizational outcomes. No
longer was survival as clear a motivator nor was there significant intrinsic
motivation coming from the work itself.

Could we have designed a more perfect way to disengage people? Since
most organizations—including a preponderance of local governments—still
operate, at least in large part, using these leadership philosophies underpinning the Industrial Model (exploitative and benevolent autocratic), is there
any wonder why virtually all surveys show low employee engagement? Today,
most US workers (almost three-quarters, according to Gallup polls[2]) are now
disengaged or actively disengaged.

Early in the twentieth century, this industrial model stimulated the growth
of labor unions to give workers a say in what affected them and a means to
resist management's autocratic behaviors. Since government at all levels has
been slow to abandon this inherited mind-set, it is not surprising that, today,
government is now one of the most rapidly unionizing sectors of the economy. Technical and professional employees are organizing today just to have
a say in the direction and processes of the organization.

The Industrial Model has survived as long as it has because it made the
United States a world-dominant economic power during the early and middle

parts of the twentieth century, but it appears to be running its course. As Larry Wilson writes in the forward of Ed Oakley and Doug Krug's book, *Enlightened Leadership*:

> *The people we used to turn to for the answers to questions, those way up in the corporate tower, no longer have the answers. The world has become too fast and too complex . . . [and] just as distressing, if they have the answers, they often cannot implement them fast enough to make a difference.*"[3]

Note that this is not an argument against the concept of hierarchy, which, after all, is about accountability. The old Industrial Model's traditional hierarchy, however, unnecessarily creates an "I'm better/smarter/more powerful than you" mind-set, limits people's ability to use their full range of talents and skills, causes disengagement, and ultimately leads to poorer performance. To quote former General Electric CEO Jack Welch, "In an environment where we must have every good idea from every man and woman in the organization, we cannot afford management styles that suppress and intimidate."[4]

WHAT IS THE NETWORKED TALENT MODEL?

Of course, neither of the two city of Montgomery stories above would likely have happened in the traditional hierarchy of the old Industrial Model. Organizations of the future will have to be more flexible, more innovative, faster, more responsive, smarter at all levels, more customer-focused, and more efficient. Forcing all decisions to the top of the organization for approval before returning to the first level for action is just too slow. The Industrial Model, founded on class stratification and exploitation of the less privileged, was immoral at best. It is also becoming both ineffective and inefficient for today's world. The Farmer/Crafts Model worked long enough to be part of our current human character. Any new model for the future will have to look more like that phase's 20,000 years rather than the past 200. Let's see how such a new model that expects leadership at all levels—the **Networked Talent Model**—might look.

CASE STUDY

The Networked Talent Model at the Village of Shorewood, Illinois

Bill McGowan stood at the podium and surveyed the faces of his audience, the six trustees and president of the Shorewood Village Board and the village administrator. He had been asked to speak on a subject of special importance to the Board, and it exemplified the transformation of Shorewood Village's government toward higher performance. To an outsider unfamiliar with the roles and work responsibilities of the people in the room, McGowan's presentation to the board may not have looked unusual. However, his role in the village organization made the event very special: Bill McGowan was a mechanic. His job description placed his work responsibilities in the fleet management unit, but he was presenting his idea, really a "business case," for outfitting police cruisers, insourcing some vehicle maintenance work, and early rotation of police vehicles; proposals that, until recently, would lay outside his "swim lane" in virtually every respect.

To village manager Kurt Carroll and the Shorewood Board, though, this presentation was exactly where they wanted the village government to be heading. Not long before, they were visited by city representatives from Montgomery, Ohio, who shared their experiences implementing the High-Performance Organization Diagnostic/Change Model. That city had adopted the HPO Model almost a decade before, and high performance was now ingrained in their work culture. The presentation that day included practical solutions to common concerns and what was implemented to instill a shared sense of ownership in organizational results at every level.

A little earlier, Carroll had attended the University of Virginia's two-week Senior Executive Institute residential program, where he got a good introduction to the meaning of high performance. Even before he returned to the office, he began imagining how he might implement the HPO Model in the village government workforce. Shorewood operated with a number of departments. Each, he felt, could benefit from this transformational work to engage the workforce with the Networked Talent Model, so he sent the department directors to UVA's shorter one-week LEAD program. Kurt then wanted to get more of his staff exposed to the HPO material, so he decided to bring the three-day Building High-Performance Organizations (HPO) seminar[5] to Shorewood. The Board supported his plan to have an HPO seminar delivered on-site for about half of the village's staff. Another seminar followed, and implementation efforts proved to be a high priority for the senior management team. By the time Bill

McGowan stood before the Shorewood Village Board to tell them about his proposals, nearly every employee had been through the HPO seminar.

As a veteran journey-level mechanic, Bill McGowan was already coming to the job every day with the technical skills to do the work required in his position description. When he learned about the Networked Talent Model, Bill fell into it naturally. He had been outfitting police cruisers with new center consoles, engaged in labor-intensive, painstaking work to install computers and communication equipment, when he discovered some problems. He took ownership of the problems, developed ways to fix them, streamlined the process, and saved both time and financial resources. He shared the ideas with his fleet management supervisor, who supported them enthusiastically. Before the village started its transition toward a high-performance work culture, Bill's supervisor might have told his mechanic that coming up with ideas on saving time and money was not his responsibility. The Board certainly picked up on the value of this new way of thinking as they listened attentively to Bill McGowan talk about his management and leadership roles.

As Bill ticked off the cost savings of his process improvement ideas, he highlighted process steps eliminated from the workflow and the wasted time and work in the process that could be cut. The presentation sounded more like that of a management consultant than a mechanic, but it was his engagement and excitement that impressed the Board and village manager most. As a line employee, Bill spent most of his day with his police partners and their vehicles. He knew what high performance meant to them, and he understood their quality expectations as well as their frustrations. The mechanic knew that his partners spent most of their time in their cruisers. He often asked them questions about the ergonomics of their typical work motions and economy of space. To him, the job naturally involved more than installing consoles, so he fully embraced the Networked Talent Model quickly.

The mechanic's recommendations covered a number of areas beyond his normal scope of work, such as making a comparison of purchase vs. maintenance costs, using data he had been tracking over time. Bill suggested that the village would avoid costs and save money and time by rotating the cruisers out at the point their warranties expired, and selling them as surplus vehicles to other police departments. He documented his recommendation by providing a cost comparison of extended maintenance costs vs. projected surplus sales revenues. Another of his suggestions provided for improved inventory control practices to reduce work-in-process and wait time, all of which translated into savings for the local government as a whole.

Bill McGowan was not the only line employee who internalized the work of management and leadership into his task job to put the Networked Talent Model into practice. Many other line employees blossomed with the new awareness that comes from embracing their expanded roles. Administrator Kurt Carroll tells of a cross-functional team of Shorewood Village line staff who compared features and costs of various health plan options and identified how to acquire an improved prescription package at a lower cost than the village was then paying. Kurt is pleased with the progress of his government's transformation, describing their work as a continuous process made possible through a strong emphasis on communication. He says he is sure that front-line staff is in the best position to know what customers want and need, and consequently, are able to derive the most satisfaction in delivering quality services in the most efficient, effective way. One of his favorite expressions is, "Let's keep our thinking caps on." It is an expression his division directors and the staff on the line enjoy hearing him say.

AN EVOLVING HIERARCHY AND THE NETWORKED TALENT MODEL

So what's in store for us in the future? Unfortunately, there doesn't appear to be a silver bullet that solves all these issues. On the other hand, on the organizational horizon is an outline of an alternative that takes the best of the past and modifies it for the future.

To be successful, hierarchies have to become more flexible, innovative, responsive, smarter at all levels, customer-focused, faster, and less costly. The notion that all decisions must flow up to the top of the organization and return to the first level for action is clearly flawed in today's environment.

This book approaches this dilemma in two ways: First, we'll look at organizations that routinely deliver high performance and identify the nature of their work and jobs. Their line of thinking seems to be:

We understand that customers want excellent technical delivery. However, we recognize that technical skills alone are insufficient because our customers also expect services and products to be on time, on budget, and with good customer relations. To do that, we must periodically evaluate our performance relative to our plans and our customers' expectations. When a gap is found, we do some root-cause analysis problem solving and take the required corrective action—that's the work of management. This work shouldn't be left to managers alone, but rather, the front-line staff should deal with it immediately, because to wait until the manager gets involved typically results in slower, less responsive, and more costly service. Moreover, in order for us to continue to deliver this higher level of performance, all the staff need to continue to develop their skills, constantly improve the organization's administrative systems and work processes, interact with customers to ensure they are meeting expectations, understand how what they do supports the larger organization, and work together to build capacity—that's the work of leadership.

MANAGEMENT
Skills, Abilities, and Behaviors
(partial list)

- Business Models; Business Plan Creation, Implementation, Measurement, Monitoring, and Corrective Action
- Systems Thinking/Causal Reasoning
- Financial Management Systems
- Project/Change Management
- Process Improvement Tools
- People Systems
- Information Technology Systems
- Open Communication Systems

LEADERSHIP
Skills, Abilities, and Behaviors

- Strategic Stakeholder Value Analysis
- Vision/Values to Strategy/ Structure/Systems
- Suprasystems Integration/ Stewardship
- Learning/Thinking/Changing/ Renewing
- Enabling/Empowering/ Engaging/Energizing

TASK/TECHNICAL
Skills, Abilities, and Behaviors

- Continuously Broaden and Deepen Task/Technical Skills and Abilities

TEAM SKILLS
Abilities and Behaviors

- Procedural, Problem-Solving and Behavioral Skills at the Personal, Interpersonal, and Team Levels

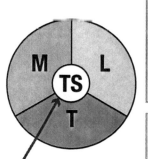

FIGURE 1.3 Employee Skills Required in the Networked Talent Model

As you can see, all levels of the workforce need skills similar to the farmer/craftsperson: leadership, management, and task/technical skills, plus one more competency area: team/networking skills. Examples of these team/networking skills include self-awareness, interpersonal/communication skills, team building, facilitation, group problem solving, and decision making. These team/networking skills differentiate the Networked Talent Model from the Farmer/Crafts Model. They are important because as work has become more and more complex, people must interact effectively with members of their own, and other, units or organizations to solve problems and improve performance. It is the combination of abilities in the Networked Talent Model that allowed the city of Montgomery to creatively develop innovative alternatives during their rock salt crisis.

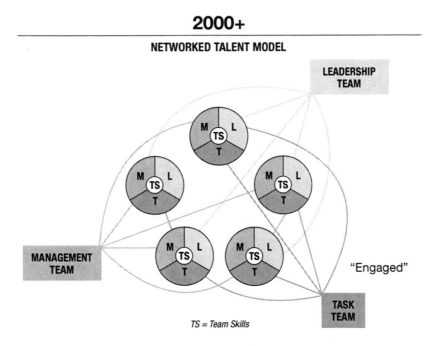

FIGURE 1.4 The Networked Talent Model

The idea is to enable the production workforce and their support partners to focus on citizens/customers/stakeholders directly with broad authority bound by a clear understanding of their vision/mission/values and expected behaviors. This networked cross-functional grouping is called a **microbusiness**. Microbusinesses have to perform all the same kinds of functions that a larger business would require. They have to understand their customers' wants, needs, and expectations; determine which of these to meet and how to do it; make sure that its work is well integrated with other relevant parts of the organization; understand and operate within its administrative, support, and financial constraints; and assure that it has the support, energy, authority, and management information to accomplish its goals. And, of course, the members have to be able to work together collaboratively and effectively using appropriate team skills. Therefore, in order to be successful, a microbusiness must accomplish the technical, management, and leadership components of its work.

Within a microbusiness, all the members are responsible for achieving the desired outcomes. While there is a team leader accountable to the larger organization in the hierarchy, she relies on all the members for success. She doesn't need to come up with all the answers by herself; rather, her job is to help smart people develop smart solutions. It should be clear that the expectations for each of the microbusiness members are a dramatic change from what most organizations expect today.

So how do we get managers and front-line employees ready to accept the responsibility to make decisions for their microbusiness? It is clear that the current job contract needs to be revised for both the workforce, including managers. To paraphrase an outspoken former senior manager in a Fortune 100 company, "When your face is to the boss, your butt's to the customer!" If an employee is focused on only the direction from the top and the rewards handed out by the boss, why would that employee care about pleasing/serving external customers? Increasingly, it will be critical that all employees—at every level—become focused on serving external customers and on accomplishing the larger organization's mission, rather than just seeing their job as a set of tasks to be performed without regard to overall impact. It also follows that other components of the human resources system will require reexamination. It will be important that behavior supporting the Networked Talent Model become expected, evaluated, and rewarded, including integrating individual behaviors, team-based contributions, and microbusiness/organizational results into the system.

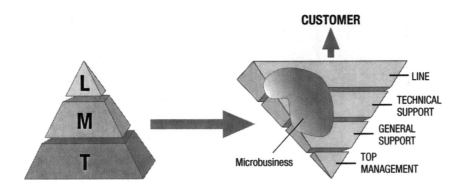

CUSTOMER

L

M

T

Microbusiness

LINE

TECHNICAL
SUPPORT

GENERAL
SUPPORT

TOP
MANAGEMENT

FIGURE 1.5

In order to make the Networked Talent Model work, another critical shift will be required: moving from exploitative and benevolent autocratic leadership philosophies to more "adult-adult" **consultative/participative** leadership philosophies. These will be discussed in more detail in the section on leadership philosophy in Chapter 4. Let's be clear about the Networked Talent Model, however: There is still a hierarchy. It is not based, as it was in the Industrial Model, on the smart ones at the top accomplishing the *thinking work* and the others just *doing* what they are directed; rather it is based on the need for smart people at all levels of the organization thinking about and doing what is appropriate in their sphere of work. Exhibiting competencies in coordinating the complex work of future organizations and supporting and growing the capabilities of the workforce will be the bases for promotions in the future. Rather than figuring out what the organization needs to do and then giving orders, future top managers will focus on involving smart people distributed throughout the organization to solve problems. Though consensus decision making has its place and its advantages, at the end of the decision process, if team members can't all agree, then management will take all the good input they've collected, make the call, and explain why the decision was made so that team members can understand it. You can't afford to miss deadlines because you can't reach a consensus.

One other implication of the hierarchy is that not everyone devotes an equal percentage of time to leadership, management, and technical work. Top managers can be expected to spend more time on longer-term, strategic leadership work than others in the organizations. The front-line personnel can be expected to spend more time on the shorter-term, more tactical technical work. Regardless of the percentages, however, each individual performs each type of work. The middle manager role evolves the most, shifting from primarily a management job to one with more leadership responsibilities—specifically, the mentoring, coaching, and development of the front-line staff so that they can participate in making informed, independent management and leadership decisions.

Changes to the front-line personnel's focus and the managers' behavior require adaptation of a variety of human resource systems, from hiring and development through performance management to promotion and retention. The kinds of changes required of the Networked Talent Model might initially be seen as threats to "old-line" unions, because the distinction between management and labor is blurred. In the Networked Talent Model, though, everyone is on the same side: focused on improving organizational performance and customer service. In a growing number of organizations, progressive unions have been open to the Networked Talent Model as a way to secure for their members the skills necessary to provide job security and satisfaction. Whether unions are involved in an organization or not, the Networked Talent Model begins to lay the basis for building trust, open communication, active participation at all levels, and transparent decision making in the organization. A natural result is increased engagement and individual commitment.

With this review of how we got to where we are and where we might go, let's now turn our attention to finding a road map to guide our improvement efforts.

---

1 Cheryl Hilvert was the City Manager of Montgomery during the period of this case study. She is now the Director of the ICMA Center for Management Studies.
2 Ibid.
3 This discussion is based on ideas from Alvin Toffler and Jared Diamond. See Toffler, Alvin, 1980. *The Third Wave*. New York, NY: William Morrow & Co. and Diamond, Jared. 1997. *Guns, Germs, and Steel*. New York, NY: W.W. Norton.
4 Gallup, Inc. *State of the Global Workforce: Employee Engagement Insights for Business Leaders Worldwide,* 2013.
5 Oakley, Ed and Doug Krug. 1991. *Enlightened Leadership*. New York, NY: Fireside (Simon & Schuster), p. 9.
6 1992 GE Annual Report.
7 The three-day *Building High-Performance Organizations* seminar is conducted by the Commonwealth Centers for High-Performance Organizations.

The HPO
Diagnostic/Change Model

In our professional work we are inundated with hot topics, crises, and the latest council or board priorities that require both time and attention. We go from solving a problem that requires an immediate fix to making an improvement in a specific process and on to the next things that consume our time. Our days are saturated fulfilling our regular, current responsibilities and handling emergencies that arise. We seldom have the time to step away from these pressing duties to examine the long-range health and performance of our organizations. And when we make the opportunity, we usually don't have a good framework to do such an analysis.

Yet many of us recognize that for our personal physical health we need a periodic systematic review to understand how we are doing in important areas and, if something is amiss, what to do about it. We turn to someone like a medical doctor to perform a diagnostic health assessment of a human body system that involves a complex set of variables that are often rapidly changing.

Consider how an annual physical exam is conducted:

I arrive at the doctor's office for my annual physical. "How are you feeling?" she asks. The doctor wants to know how I think I am doing. She is beginning a diagnostic process to compare my current state— starting from my perspective—to her understanding of how a fully functional person at my age would be feeling and performing, to get a clear sense of my current health against the standard that I could achieve: my full physical potential. She has in her mind several sets of indicators that she'll be using during the exam to measure what she finds against that standard.

*We've talked before of some goals for me to get closer to my healthy potential. If I say that my back is hurting, she will begin her examination focusing on the area that needs most attention. She'll ask where it hurts, what kind of pain it is, whether it is severe, and how it might have happened. She will touch, push, and prod to get a sense of the extent of injury. She may conclude from this that there are several options for next steps that could be used to make me better. She'll decide if more diagnostic tools, like an X-ray or MRI, are needed. When she feels she has a handle on the problem, she can then turn to treatment options or "**change levers**" to do something about it. She could recommend simple steps, such as an exercise program or physical therapy, or more complex tools, like injected steroids or surgery. Whatever the course, we'll agree on a plan, set the short- and long-term goals for the treatment, and decide on a date to measure progress.*

Of course, since this is my annual physical, the doctor will be doing a thorough examination of my whole body: vital signs, physical systems, internal organs, including drawing and analyzing all those endless vials of blood. If she sees things that need follow-up, she'll order them, as she identifies areas where additional treatment is necessary. And finally, we'll have mutual expectations for the progress to be made and when we'll check in on it. At that time, we'll see whether I have moved closer to my full, healthy potential.

A good health assessment of a local government uses a similar diagnostic approach for its dynamic system, but with different tools for its unique environment. Each high-performing organization should have a way to routinely diagnose how well it is doing and then use levers and tools to adjust its operations and culture to be sure it stays on track to fulfilling its potential. The **High-Performance Organization Diagnostic/Change Model** (the HPO Model) helps organizations identify key areas to look at their performance and levers to use to improve it.

To set the stage for describing the HPO Model in more detail, let's look at a case study of a local government's multiyear journey toward higher performance. As you read, think about the plans, actions, actors, cultural environment, and systems that helped them become more successful.

CASE STUDY

The "One-City" Approach to Development Services in Bellevue, Washington

—Mike Brennan, the director of development services for Bellevue, Washington, served in that capacity through the period discussed in his case study

The city of Bellevue, Washington, located across Lake Washington from Seattle, is a growing high-tech and retail center. While business booms downtown, much of Bellevue retains a small-town feel, with thriving, woodsy neighborhoods and a vast network of green spaces and recreational facilities that have earned it the nickname "a city in a park."

As a growing city, Bellevue faces the challenges confronting many local governments, including the community pressures that accompany change. Many of the gleaming high-rise buildings that now define Bellevue's prominent skyline arrived during the dot-com building boom of the late 1990s and during the more recent development cycle that ended in 2008. Both development peaks delivered great new projects, but the customer experience was dramatically different between the two periods.

In 2001, the dot-com development boom came to an abrupt halt. The local government had survived the largest development peak in the city's history, but it was hard on the city's customers, especially developers, and they let us know. They complained that our processes were fragmented, our codes were in conflict, and the city was slow in delivering the permits and decisions necessary for successful projects. Equally disturbing, the city council was unhappy with Bellevue's performance, because that's what their constituents were telling them. Something had to change.

Many jurisdictions have jumped on the bandwagon of reform to make their development services function in a more predictable and customer friendly way. When Bellevue set out on such a reform initiative in 2002, our aim was to move beyond making improvements in individual departments or simply focusing on business processes. Our goal was to re-create the entire development services function and realize a vision of a single line of business, spanning across multiple departments and divisions including building, fire, land use, transportation, and utilities. The effort would be based on a common set of management principles—an accountability model built on performance measures and a financial structure that would sustain performance through development cycles. We called it the "one-city" approach to delivering services.

It has been a long, continuing journey, but the results have already been dramatic. Timelines for issuance of permits have decreased significantly, and a new culture has emerged across departments focused on an ethic of collaboration and delivering high-quality customer service. The delivery of fast, predictable, one-city services has become a positive factor in the city's economic development strategy. Most significantly, departments that in the past had been operating as standalone units that took little ownership for the system as a whole now see themselves as part of a broad, cross-departmental line of business. These departments now embrace responsibility for, and take pride in, the reputation and work products they collectively deliver.

GETTING STARTED

We had already implemented many of the standard development reforms, including establishing a permit center where customers could meet with staff from departments with a role in development services, and completing efforts to map and streamline business processes. To bring about substantial and lasting improvement would require staff to find innovative solutions to generate fundamental changes in defining both this development process and the staff role in creating it—in a way that addressed problems and issues cutting across all departments. We needed to redefine our culture and change the organization to allow development services to operate as a single line of business, not as disjointed independent departments.

Given the complexity of this line of business, project managers realized that solutions needed to come from the people who actually did the work on a daily basis and that the voice of the customer had to be a primary driver. Staff teams were developed around specific goals, for example

- developing a plan for customer information that allows the customer to succeed the first time when attempting to obtain permit and inspection approvals
- aligning how we use technology in all departments, giving customers the same experience and level of access when seeking information or services
- creating a fiscal model and fee structure that sustains the level of service defined by our performance measures through development cycles

To bring the voice of the customer into the organization, a Customer Advisory Committee (CAC) was formed with members representing a variety of customer groups and perspectives; some members were among our greatest critics—at least in the beginning. Over time, the CAC's influence and credibility grew and, when discussing proposed changes, staff routinely asked, "What would the CAC think?" As improvements responding to customer interests mounted, members of the CAC became new advocates, and the stories in the development community about Bellevue began turning toward the positive.

ORGANIZATION AND LEADERSHIP

In the beginning, problems and issues identified by managers, staff, and customers were so varied that one of the biggest challenges was to organize them to develop solutions. Eventually, the problems were grouped into six unique categories aligned to form the Development Service Improvement (DSI) initiative star:

- Organization, Oversight, and Accountability
- Building a Better Customer
- Doing the Right Thing
- Customer Services and Facilitation
- Providing the Tools
- The Smoothest Path

Together, these six categories represented a comprehensive strategy that captured all aspects of how Bellevue delivered development services and how customers engaged with us. This helped to frame the project in understandable terms and formed a new language. Every staff member and staff team knew which triangle of the star they were working on (e.g., "Today my efforts were focused on *building a better customer*").

FIGURE 2.1

MANAGEMENT PHILOSOPHY AND CULTURE

The management philosophy supporting this change effort came from the city manager,[2] who voiced at the outset his expectations for performance goals, monitoring against those goals, and accountability for outcomes. The key concept behind his philosophy was based on mission and operations alignment: "If everyone is clear about what he or she is working toward, success will follow."

Culturally, the project required a shift in the way we thought about our work. Bellevue development services staff have always prided themselves on their exceptional technical abilities and knowledge. However, customer service and timeliness were inconsistent, as some clung to the belief that technical quality, speed, efficiency, and customer service couldn't be accomplished simultaneously and that trade-offs would always be necessary among them. Early on, it was clear that success would require the staff to focus on multiple goals at the same time—an individual's singular focus on the technical integrity of his or her work would no longer be enough. Now, each city staff member would be responsible for performing in a way that reflected the broader goals of exceptional customer service and efficiency. Even more, as members of productive work teams, they would be expected to act as facilitators and problem solvers.

An early and important step in the process was creating a new mission statement to provide the purpose and goals to guide improvement efforts and set the framework for future decision making and investments reflecting the new shared values. The conversation to create the new mission statement was broad and involved managers and other staff from all involved departments, including supervisors, inspectors, engineers, and administrative staff. In the end, a consensus was reached on a mission statement that reflects a balance of respecting the needs of customers, how we wanted to be viewed as an organization, and the broader value that our work and service products offered the community:

"Facilitate appropriate and timely development"

- Deliver a process that is predictable, efficient, and understandable to the people who use it.
- Act as a single organization in the delivery of development services, not separate departments working independently.
- Preserve the quality of the end product.
- Ensure we continue to protect the quality of the public and private infrastructure, the safety and integrity of the built environment, and the livability of the city.

FAST, PREDICTABLE, AND ONE-CITY
Key Changes That Let a Single Line of Business Emerge

The public views the city as a single organization. Citizens become confused and frustrated when they get the runaround or responses like "I can't help you, that's not my department." Broadening responsibility for the coordination, communication, and information offers customers a single point of entry and convenient access to services they need. Starting from a place of siloed departments, inconsistent technologies, separate budgets, and independent management structures, the realization of a single line of city business was a long way into the future.

1. **Building an organization and governance structure providing system-wide leadership and management.** In Bellevue, as in most city organizations, responsibilities for permit review and inspection services are dispersed throughout multiple departments. Permit review and inspection functions were located in five separate departments or divisions, including fire, utilities, transportation, building, and land use. Such a fragmented approach poses

challenges—for example, varying priorities can change according to short-term demands and impact permit review and inspection, cause inconsistent staffing levels, create disjointed processes, and introduce barriers to timely decisions. Aligning and coordinating disparate functions would allow us to behave as a single line of city business. Now all that was needed to support the new mission and sustain performance over time was finding a way to come together organizationally in a holistic way.

We chose cross-functional management committees to connect management and accountability for development services. (The table on the next page shows the committee organization and membership.) The leadership team, made up of department directors, engages in policy direction and budget strategy and monitors performance. The Permit Services Oversight Committee (PSOC), comprising assistant department directors and the director of the development services department serving as chair, is responsible for establishing performance measures, monitoring performance, developing and managing budgets, and ensuring resources are adjusted according to shifts in development activity. The PSOC members are accountable for the overall performance of the development services line of business. Similar cross-departmental management committees made up of supervisors oversee permit review and inspection services. These committees oversee day-to-day operations and manage according to performance measures established for permit review or inspection. Together, these committees hold responsibility for management and oversight of all development services functions and are held accountable for their performance.

Management with committees is not a new concept, but integrating a shared obligation for performance and accountability elevated the need for mutual commitment and support—members of the committees succeed or fail together. Charters drafted by each committee gave clarity of purpose and oversight responsibilities, explained how they would operate, and defined how decisions would be made. Decision making was done primarily by consensus; when consensus could not be reached, the issue was presented to the PSOC for resolution.

Not surprisingly, the mandate to pull together management and staff from all departments was met with some resistance—it meant change, more work, and an uncertain future. However, as cross-functional management and project teams achieved near-term successes and began to win broad support, a positive buzz about development services became noticeable with the public and political leaders. Staff began asking how they could get involved to help support this transformation. Our capacity to implement fundamental change was taking hold. We had broken free from the organizational inertia that prevented real and sustainable change, but the hardest work was still ahead.

Development Services Management and Leadership Matrix					
	Fire Department	Development Services Department		Transportation Department	Utilities Department
Leadership Team	Fire Chief	Director		Director	Director
Permit Services Oversight Committee (PSOC)	Fire Marshal	Director—Chair		Assistant Director	Assistant Director
		Building Assistant Director	Land Use Assistant Director		
Permit Services Management Committee (PSMC)	Assistant Fire Marshal	Plan Review Supervisor	Planning Manager	Development Review Supervisor	Development Review Supervisor
Inspection Services Management Committee (ISMC)	Assistant Fire Marshal	Inspection Supervisor		Inspection Supervisor	Inspection Supervisor

TABLE 2.1

2. **Developing high-performance ideals.** To give more depth to the meaning of the mission statement and describe in more detail the behavior of the organization we were striving to become, we created the development services high-performance ideals. This work occurred several years after creating the mission statement, as part of the ongoing continuous improvement efforts. Using a process similar to that used to create the mission statement, staff engaged in a broad discussion to reach consensus, refine direction, and create a touchstone for evaluating our individual and collective behaviors. It describes both our philosophy of leadership and the expectations we have of each other in our mutual interactions and in our engagement with our customers. These values have come to guide where we place our time, energy, and resources; our high-performance ideals have proven to be a valuable tool and continue to define the path to become better.

DEVELOPMENT SERVICES HIGH-PERFORMANCE IDEALS

Development services is a high-performing organization committed to providing exceptional customer service, upholding the public interest, being effective stewards of our financial and environmental resources, and advancing the community vision. Our work is essential for creating a safe and sustainable city. We endeavor to make the following ideals a reality:

We are proud to work for development services.	Those we serve appreciate our efforts.	We constantly strive for high performance.	We share leadership.
Bellevue is a vibrant, diverse, and livable city.	We strive to understand their needs and concerns.	We are team-oriented, and we have a city-wide focus.	We remove roadblocks and create a climate where everyone can excel.
Bellevue attracts and seeks a variety of interesting and exciting projects.	We treat them with respect.	We make informed decisions by involving the right people at the right time.	We motivate, inspire, mentor, and support each other.
Bellevue offers attractive compensation and benefits that reflect the challenges and complexities of the work.	We keep them informed.	We think strategically to balance the short-term and long-term view.	We provide resources and opportunities for leadership development.
We are talented, trained, and engaged.	We listen and are open to considering new ideas.	We use technology to its full potential for our customers.	We take personal responsibility to recognize and cultivate our own leadership abilities.
We use our talents to make a difference.	We partner with them while upholding the city's interests.	We seek creative solutions and encourage innovation.	We share our experiences and learn from the experiences of others.
We understand our role in achieving what is important to the community.	They understand and can rely on our decisions.	We have challenging, relevant, and achievable performance measures.	We anticipate change and create a strategy to realize our vision for our team and community.
We have the facilities and tools to do our jobs to the best of our abilities.	Our procedures are predictable and our systems are easy to use.	We communicate in a relevant, timely, and candid manner.	We model integrity, trustworthiness, and service.

TABLE 2.2

We are proud to work for development services.	Those we serve appreciate our efforts.	We constantly strive for high performance.	We share leadership.
We have opportunities to develop our professional knowledge and skills.	We provide exceptional, dependable, and equitable service.	We are accountable for the quality of our work and the service we provide.	
We value and respect one another.	They see the value in our involvement.	We recognize the need to be agile and adaptable.	
We take time to celebrate success and learning.		We evaluate where we have been and continue to learn and improve.	
We recognize each other's contributions.		Our work reflects our strong bias toward action.	
We have fun.			

TABLE 2.2, cont.

3. **Moving to common technologies.** To create a common online experience for customers and to align permit and inspection management, the multiple legacy systems used in each department were abandoned. This was accomplished by moving all services to a single, common technology platform and permit management system, and applying a common set of performance mea sures. Permit and inspection information for all functions are now stored and managed within a single system. This single system allows comprehensive performance management and easier integration with the city's geographic information system and other property information. The result: simplification, better coordination, consistency, and lower cost.

4. **Aligning business practices.** The centralized permit tracking system required large-scale changes in business practices. For example, each department had its own system, which meant that to schedule inspections, customers had to understand four different inspection request processes, and it was their burden to coordinate the timing of inspections. Creating a common approach offered significant challenges, but the rewards associated with customer service proved to be worthwhile. Now customers can schedule any city inspection by calling one number or visiting the city's website, and inspectors show up the next day.

5. **Implementing performance management.** A key driver in this high-performance transformation was a focus on measurable outcomes. Before 2002, city employees could not answer the simple question, "How are we doing?" Complaints and (often negative) anecdotes were the main source of information for policy makers and managers. Without reliable data and facts to tell the real story, people believed what they heard. The construction and development community grapevine was a well-connected network, and it didn't take long for a bad story, true or false, to get around. We knew that only performance improvement would change the tone of those stories.

New and clear performance goals for issuance of permits now measure the speed and predictability of the permit review process. To track customer service performance, measures were also created to capture the number of revision cycles a permit application experienced before final approval. Determining performance goals proved challenging because the time required to issue different permit types and the variety of processes used to move them through the system vary widely. In the end, we agreed on a common set of measures and allowed the creation of real-time reports that let managers and staff monitor progress toward these goals and realign priorities to achieve the best outcomes.

In addition, it was important to define the performance expectations for the people operating within those systems. A key step in changing and sustaining the culture was creation of a common set of specific performance expectations and behaviors for all staff—within the framework of the high-performance ideals—and aligning the performance evaluation process across all functions. It was a difficult task that required negotiation with unions and a significant investment of time with all staff to reach the goal. Most people agreed that clarity in what was expected on an individual level was generally viewed as a positive step.

As mentioned above, the voice of the customer is a critical element in defining and leading any transformation effort for service providers, and structured feedback from customers is an important success measure. Customer surveys proved to be the most effective way to obtain ongoing feedback. To capture this feedback, comment cards and an annual survey of departmental customers helped to identify areas for improvement and excellence. In the 2010 customer survey, 86 percent of the respondents said that Bellevue does a good job inspecting projects and reviewing permit applications. While this is a respectable response for a regulatory function, we are convinced that performance will continue to improve in the years ahead.

6. **Creating financial policies and a fee structure to consistently support all business functions.** Another large challenge in achieving predictability was finding a financial solution to support continuity through the highs and lows of service levels during development cycles. The city council and the development community agreed that the outcome of fast, predictable services was of great value, and developers were willing to pay for it. That commitment came with the expectation that the city would be able to consistently deliver. The goal was achieved by developing a budget and rate model that supported the entire line of business, charged customers based on the costs of the services they received, and established financial reserves to support core staffing levels during economic downturns. Like private business, staffing and investments increase with workload and fee revenues and must be reduced during development downturns.

7. **Co-locating staff around business functions, not departments.** City operations moved to a new city hall building in 2006. Constructed in the heart of downtown, the new operations location pushed the one-city single line of business concept to yet another level. Large floor areas allowed the co-location of most staff working within the development services line of business. Not all staff accepted the co-location immediately. Their worries over the possible loss of departmental identity, inefficiencies brought on by the move, communication breakdowns with home departments, and severed working relationships with department colleagues made the move's implementation difficult. These problems notwithstanding, new relationships formed, the inefficiencies were addressed and mitigated, and co-location ultimately created physical and visible change that emphasized the concept of operating as a coordinated line of city business.

RESULTS

The benefits of the improvement initiative have been significant for homeowners, builders, and developers. Speed and predictability were repeatedly cited as the issues our customers cared about most; homeowners were more concerned about speed, and developers largely focused on the need for predictability.

Our dramatic improvements in the speed of review and issuance of permits for interior remodels and additions impressed homeowner customers. In 2002, the median time for approval of an interior remodel was twenty-one days. That number was reduced to one day. Median timelines for additions dropped from thirty-five days to twenty-one in one year, representing a significant reduction.

For developers, timelines were still important, but we also sought to improve the predictability of the process, especially for large, complex projects that involved significant back-and-forth between the city and the developer. Re-crafting many of our more complex permit types around a project manager model and developing negotiated timelines on a project-by-project basis helped to establish performance expectations and commitments for both the city and the applicant.

These changes have improved customer service for homeowners working on their houses and have served economic development in the value added to the community through quality development. With office vacancy rates in Bellevue as high as 30 percent during the course of the improvement project, the city marketed its streamlined process for reviewing and approving tenant improvement plans to invite relocations into Bellevue. This process reduced the median days for approval for office tenant improvement permits from fourteen to two.

REAL-WORLD ADVICE

This cultural shift has been broadly noticed both internally and externally. Bellevue has successfully shifted its original emphasis from regulator to facilitator and problem solver. The roles of regulator and code enforcement are not lost, but the strategy to gain code compliance has changed, with positive results. Our initiative had several false starts, largely because staff at first resisted the idea that there was a problem, and those who believed a problem existed could not agree on what that problem was.

Looking back at our shared experience, we offer this simple advice:

- Make sure that there is agreement on the problem being addressed.
- Define the project goals and a mission that reflects the new way of doing business.
- Listen to your customers, as their input and support are key factors to success.
- Build and support a culture that emphasizes collaboration and shared leadership and stays persistently focused on the vision.

Managers and staff spent a lot of time developing the definition of the problems and issues we were trying to tackle and creating a clear mission statement for the function. Once we agreed on the issues and where we wanted to go, the rest of the project fell into place. From that point, a huge amount of work was still required, but a strong consensus on the direction and vision made excellence possible.

Bellevue is a rapidly changing city that experiences the pressures and benefits of growth. Achieving development that is of a high quality, reflects the appropriate land uses, and is consistent with the vision for the city is critical in creating a great city. Our improvement effort established a balance to support our shared vision of being a great city and serving the needs of our customers. Deliberate and predictable application of codes, speed in the delivery of services, and a continued focus on quality combined with a one-city culture that values collaboration and exceptional customer service have resulted in great success.

The Bellevue story demonstrates that an organization can step away from the daily work to assess how it is doing, diagnose its performance, identify areas to improve, and then use the appropriate levers to change its direction. This process is at the heart of the HPO Model. So let's take some time to examine the model and then see the connections between what Bellevue did and what the HPO Model suggests.

The HPO Model was developed at the US Office of Personnel Management's Federal Executive Institute and at the University of Virginia's Weldon Cooper Center for Public Service by John Pickering, Bob Matson, Allen Hard, and later, Gerry Brokaw, Phil Harnden, and Tony Gardner. Based loosely on Rensis Likert's Causal Model, Marvin Weisbord's Six-Box Model, the McKinsey Company's Seven S Model, and others in the management literature,[3] it is a road map for practitioners to use in improving their organization's performance. The HPO Diagnostic/Change Model has been refined and expanded over the years, through work with scores of federal, state, and local government organizations, nonprofit agencies, and a few private sector entities (see Figure 2.2, The HPO Diagnostic/Change Model).

The HPO Model is a classic systems model that moves from the three conceptual change levers of leadership, vision, and values, through the three applied change levers of strategy, structure, and systems, to impact organizational performance—with a feedback loop to the organization's environment, which creates new demands on the organization. Seven key diagnostic questions need to be asked at all levels of the organization because they apply to people personally, to their immediate units, to the intermediate units above them, and to the organization as a whole.

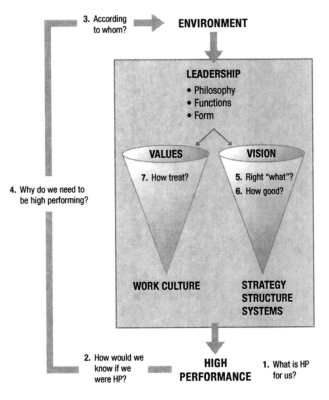

FIGURE 2.2 The HPO Diagnostic/Change Model

THE SEVEN KEY DIAGNOSTIC QUESTIONS (KDQs)

The best way to get started in understanding the HPO Diagnostic/Change Model is through the seven **key diagnostic questions** (KDQs), which help to evaluate foundational assumptions and causal reasoning. The seven KDQs are

KDQ 1: "What is high performance for us?"
KDQ 2: "How would we know if we were high performing?"

KDQ 3: "According to whom are we high performing?"

KDQ 4: "Why do we need to be high performing?"

KDQ 5: "Are we doing the right 'what'?"

KDQ 6: "How good are we at it?"

KDQ 7: "How are we going to treat each other and our stakeholders?"

Tackling these questions leads an organization or unit to define which change levers to use and the work required in each of them. These are among the most important conversations your organization or unit can have. Let's examine each of the questions:

KDQ 1: "What is high performance for us?"

Applying the HPO Diagnostic/Change Model requires that members at all levels of an organization assess whether there is agreement on what high performance is—for the organization as a whole, for their individual units/ microbusinesses within the organization, and for themselves individually. Without a clear understanding and common agreement at all levels, there is little chance that individual members or units of the organization, acting alone and in isolation, will coincidentally arrive at a common understanding of what high performance is or how to achieve it. If all parts of an organization are not aligned on what high performance is, then no matter how talented or committed the individual members are, the organization will be unlikely to achieve the outcomes and impacts it seeks.

Further, it is not enough for an organization to define high performance in a general way as just "wanting to be the best." High performance needs to be defined much more specifically and compared with the top performers we can identify. In this respect, high performance seems similar to what Jim Collins describes as "great" in his book *Good to Great: Why Some Businesses Make the Leap . . . and Others Don't.*[4] It takes a great deal more to be "great"— or, in our language, high performing—than simply being better than a lot of mediocre competitors.

People generally have a sense from their own experience of what high performance means for them personally—a generic definition of high performance regardless of the type of organization (public, private, or nonprofit), which invariably includes the following three elements:

- **Quality of products and services.** These are appropriate design and features delivered with excellent process execution. (See Chapter 3 for a more thorough discussion of the definition of quality.)
- **Outstanding customer value.** This includes dependability, responsiveness, service, timeliness, convenience, courtesy, competence of staff, and problem-solving ability. (See KDQ 3 and Chapter 3 for a more thorough discussion of the different "flavors" of customers.)
- **Sound financial performance.** This means having a robust business model that can generate revenue, minimize costs, and meet financial objectives.

These generic factors are common in almost every organization. What differentiates high-performing organizations from the others is that they simultaneously deliver all three elements—they **Pick 3**. And since these three factors need to be delivered and improved over time, the expectation for high performance is really **Pick 3+**, where the "+" refers to the consistent, sustainable, and constantly improving performance of all three over time.

KDQ2: "How would we know if we were high performing?"

This question asks if we have an effective system of measurements to let us know if we are moving in our intended direction. Such a system focuses us on the purposes and outcomes we seek from our work, the logic model that determines our efforts to achieve those results, and the measurements for us to know—throughout the levels of the organization—that our actions are indeed leading to accomplishing our worthwhile goals.

If we are to contribute effectively to these purposes and outcomes, each of us needs to understand how what we do adds significant value to our achievements and that our actions are on target and properly aligned with others (in sufficient quantity and quality), our stakeholders are well served, and we are using our resources wisely. Only a reliable and relevant system of measurement that is clear to us and not administratively burdensome can do this. It must create a "line of sight" from our personal efforts to our organization's vision and purpose. At every level of the organization, members must be able to readily assess the effectiveness and the impact of our work.

KDQ 3: "According to Whom Are We High Performing?"

This KDQ asks us to do a thorough analysis of the environment inside and outside our unit/microbusiness/department/organization. This includes an array of stakeholders who can affect us as an organization. In the public and nonprofit sectors, the concept of "the customer" appears especially complex compared to the private sector. Our stakeholders tend to fall into the following categories:

- **our business partners**—people and entities inside and outside of our unit/organization with whom we must work closely to produce "value" for our beneficiaries
- **our chain of beneficiaries**—those who use our products and services (e.g., consumers, citizens, clients, patients, end users)
- **our "food chain"**—those who provide funding, resources, and/or policy direction (e.g., councils, boards, grant sources, other governmental agencies like states and the federal government)
- **our competitors**—those with whom we can or do compete
- **other stakeholders**—those not included in the preceding categories who can influence us in sometimes positive, but more often, potentially negative ways (e.g., the media, regulatory agencies, legislative review or audit functions of other levels of government)

See Chapter 3 for a more thorough discussion of these players in our environment.

KDQ 4: "Why Do We Need to Be Higher Performing?"

This question concerns the need to generate organizational energy to sustain improvement efforts over time. Without answering this question to the satisfaction of ourselves and our workforce, it will be difficult to sustain long-term performance improvement.

People usually identify a number of elements that energize them to perform well. We've certainly seen in the past few years that organizations can improve when faced with imminent danger. When employees are faced with threats to their survival, as an organization or for their continued employment, they often rise to the occasion, meet new challenges in different ways, etc. But this is, in the end, negative energy and, if endured for a long time, actually leads to lower, rather than higher, performance. Threat to survival may "shock" an organization that is complacent into action, but it can't be repeated often; it is a short-term, nonrenewable energy source.

A more personal energy source is self-pride (e.g., "I need to be part of something high performing for my own sense of pride and well-being"). While positive and renewable, self-pride can be injured by an organization, especially in a culture with an autocratic leadership philosophy. The good news is that even if their self-pride has been injured, most people's energy will return when they are allowed to experience it again.

Perhaps the most powerful and sustained positive energy comes when it matters to us whether we are high performing because the missions we have are important: They are critical to the betterment of society—creating sustainable communities, healthy business environments, clean air and water, public safety and health, educated citizens, and many more. For public and nonprofit sectors, these purpose-driven energy sources can be readily apparent: higher moral purpose in abundance. Unfortunately, these are too often taken for granted, rather than articulated clearly and often. People lose sight of them in the detail of their daily work; connection to the bigger picture and purpose is often forgotten. This KDQ examines how an organization identifies its higher moral purpose and communicates it in a meaningful and frequent way so that it energizes and sustains employees toward higher performance even in the face of very difficult times.

KDQ 5: "Are We Delivering the Right 'What'?"

With this question, we evaluate whether the quality of our products and services is appropriate for our customers and how they feel treated by us. We need to clarify

- Who are/could be/should be our beneficiary customers? (We use the results from KDQ 3 here.)
- What are/should be our key products and services to meet the wants, needs, and expectations of our customers, now and in the future?
- Are we delivering excellent customer value?

- Are we effective with our customers? In the stakeholders' opinions, do our products, services, and relationships meet their expectations?

One of the most powerful discussions in units and organizations can be how each of us defines quality. Unfortunately, this discussion rarely takes place. The lack of an explicit consensus on what quality means to us in our context often leads to higher costs, "gold plating," irritation within organizations, and unhappy customers. (See Chapter 3 for a more thorough discussion of **design and features quality**.)

KDQ 6: "How Good Are We at Delivering Our Products and Services?"

In examining a second dimension, **execution quality**, we assess how efficient we are in planning, designing, producing, and delivering our key products and services. Do we have the right (i.e., best-practice or world-class) business strategy, organizational structure, and administrative support systems/work processes, and are they being executed flawlessly?

Many local governments expend their managerial energy on ensuring that established processes are done well rather than that they are efficient. Often, employees report that a significant portion of their effort is wasted due to overly bureaucratic, overly controlled business systems and work processes. Many tools and concepts are available to improve execution quality, but have we brought these skills into our organization and applied them with consistency and discipline? See Chapter 3 for a more thorough discussion of execution quality.

KDQ 7: "How Are We Going to Treat Each Other and Our Partners, Beneficiary Chain, Food Chain, and Other Stakeholders?"

Here, we assess the values foundation of our work culture and resultant way the culture operates in our organization. This often does not get serious attention, because it is dismissed as "soft" or "touchy-feely." But if we care about creating and sustaining a culture of customer focus, continuous improvement, accountability, and mission accomplishment, then we must focus on both ends values and means values. If we have clear desired **ends values** (why our higher moral purpose is important), it will be the means values that guide how we achieve them. Means values must be identified, translated into well-understood criteria, and implemented; they will shape and even set boundaries on our decisions, actions, and behaviors. It is, after all, these means values (the ones actually reflected in everything we do organization-ally and individually, irrespective of what we say they should be) that create our organization's work culture—a leading indicator of future results. How we act is who we are—a change lever doesn't get any harder than that. The discussion on Values to Work Culture in Chapter 4 delves into this question in more detail.

THE SIX CHANGE LEVERS IN THE HPO DIAGNOSTIC/CHANGE MODEL

The HPO Diagnostic Change/Model moves from the three conceptual change levers of **leadership** (philosophy, functions, and form), **vision**, and **values**, through the three applied change levers of **strategy**, **structure**, and **systems**, with the ultimate effect of improving performance. Let's look more closely at these six change levers.

Change Lever 1: Leadership

The first, and most critical, change lever is leadership. In Chapter 1, we saw leadership as a set of functions that everyone at every level of the organization has to help get done. It is not an individual's charisma, vision, or any other trait that makes her a leader; it is causing and helping her unit/organization get the work of leadership done. While the scope of leadership work differs at top-management, mid-management, and line levels, every person at every level has to do his leadership work well if the organization, overall, is to be high performing. Let's be clear: Unless an organization makes full and cor-rect use of the leadership change lever, little else matters, because the change effort for performance improvement is unlikely to be successful. The leader-ship change lever is divided into three parts for examination and discussion.

Change Lever 1.1: Leadership Philosophy

Leadership philosophy is a critical factor determining whether almost any change effort we attempt will be successful. It is a major determinant of our work culture, of the trust level between the workforce and management, and, ultimately, of whether we will be high performing over time. In the roughly left-to-right flowing sequence defined by the HPO Model, leadership philosophy is in the number one position: If we don't get it right, almost nothing downstream in the model works as it should.

An organization's leadership philosophy is the result of the beliefs held by and behaviors of the organization's managers, support systems, and work processes. What does our organization believe about the following and how have those beliefs been implemented in the business systems and work processes we have established?

- the nature of people and their attitudes toward work
- what motivates most people (once basic needs are met)
- the distribution of knowledge and creativity among people in the organization and, as a result, how decisions should be made
- the nature of work—i.e., how work should be designed as a result of answering the previous questions

In Chapter 1, we touched on the exploitative/benevolent autocratic leadership philosophies of the Industrial Model compared to the consultative/participative philosophies underlying the Networked Talent Model. Even from that brief discussion, you might be able to see the connection between how you answer the above questions and the behaviors that would result from those beliefs. For example, if you don't believe that people want to work and do a good job, then you are more likely to want to control them and not give them any significant autonomy, as in the traditional Industrial Model. If, on the other hand, you trust that the vast majority of people want to be part of something important and will work to achieve it, then you are likely to engage them to take on more leadership, management, and task/technical responsibilities, as in the Networked Talent Model.

The development and implementation of a common organizational leadership philosophy is not commonly undertaken. Its absence is a significant barrier to high performance, because it leaves individuals throughout a government free to adopt whatever philosophy they choose. This means that within the organization, people can be treated very differently and the level of engagement can vary widely, hurting both morale and performance levels.

To remedy this, the organization needs to confront the questions above, reach agreement about the shared beliefs, create a statement that describes the leadership philosophy that follows from those beliefs, show examples of the behaviors that are consistent and inconsistent with it, and then take action to see that it actually guides how people act in practice. See Chapter 4 for a more thorough discussion of leadership philosophy, its impact on organizational performance, a set of diagnostic tools for assessing your leadership philosophy, and how to develop and implement a leadership philosophy in an organization.

Change Lever 1.2: Leadership Functions

The second part of the leadership change lever focuses on the five leadership functions that define the work of leadership, and are expected to be performed by every employee at every level of the organization. These are the leadership skills, abilities, and behaviors in the Networked Talent Model (see Figure 1.1). The five leadership functions are:

1. **Strategic Stakeholder Value Analysis (SSVA).** The discussion of KDQ 3 (According to whom are we high performing?) identified some of the specific aims of this leadership function: Who are/should be our customers? What do they want, need, and expect now and in the future? Can we map who our partners, the beneficiary chain, the food chain, and other stakeholders are, and what is the quality of our relationships with them? How well do they feel our products, services, and relationships meet their expectations? Have we completed an environmental scan, market analysis, and political analysis/feasibility review?

2. **Vision/Values connected to Strategy, Structure, and Systems.** When performing the second leadership function, we assess and "pull" the other five change levers: vision, values, strategy, structure, and systems. In brief, this function involves causing a shared vision and values for the unit/organization to be articulated and lived; the vision/values of each unit must "nest" within the next higher level's vision/values.

Activities in the vision work include visioning, strategic thinking, strategic planning, tactical or operational planning, and monitoring/ recovery. The values work includes articulating our leadership philosophy, individual behavioral values, and operating systems values, specifying the behaviors that are required and those prohibited based on the values. To make the values "stick," we also want to create a feedback, coaching, and resolution process to implement and enforce the values across the organization.

3. **Suprasystems Integration/Stewardship.** After dividing an organization into departments, offices, units/microbusinesses, and so forth so that work can be accomplished, we also need to "glue" the parts of our organization back together to accomplish the organization's vision and create mechanisms that align the parts to form a whole. It requires a **stewardship mind-set** among all employees, rising above "turf" to serve and be responsible for the larger whole. We must all be "stewards of the whole, rather than just owners of the pieces," and it requires linking with others to address crossorganizational issues. This is critical because in the absence of a stewardship mind-set, focusing only on "my part" as the most important part of the organization becomes the norm. No organizational structure can overcome a self-centered, "Me and my unit first and to heck with everyone else!" mind-set.

4. **Learning, Thinking, Changing, and Renewing.** How do we ensure that we stay on the cutting edge both individually and organizationally and build a **learning/renewing organization**? At the personal level, this function requires each of us to stay current in our technical field and grow in competencies that will help us run the microbusiness of which we are a part. At the organizational level, this work involves benchmarking, best practices analysis, reengineering, and continuous improvement; it is similar to the learning organization concepts in Peter Senge's book, *The Fifth Discipline*.[6]

5. **Enabling, Empowering, Engaging, and Energizing.** The previous function is about learning; this one is about teaching, mentoring, motivating, engaging, and bureaucracy busting; providing knowledge, skills, and information required to make good decisions; being proactive; and removing barriers to participation and empowerment. What should be our organizational systems and mechanisms that ensure this function is performed?

These five leadership functions are explained in more detail in Chapters 3 and 4.

Change Lever 1.3: Leadership Form

In examining and discussing the five leadership functions as an executive team, a local government on the road toward higher performance will look at whether these functions are getting done effectively at all levels in their organization, and, if not, why. Generally, most find the functions are not getting done well uniformly across the organization, but they are less clear as to *why* they aren't getting done. Most traditional hierarchies run with cultures and management systems intended largely to get pressing, near-term tasks done, even when many of these near-term issues are not very significant to the long-term improvement and success of the organization. This near-term mind-set moves them from one crisis to the next, leaving little time for addressing many significant but less-pressing, longer-term issues. Although dealing with such issues could have prevented many crises from occurring in the first place, many still ignore the longer-term focus on more efficient operations. This "busy work" environment produces a sense of urgency and a constant pressure to meet commitments or deliver short-term outputs. The remedy, building a disciplined change mechanism, ensures that the significant-but-not-so-pressing **work of leadership** gets done.

This final part of the leadership change lever relates to building such change mechanisms at all appropriate levels of the organization to ensure that the work of leadership is done with discipline and continuity. The vast majority of leadership work gets done best by shifting from individuals in positions of authority acting alone to employing networks—**leadership teams**—where authority is shared and actions are collaborative. Individuals at all levels of an organization must join with their colleagues to become stewards of their microbusinesses and of the larger organization. There is still a hierarchy and chain of command in this approach; if we can't all agree, the person in authority will take all the good input from team members and make the call. But the role of people in management positions shifts from command and control, in most instances, to consultation and participation—i.e., engendering smart decisions out of a network of smart professionals.

Because many organizations seem to have an ingrained functional hierarchy and a top-down, benevolent autocratic leadership philosophy, creating a protected environment—a mental space—outside the traditional hierarchy in which leadership teams can learn to do the work of leadership is essential. This space is called a **parallel organization** because it depends on the same people as the hierarchy but asks them to operate in leadership teams under different rules and relationships to each other in a space parallel to the current traditional hierarchy. Here, team members learn and practice new behaviors, relationships, and skills with colleagues who are committed to each other's individual, as well as collective, success. From this new space, the trappings of the traditional hierarchy (including silos) can actually be changed. Leadership teams do this developmental work at the same time as they are tackling the issues of the second change lever, vision and values connected to strategy, structure, and systems. Leadership form is discussed in more detail in Chapter 5.

Change Levers 2 through 6: Vision, Values, Strategy, Structure, and Systems

The remaining five HPO Model change levers represent a movement from the **conceptual** (vision and values) to the **applied** (strategy, structure, and systems). Two pieces of work need to be done at every level of the organization: **vision work** and **values work**. They are not the same (although they interact), and they require different thought processes. Both are critical to high performance; doing either one without the other is insufficient in sustaining performance improvement. Let's take a look at vision work first:

Change Lever 2: Vision

Vision work is, perhaps, the most time consuming of all the change levers, since it addresses six of the seven key diagnostic questions (all except KDQ 7). It is important to understand that vision work is *not* just about developing another vision statement. Let's face it: Most units and organizations have enough vision statements. What they often don't have is a shared vision—that is, when members of the organization are asked where the organization is headed, they all point in the same direction. Do members of the organization test what they do daily against a mutually agreed upon causal sequence of actions designed to move the organization toward the shared vision?

Visioning moves from a more abstract, broad, and long-term perspective, through an increasingly focused set of activities, including strategic thinking and planning, tactical/operational planning and execution, and monitoring and recovery. We call this process the **Vision to Performance Cycle.** This funnel-like process cycles down from broad and general at the top to near-term and specific at the bottom. The objective at the end of the process is for all individuals to be aligned on what they are going to do each day, with whom, and using which resources to move them individually and the organization toward accomplishing the vision. Each level of the organization—from microbusinesses to the whole—needs a vision that nests into the next higher level. Visioning does not come from the top alone; it also wells up from units to create organization-wide alignment. We explore vision work in more detail in Chapter 3.

Change Lever 3: Values

The second main piece of work for units and organization, values work, is qualitatively different from the preceding vision work; it focuses on KDQ 7 (How do we treat each other and our partners, beneficiary chain, food chain, and other stakeholders?). Typically, some are challenged by this work; those who have dedicated their careers to technical fields may be less comfortable with what they see as the "touchy-feely, people side" of organizational performance improvement. The fact is that people *are* the organization. The values work is about creating a work culture that releases each individual's discretionary effort: the choice of individuals to be fully engaged and work at their highest level of capability, rather than just hard enough to get by.

Like the Vision to Performance Cycle, the **Values to Work Culture Cycle** proceeds from high-level, conceptual values work downward, with each lower level becoming more near-term and more specific. The values work begins by addressing the three means values that are the building blocks of our organization's work culture:

- **Leadership philosophy.** How do we want individuals with hierarchical authority over other individuals (e.g., managers and team leaders) to treat those they supervise? As described earlier, we ask teams through-out the organization to participate in producing a leadership philoso-phy, explaining the assumptions upon which management actions are to be based and judged.

- **Individual behavioral values.** These are a larger, overarching set of val-ues describing how we treat each other—and, by extension, our stake-holders—whether we are managers or not. These values help define the human side of the organization's work culture; they provide a standard for judging interpersonal behavior.
- **Operating systems values.** The third part of values work states how we want the organization's systems and processes (e.g., support systems like HR, purchasing, and IT, as well as technical work processes) to treat us. These values define the technical side of the organization's work cul-ture and provide a standard for judging the values embedded in the organization's strategies, structures, and systems/processes.

We explore the values work in more detail—including how to implement the values so that the organization's work culture begins to improve—in Chapter 4.

Change Lever 4: Strategy

Using this lever, we examine and ensure that our overall **business strategy/ business model** is sound and that our service delivery approaches and strat-egies support us in accomplishing our vision and mission effectively and efficiently. We verify that they encompass the leading practices available to achieve the results we seek. We want to be sure that we have a sound approach to strategic outsourcing decisions and an efficient way to handle a surge in demand and surplus production capacity.

Change Lever 5: Structure

Our **organizational structure** should reflect an organizing principle that allows us to support the accomplishment of our vision and strategy. Most organizations have inherited a siloed structure from their traditional Indus-trial Model past. Even though examining structure might be threatening to the established order, we need to consider whether shifting to a Networked Talent Model might suggest alternative structures that would help to improve performance. For instance, what are the microbusinesses that should be operating to achieve our goals? Are there appropriate macrobusinesses that should bring together the network of resources, irrespective of home departments, who are required to think through, organize, and deliver the results that our customers seek?

Change Lever 6: Systems

Finally, we must review each of our **administrative support systems and work processes**. We assess the extent to which the systems and processes aid us in improving our performance. Are they leading-practice or world-class? Are we executing them flawlessly? How would we know if we were? Too often, we assume that these systems and processes are givens and that there is little we can do improve them—they work pretty darn well. This may sometimes be true, but we'd want to test carefully whether they can be improved before reaching that conclusion. Typically, organizations are seriously deficient in the knowledge, skills, tools, and discipline to examine and improve their systems and processes, squandering valuable organizational resources on continuing ineffective and inefficient ones and frustrating the workforce.

This chapter outlined a great deal of work that is required for an organization progressing toward its full potential and becoming high performing. Think back to the story of Bellevue. While the city was not trying to implement the HPO Model in any formal way, the city manager, Steve Sarkozy, had attended the Senior Executive Institute at the University of Virginia and brought back to Bellevue a consciousness of the elements of the model and good business practices. He used them to frame for the staff the outcomes that the city needed to achieve in development services. In this case, you saw the new line of business (a macrobusiness) thinking through with the help of its customers what high performance should be and being diligent about the measurement systems to know if they were achieving it. They assessed whether they were delivering what the customers wanted, needed, and expected, and how good they were in providing it. In a parallel organization, they spent the strategic thinking time doing the work of leadership to create a compelling mission/

vision and values to focus on the higher purpose they sought. They created an organizational culture that engaged employees in the evaluation and improvement of their systems and processes. They created a structure that integrated the efforts of several departments into a macrobusiness that served a unified city purpose.

The next three chapters of this book take a more detailed look at the Vision and Values Cycles and the leadership teams needed to accomplish them. We'll see several good examples of how localities used the principles in the HPO Model to improve their own performance. This will not only help to make the necessary work clearer; it might also point you to some places in your own government where similar work is occurring and which can be built upon to accelerate the larger organization's progress.

---

1   Steve Sarkozy was the city manager during this entire period. He attended the Senior Executive Institute at the University of Virginia and became acquainted with the HPO Model. He applied a number of the model's principles in Bellevue without making explicit references to the model.

2   Likert, Rensis. 1961. *New Patterns of Management.* New York, NY: McGrawHill; Weisbord, Marvin. "Organizational Diagnosis: Six Places to Look for Trouble with or without a Theory." *Group & Organization Studies*, Volume 1, Number 4, December 1976, pp. 430–447; and Peters, Thomas J. and Waterman, Robert H. Jr. 1983. *In Search of Excellence*, New York, NY: Harper & Row. Note: we prefer to use the "older" seminal works in the Organizational Development, Change Management, and other literature in our HPO Diagnostic/Change Model, and then, if the client is interested, show how more modern material builds on the base laid by the "giants" in the fields we cover.

3   Collins, Jim. 2001. *Good to Great: Why Some Companies Make the Leap . . . and Others Don't.* New York, NY: Harper Collins.

4   Senge, Peter M. 1990. *The Fifth Discipline.* New York, NY: Doubleday.

From Vision to Performance

The seven key diagnostic questions (KDQs) align our organization's purpose, the work we do, how we accomplish it, and the work culture that encourages high performance; these are the areas Chapters 3 and 4 address. This chapter describes in more detail the first six key diagnostic questions that make up the Vision to Performance (V2P) work in the High-Performance Organization Diagnostic/Change Model. Moving from visioning through strategic thinking and multiyear strategic planning informs a series of discrete, short-term actions that move the organization in the proper direction—from the things we *could do* to a fewer number of things that we *must do* and, ultimately, to plan for those things we, in fact, *will do*. In Chapter 4, we will look at situations people have encountered based on the seventh KDQ, the essential nature of values and work culture, known as the Values to Work Culture (V2WC) work.

These two bodies of work represent somewhat different efforts and are separated here primarily because it is easier to understand them as separate cycles. However, while we can work with them in partial isolation, neither Vision to Performance nor Values to Work Culture can function separately. They are, in fact, elaborately linked. We cannot improve processes, change human resource systems, or create new products and services without considering how they support workforce alignment with our values. But if we are to align behaviors and organizational systems with our values, we must have strategies and tactics that are supportive of, and perhaps even focused exclusively on, that effort. In spite of our best effort at reductionism, we must constantly be aware of the need to understand the organization as a system and reflect upon its integration and alignment. As a result, we will need to insert the Values to Work Culture efforts in our Vision to Performance analysis.

CASE STUDY

Fire Plan Review Unit Improvements in Prince William County, Virginia

Prince William County, Virginia, has a population of more than 400,000, covering a 348-square-mile suburb of Washington, D.C. The fire and rescue department includes twenty fire stations, with more than five hundred uniformed and civilian personnel and hundreds of volunteers. Within the community safety section, the fire marshal's office has a unit responsible for reviewing fire protection systems plans to ensure new commercial and residential developments meet the fire code requirements.

This unit was seen by stakeholders both inside and outside the county government as actively restraining the larger enterprise's accomplishment of its vision and mission. Their actions were causing a misalignment between critical processes and desired countywide outcomes. Their work outcomes might even have been at cross-purposes with the outcome needs of the county. They were oblivious to this conflict as they pursued their understanding of their technical work. This reminds us of the "boiling frog" story: If you put a frog in a pot of scalding water, it will jump out immediately. But if it is placed on the stove in a pot of room-temperature water that's heated slowly, it will be oblivious to the change of its environment, fail to perceive the rising temperature, and meet a sad ending.

From their point of view, however, the Prince William County fire marshal's office plan review unit felt overworked, and their morale was low during a peak development period. The most common complaints about the unit were that permits were taking twelve or more weeks for review and rejection rates were high. In some cases, plans were rejected three or more times before approval. Developer reaction wasn't a big problem in their eyes because they saw themselves as stern, tough, effective regulators who existed to keep the community safe. They saw their charter as far removed from economic development of the county. Ninety percent of permits applications were rejected after initial submission. Interestingly, they did not know this metric until their chief asked them to compile it. Like the frog's boiling water, this gradual increase in economic development-related workload and the unit's lack of attention to stakeholder views was too incremental for the staff to realize the scope of the problem. They were simply too close to the issue to see it.

As the high rejection rate and the slow approval process hampered economic development in the county, the fire marshal's office was being hammered by developers and other customers, economic development staff, and the county executive. The county elected officials were highly concerned. Fire marshal personnel were in the way without knowing it until the pressure became untenable during a time when development was an important part of the county's health and future, not to mention its tax base. Now they were in boiling water and actually beginning to feel the heat—not an ideal time to be doing vision to performance work. A quick reboot of the system was required.

Around this time, Assistant Fire Chief Kevin McGee was appointed as the new fire marshal. He declared an emergency to show the importance of the situation. To get people's attention and initiate work on the problem, he instituted the "Incident Command System." He knew that the solution required the entire staff to work on the problem with their stakeholders, using focus groups to gather information and outsiders to introduce new perspectives to further understand the situation. He first asked the county executive to extend enough time to allow the office to identify and implement improvements. He also sought out and received the support of major external stakeholders, including developers, many of whom were aware that the situation might become worse by diverting resources to finding solutions before it could get better. This relieved some immediate pressure and made some new staff resources available.

Transferred from the operations section of the department, McGee wanted to better understand the work processes, leadership philosophy, and level of staff engagement in this unit. When the staff analyzed the "nature of work" within the unit, they found that the most time (90 percent) was dedicated to task/technical work, with 8 percent spent on managing the daily routine, about 1 percent doing leadership work, and about 1 percent working as a team using their team skills. McGee was determined to change this short-term task focus to one that would engage all the talents, skills, and abilities of his staff.

First, McGee scheduled meetings to address review backlogs and needed process improvements. But the staff were so entrenched in their task work that many simply ignored the meetings, justifying their actions with the perceived importance of their technical duties and working through an enormous stack of fire protection system plans. So McGee personally escorted the employees to the first few meetings. He assured them that their involvement was critical and that finding ways to improve service was, especially in the immediate future and for short periods, more essential than performing task duties.

Next, he administered a short version of a leadership philosophy assessment instrument based on the work of Rensis Likert. The instrument showed that, in practice, the unit operated predominantly in a benevolent autocratic philosophy inherited from their earlier Industrial Phase roots as described in Chapter 1. It also showed, though, that such a broad range of philosophies coexisted in the unit that there could be no common agreement on how the unit would operate. When this became clear, they quickly laid out common expectations based on the Networked Talent Model and operated in a consultative/participative leadership philosophy—the two systems Likert found that support sustained high performance. Their vision to performance work was dependent upon the creation of an engaging work culture, a primary determinant of which is such a leadership philosophy. After doing much of the work described in this story, a second round of the Likert instrument revealed the results shown in Figure 3.1. (See Chapter 4 for a more detailed explanation of the instrument and the four leadership philosophies.) The declaration of expectations and the consequent actions had radically shifted so that the desired leadership philosophy had been realized.

Another early step involved developing a shared vision for the unit that would nest within the overall county vision and the county government's internal vision. The overall vision for the county is

> Prince William County is a premier community where we treasure the richness of our past and the promise of our future. We are diverse and dynamic with a thriving economy where citizens and businesses grow and succeed together. We are a global technology and business leader for the 21st century.

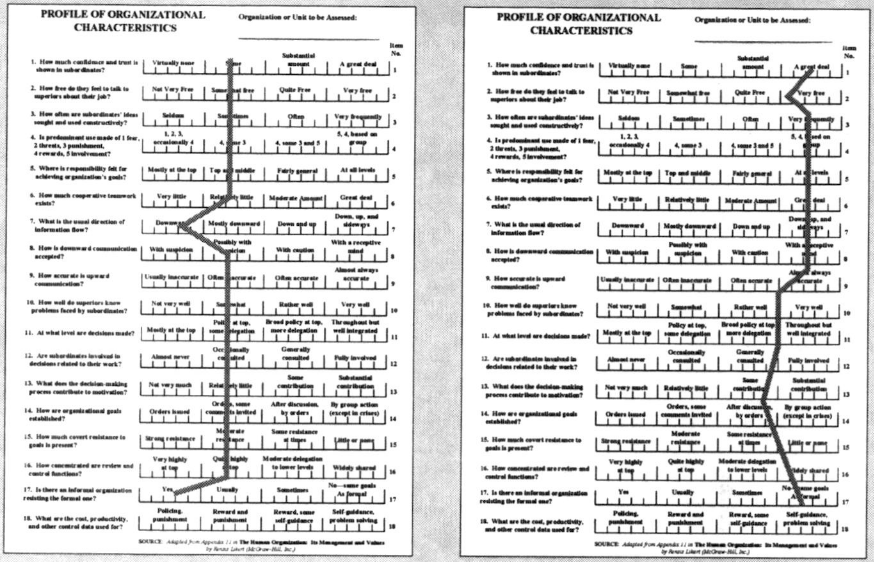

BEFORE **AFTER**

FIGURE 3.1

The county government's internal vision, which nests into the larger county vision, is

> Prince William County Government is an organization where elected leaders, staff and citizens work together to make our community the best.
> We, as employees, pledge to do the right thing for the customer and the community every time.
> We, as a learning organization, commit to provide the necessary support and opportunities for each employee to honor this pledge.

The unit had seen itself contributing to the county's vision primarily through its emergency and hazard prevention services. When it refocused its understanding of the county's and the government's visions and how its own vision nested within them, the unit realized that it was underachieving in two areas: contributing to a thriving economy where businesses grow and pledging to do the right thing for the customer and the community every time. They now understood that they had seen their contribution just as strict enforcement of safety standards for the broader community, not also serving the individual customers at their counter. This realization created the motivation needed to reshape their vision and goals so that they would align with the larger organization

The vision created by the fire marshal's office to align with the county and government visions held that "customers would know as much about how to prepare a code compliant fire protection system plan as does our fire marshal's office staff." This vision required a change in philosophy from their earlier strict code enforcement approach (under which developers were not to be trusted and needed to be regulated, and it was the staff's job to find what was wrong with the developers' plans) to a more collaborative code compliance approach (where developers were seen as the customer, thus seen as having every intent to comply with the building and fire prevention codes and could do so if they knew as much as a fire marshal about what was required for plan approval). This philosophical shift meant that the fire marshal's staff was not responsible for finding fault with customer plans. Instead, they devised a process to help customers make improvements in the quality of their plans. The result was a new regard for stewardship of the countywide mission and for the success of residential and business customers while ensuring fire safety for the community.

The unit then undertook an improvement effort refocused on how to help their customers submit complete and safe permits the first time, rather than simply rejecting the unsafe or marginal ones. This process involved long, frequent meetings with the permit review staff, development community representatives, other fire and rescue department members, county economic developers, and other key stakeholders. The fire marshal's staff sought input from these customers, partners, and other stakeholders, demonstrated that they understood the needs of each, and pledged to improve the review and permitting process. Focus groups helped elicit the primary concerns, explore alternatives, and map out solutions. When it became clear that the customers were not adversaries and could actually be advocates, opportunities for agreement expanded.

In the end, a radically different strategy to guide process improvement emerged, as did a new appreciation among the staff toward the willingness of the development community to take on more responsibility for achieving an acceptable set of fire protection system plans. The fire marshal's unit had ultimately switched their mind-set from an enforcement only mentality to a belief in collaborative building and fire prevention code compliance.

The system changes were dramatic. First, the staff sought to assure that their customers could become sufficiently adept at submitting successful plans. They created well-attended training seminars and sessions in which they shared significant technical knowledge with those who would become responsible for developing and submitting the plans. They created a walk-through process where the staff could provide constructive advice and customers could make on-the-spot corrections. They developed a code compliance manual showing how to prepare a plan and made it accessible through their website. They also encouraged predevelopment meetings for major projects that initiated a dialogue before the developer began drawing the plans.

The working relationship and trust developed to a level where, after the first year, two new services were created: Sprinkler Express and Fire Alarm Express. These allowed for automatic permit approval for certain types of work without presenting a plan until after the work was done and the final inspection was requested. The staff reconfigured their task from a primarily enforcement-based focus to coaching the system plans designers through knowledge transfer. When a plan arrived in general compliance with requirements, the review process would be smoother, quicker, and more efficient. Further, the staff realized that the one-size-fits-all permit review process had treated simple submissions the same way as complex ones and reviewed all plans sequentially. Seeing a new opportunity, the staff, in consultation with its customers, devised a radically different process to triage new plan submissions, differentiating among the kinds of applications and establishing alternative review processes and timetables. These process improvements were made entirely through ideas offered by the permitting staff—those who were closest to the work, as opposed to the fire marshal or higher-level authorities of the county government.

The results were remarkable: From a base of twelve weeks, the staff reduced average plan review time to four weeks and then to two weeks. Some applications were approved in a single walk-through process. Later, some plans even had automatic approval so there was no wait time at all. The former 90 percent rejection rate became 90 percent acceptance on first submission. In consulting customers for their expectations and engaging line employees as consultants rather than as just implementers of a management-designed system, the fire marshal's unit was able to refocus to achieve a clearer vision and institute multiple cost-saving and process streamlining initiatives that might otherwise have been impossible to develop or achieve.

In the Prince William County case study, the power of connecting the plan review unit's work directly to both the county's overall vision and the new subordinate vision within the unit accomplished two feats: It clarified and focused the purpose of the unit's work, and it led to a total restructuring of the way it operated to achieve high performance. Through a radical shift in the work culture, the line employees were enabled to create solutions that led to dramatic results.

As noted earlier, an organization's Vision to Performance work is often the most time consuming of all the leadership work because it has to deal with six of the seven key diagnostic questions and four of the six change levers. Figure 3.2 ties together the six KDQs and four change levers that are addressed in vision work.

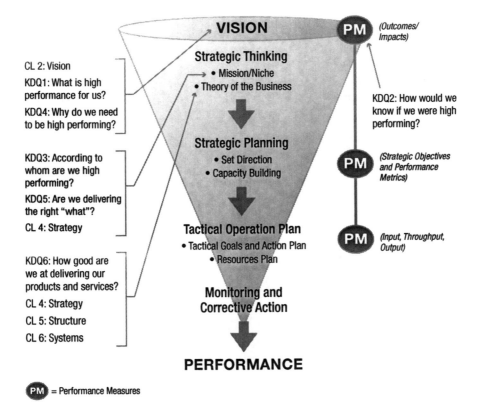

FIGURE 3.2 The Vision to Performance Cycle

The Vision to Performance Cycle is both flexible and scalable: One can start anywhere in the process and choose the right pieces and parts to create a number of approaches, and any or all levels from the individual to the top of the organization can do the work. For example, if the organization is interested only in improving the way work is currently performed ("Let's do more or less" or "We need to be better at what we're doing now"), the lower part of the model (Tactical Operational Plan) may be all that is required at the moment. If the interest is in moving from one set of priorities to another without a fundamental rethinking of who we are and why we exist ("Let's move from here to there"), the middle of the model (Strategic Planning and Tactical Operation Plan) might be all that is required. However, if one is looking for something more transformational, like improving overall performance and culture ("We should work on who we are and what we do in the future"), the entire model will need to be employed. The Vision to Performance (V2P) Cycle as a thought process versus a prescriptive set of steps allows for any one of these. On the other hand, in a world where taxpayers want more services and lower taxes while other revenue sources are static, where old models of economic growth and job development no longer seem to apply, and where technologies continue to evolve at an unprecedented rate, anything short of transformational thinking is all too short-sighted.

VISION

At the top of the Vision Cycle, units at every level of the organization begin their strategic thinking by addressing KDQ 1 (What is high performance for us?) and KDQ 4 (Why do we need to be high performing?). This directly addresses the work of Change Lever 2 (Vision). These discussions focus on what our end values should be (what higher moral purpose we seek, our desired future state, and what outcomes and impacts we want).

We noted earlier that members at all levels of the organization must agree on what high performance means. They must understand this for the whole organization, for their unit, and individually. The definitions are nested and aligned with the level above. In the Prince William County fire plan review unit, the vision refocused on how it could contribute toward the achievement of the county's vision of having a thriving economy where citizens and businesses grow and succeed together while still fulfilling its public safety mission.

They reasoned that if customers knew the applicable codes well and how to create effective fire suppression systems, the plan review process would flow much more smoothly and safe development could proceed more quickly.

Recall that the basic definition of high performance is the simultaneous efficient delivery of (1) quality products and services, (2) outstanding customer value, and (3) sound financial performance—or "Pick 3." The need to deliver these consistently, sustainably, and with continuous improvement over time pushes our definition from Pick 3 to Pick 3+. When answering KDQ 1 (What is high performance for us?) and defining our vision, we must state clearly what Pick 3+ means for our stakeholders, the organization as a whole, and for our units, ensuring that we have articulated our desired outcomes in all three categories.

KDQ 4 (Why do we need to be high performing?) is generally answered early in the visioning process, as it is a critical factor in successful change efforts. This question is looking for organizational energy to sustain our improvement efforts over the long time period required. If we can't answer this question to the satisfaction of ourselves and our workforce and don't get something personal out of the change, then they may not support the change effort long enough for performance to improve. Noel Tichy argues that each of us needs to develop a "teachable point of view": a succinct, personal, and compelling set of arguments delivered with passion to ourselves, our coworkers, and others, reminding us of the importance of our efforts[1]. If we aren't motivated at this early stage, very little of the rest of the work will be done with the drive, determination, and desire that is required. In order to generate the high levels of commitment needed, the answer to "Why do we need to be high performing?" should appeal to our higher moral purpose, as described in Chapter 2. Though some organizations have difficulty identifying their higher moral purpose, local governments typically do not. We are often directly linked to our purpose in all our direct service delivery activities. If we don't do a "great" job, people suffer. People on the line, especially in public safety positions, see this connection more easily than others. The organization's challenge is to make clear to all workers, including those in support agencies and administrative positions, that they are significant contributors to the community's well-being.

Answering KDQs 1 and 4 definitively compels us to address KDQ 2 (How would we know if we were high performing?) and KDQ 3 (According to whom are we high performing?). KDQ 2 adds specificity and clarity to our definition by requiring us to spell out how we will measure what we mean by high performance, and KDQ 3 gets the "voice of the customer" into the discussion.

KDQ 2 helps us chart the future with landmarks that everyone can understand, asking, "How would we know?" This opens the discussion of measurement, and it applies at every level of the V2P Cycle. We need to be certain that our efforts are actually achieving the intended direction.

At the top of the Vision Cycle, where we are future-focused, we can't measure *now* whether we are *there*; but we should be able to say what *there* looks like. Think of it this way: If we are using a GPS to get to a place, we need first to enter the location so it knows where we are headed. Later, as we travel along the way, we can determine whether we're on the right track or need a course correction. The indicators at the top of the cycle are often called "trailing" or "lagging" indicators. Since these indicators measure the end we are seeking (e.g., did we get the longer-term results we wanted?), they are also called outcome or impact measures.

We want to identify these measures early in order to focus our thought process on what actions we must take both strategically and tactically to move them in the right direction. The measures can also help us evaluate the effectiveness of our planning process. If we are executing perfectly and our outcome measures are not moving in the direction we expected, there is likely a flaw in our causal reasoning, in the strategies we are employing, or both. Without a good measurement and management review process, we cannot be certain that our strategy and our actions are correct. The measurement system helps identify early on what is working and what needs revision. It also offers the clarity necessary to truly understand the vision statement, being clear about what it means at every level of the organization, and what performance criteria should be for individuals and groups.

For example, here is the customer service vision for a certain Southern city in the US:

> "The vision of the city . . . is to be recognized as the prevailing provider of city services through its progressive organization and strategic partnerships with, and for the aid of, the local community, including our city employees, residents, and the business community. City employees strive to offer the best customer service to the citizens of the city . . . by providing exceptional value and quality."

You be the judge. As one of this city's employees, would you know what you should do and what you shouldn't do based on this statement? If not, two things must be done:

(1) You must be a part of a discussion of what this statement means for you personally, as it relates to your job function. This is part of vision work at every level—truly understanding what words mean and translating them into boundaries for the actions we are going to take.

(2) We must break this statement into "vision elements"—that is, deconstruct it into specifics that represent the desired future state and that are measurable. Look closely at the statement above and you can see the following strategic elements:

"The vision of the city . . . is to be:

(1) recognized as the prevailing provider of city services through its

(2) progressive organization, and

(3) strategic partnerships with, and for the aid of, the local community, including our city employees, residents and the business community.

(4) City employees strive to offer the best customer service to the citizens of the city . . . by providing exceptional value and quality."

These, then, are the items in the vision statement that we should measure, because these are the outcomes we want to deliver. If we can measure these things, then we can develop strategies for improvement, and we can be assured that the actions we take will have the desired effect—or at the very least, we will have an early-warning system indicating when we must reenter the strategic thinking process.

For each of these vision elements, we must then ask KDQ 2 (How would we know if were high performing?). We want to have a good grasp of our trailing indicators—our outcome and impact measures—demonstrating (after a predicted time delay) that our causal thinking—our logic model—works and is producing the results we predicted.

This entire process is iterative which is why it is called a "cycle." We are never finished thinking strategically, though we will temporarily suspend changes to our vision in order to create and implement our plans. This means, as it relates specifically to vision, that we can expect the subsequent strategic thinking processes to inform our thinking and influence the vision as we move forward. We should imagine a feedback loop between the subsequent strategic thinking processes going back to the vision and, perhaps, altering it. We have now answered, at least preliminarily, the first four KDQs:

1. What is high performance for us?
2. How would we know if we were high performing?
3. According to whom are we high performing?
4. Why do we need to be high performing?

With the destination defined, we can now begin thinking about how we are going to get there. As we drop down a level in the V2P Cycle, we come to **strategic thinking**. Larry Bossidy and Ram Charan write that "You cannot have an execution culture without robust dialogue—one that brings reality to the surface through openness, candor, and informality." In keeping with the organization's leadership philosophy—recognizing the value of collaboration and ownership of the results—strategic thinking is an opportunity, as they further note, to create "truth over harmony."[2] These discussions must be open, honest, and perhaps contentious, for part of their value is creating shared stewardship of the entire effort and alignment of our thinking and goals. Chapter 5 will discuss the need for stewardship and how to create mechanisms to achieve it.

Strategic thinking has two parts: **mission/niche thinking** and **theory of the business thinking**. We want to explore these areas before moving to the closing activity, strategic planning, which commits us to a course of action. Strategic thinking, by contrast, is an opening up activity. Organizations should think before they plan and open up before they close to be certain that they have considered all the conditions and options before making binding decisions. On the other hand, organizations should not let *perfect* get in the way of *good enough*. Since visioning is a cyclical process and will come around again in a year (or more frequently if needed), we don't have to be flawless in our execution of these steps the first time through the cycle—we just need to be better next year than this year and to start preparing now so that next time we have what is needed to improve the process. If strategic thinking dramatically changes our view of the desired future state, however, we may need to revise the vision immediately. Let's look at the two parts of strategic thinking:

- Mission/niche thinking looks at KDQ 5 (Are we doing the right 'what'?) and KDQ 3 (According to whom are we high performing?). It is an interactive analysis, working back and forth between these two questions. In the course of this analysis, we will explore our key products and services, the appropriate level of design and features quality required, and our strategic stakeholders.
- Theory of the business thinking looks at KDQ 6 (How good are our processes at delivering our mission/niche?). We also need to ask: Are we as efficient as we can be in delivering our products and services? How good is our execution quality? Do we have the right business strategy (business model), organizational structure, and support systems and work processes?

STRATEGIC THINKING: PART 1—MISSION/NICHE THINKING

There are a variety of mechanisms and tools in the mission/niche approach. In addition to the key products and services, design and features quality, and strategic stakeholders value analysis, we may also use tools such as an environmental scan, a **SWOC/T** (strength, weakness, opportunities, and constraints/threats) analysis approach, a benchmarking and leading practices review, a gap analysis, and a force-field analysis. All of these approaches pose a series of questions to be explored to better understand where we are today and where we want/need to be in the future. These exercises will inform our strategic planning activity in the next step of the V2P Cycle. As a result, we can expect that the answers will influence and be influenced by each other.

Paradoxically, it can helpful to begin the strategic thinking process by thinking in a tactical and problem-focused way with a challenges review. Challenges are the critical forces in the larger environment (internal and external) that currently significantly do or could affect our business in either the near or intermediate term. They are often categorized into specific types: **organizational** (structure, knowledge management, human capital, and work culture issues), **performance** (budget, customer satisfaction, and work and administrative systems and processes), **market/business** (products, services, and business niche), and **technical** (information, infrastructure, and technology). This early discussion about things we know about now rather than things we are imagining for the future is significant in beginning the more difficult discussions to come and in prioritizing actions later in the process.

KDQ 5 (Are we delivering the right "what"?) engages us in an analysis of what we deliver—our products and services, whom we deliver them to, and how we treat them in the process. It is an assessment of our core competencies and how they translate into products and services. We integrate the thinking and analysis into a concrete set of specifications. Some of the questions to be explored are

- What is/should be our major impact or outcome?
- What should we take responsibility for accomplishing in the near term (three to five years) and the longer term (six to thirty years)?
- What is or should be our organization's unique niche?
- What are our key products and services?
- Are we delivering these key products and services at the appropriate level of design and features quality (DFQ) to meet the wants, needs, and expectations of the customer? Do they achieve the results they aim for? Are these products and services the right ones for the future or will they change as a result of customer requirements and changing technology? What are the implications of this for the competencies we will require in the future?
- Are we providing the right products and services to the right customers? If we have the right products and services but the wrong customers, are there other customers that could benefit from the products and services that we deliver? If we have the right customers and wrong key products and services, then let's change the products and services. Are we effective in serving our customers?
- Do we produce excellent customer value (in the customers'

eyes—according to the beneficiary chain, food chain, partners, and other stakeholders)?

One of the more powerful necessary discussions surrounds how we individually and collectively define quality. Our quality definition brings focus on both the customers' wants, needs, and expectations and on the organization's support systems and work processes. These are two very different perspectives and result in two dimensions of quality. Let's look at the first dimension, design and features quality (DFQ). (The second dimension, execution quality (EQ), is addressed in the following discussion of theory of the business.)

To produce the design and features quality in our products and provide services that meet the customers' wants, needs, and expectations, we must have enough interaction with our customers to understand what they require and for them to understand what we will deliver. Looking at Figure 3.3, we can demonstrate on a vertical scale, with the bottom labeled "modest" design and features quality—using a Toyota-made automobile analogy, think Corolla-level features: outstanding fit and finish, reparability, and reliability but modest design and features—and the top of the scale labeled "complex" design and features quality—think Lexus-level features: outstanding fit and finish, reparability, and reliability but more complex design and features, more bells and whistles. This doesn't mean that the Corolla is a poor choice; it simply has fewer features and thus costs less. The question, then, is what is appropriate? The determination of whether to deliver a Lexus, a Corolla, or something in between (like a Camry) is a decision for the purchasers based on their needs, preferences, and budget.

If we deliver too low on the scale, below the customers' design and features requirements, we get dissatisfied customers who say we are delivering "poor quality." On the other hand, if we deliver too high and try to charge the customer for the additional features, we get dissatisfied customers who say we are forcing them to accept more than they bargained for and more than they want to pay for. If we exceed their expectations and do it without direct charge to them, we may have "delighted" our customers, but we run the risk of inflating their expectations beyond our ability to deliver in the future. Moreover, if we provide more complexity than required, we have created products and services that may be cumbersome, too hard to use, and not intuitive enough.

If we are going to make a decision to raise the level of DFQ, we should do so strategically, understanding the implications of doing so.

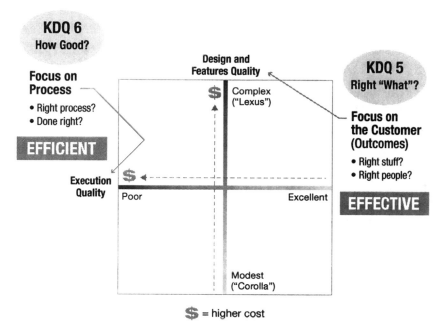

FIGURE 3.3 The Definition of Quality

Interestingly, this over-delivering on design and features quality will likely also inflate our costs and extend our schedule, both of which make us less efficient. Because the customers' wants, needs, and expectations, and often the cost of producing higher levels of features, are frequently unknown to the technical individuals performing the work, they may unintentionally deliver too high a level. Or they may do it because it lowers the risk of dissatisfaction from producing below what is expected by the customer, they take pride in producing high-quality work, they (mistakenly) believe that it is always correct to "delight" the customer, or because it is just more interesting to do so.

The term that describes this mind-set is the *gold-plated factor,* and it is one of the biggest sources of waste in government. If we are gold plating, we are delivering "less with more"—the opposite of what we ought to be doing. One way to do "more with less" is to stop gold plating and apply the savings to doing more.

From a government perspective, especially, the issue of gold plating has significant consequences. With limited resources, every time we build in higher than necessary designs and features that cost money for service A, those funds are not available for other programs, services, or products. That likely means that someone else either does not get key products and services or has to wait a longer period of time to get service B, because we have chosen to have higher DFQ for service A.

Of course, if we've made a conscious strategic choice to increase the design and features of a product or service (for example, because we determine that a high-priority need requires a higher level of DFQ) and we are aware of the consequences (not being able to provide another product or service to others), then we've made a considered business decision. If, however, the decision to increase DFQ above the appropriate level is done unconsciously or is the result of just doing what we always have, then focusing on the appropriate level of DFQ in our products and services has the potential to free up significant resources and produce citizen satisfaction at the same time.

The city of Round Rock, Texas, used the DFQ line as an analytical tool to engage its community in defining the level of goods and services to provide among several competing priorities in the face of limited funds. It is a good example of an innovative way to conduct a strategic stakeholder value analysis, which is described after the case study.

CASE STUDY

Engaging Citizens in Service and Revenue Decisions in Round Rock, Texas

"We've got a problem."

This was the opening line in their briefing slides when the mayor, city council, and city manager of Round Rock, Texas, began a series of meetings with their citizens to seek advice on how to address a serious challenge: Their revenues and expenses were both growing, but expenses were growing faster than revenues.

Round Rock, a fast-growing city of 90,000 just north of Austin, has a council-manager form of government; is politically conservative; has low property tax, utility, and crime rates, and is the home of Dell. It has always been a place committed to learning, as evidenced by the high value placed on continuing public administration education. A former city manager had attended the Weldon Cooper Center's SEI program at the University of Virginia in 1999, and more than seventy Round Rock employees were UVA LEAD program graduates. The city runs an innovative new-employee orientation program, in which new employees are encouraged to understand the relationship between an individual's job and the city's mission, vision, and values.

Paraphrased, the briefing slides continued with:

> The Round Rock City Council is confronted with a problem. Spending growth is outpacing revenue growth.

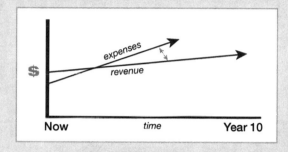

FIGURE 3.4

> If left unchecked, the potential deficit will grow over time. If not dealt with now, the city council will be forced to make budget cuts in a knee-jerk, crisis-management fashion. The city will manage modest deficits by implementing cost controls and improving efficiency both organization-wide and in our various core services.
>
> The problem also gives us an opportunity. We've never asked citizens to look at the big picture of all the core services we provide and give us input on what levels of service we should provide among those core services. Service-level discussions in the past have always focused on single issues.
>
> There are various ways to tackle the problem. We can raise revenue, cut services, or do a combination of both. The city council will make the final decisions on how to deal with the problem and would like informed public input when making those decisions.
>
> To help inform the public, we have analyzed population-growth trends and the associated financial capacity we can expect over time. We have

also taken a top-to-bottom look at the services we provide and how we
pay for them. We have identified cost drivers—things that drive costs
up—as well as cost controllers—things that can save money.

Now, we're asking for citizens' advice on their preferences on the levels of service we provide and how they would like to pay for them.

One might imagine what would have happened in Round Rock if the council had
decided, without consultation with citizens and stakeholders (e.g., the press), to
pursue either a tax increase or service level reduction (or a combination of these).
Instead, the council and city administration decided on a transparent, fully involved
citizen engagement process. The council followed a six-step, nine-month process:

Steps	Timeline
Forecast financial capacity	Aug.–Sept. 2005
Identify things that drive costs up	Fall 2005
Identify opportunities to control costs	Fall 2005
Listen to public advice	Jan.–Feb. 2006
Public input presented to city council	Feb. 22, 2006
Council decides policy direction	Spring/Summer 2006

The planning team's goal for the engagement process was to hear from 400
citizens during a series of community-based presentations and an online feedback
process. However, they exceeded expectations during thirty presentations to civic
and neighborhood groups, ten "open house" meetings, a two-week "online open
house," and a public forum, in which more than 575 residents participated, with many
expressing high levels of satisfaction with—and even expressing gratitude for—the
engagement process.

In this case study, we focus on Step 4 of the process: Listen to public advice. In
designing the citizen engagement forums, it was decided that each meeting would
use an identical template, asking the citizens to focus on seven core city services:

- Provide Library Services
- Maintain Order, Enforce Laws
- Provide Fire Response
- Provide EMS Response
- Provide Open Space, Parks Facilities
- Provide Recreational Facilities, Activities
- Provide Urban Infrastructure

Citizens would rotate in small groups to each of seven briefing stations, receiving a background presentation on (1) key issues in the service area, (2) cost drivers, (3) cost controllers, and (4) information on how the level of service in Round Rock compared to similar Texas communities.

The meeting planning team, however, encountered a problem. In their words, "How do we describe different service levels for each Core Business? High, medium, low just [doesn't] cut it." They made what they described as a "911" call to John Pickering, president of CCHPO, Inc., and adjunct faculty member at UVA's SEI/LEAD programs. During the conversation, Pickering suggested using the CCHPO definition of quality materials. Here's what resulted:

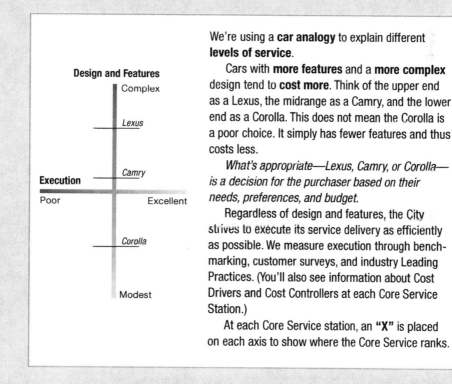

FIGURE 3.5

Here's an example of the presentations for Library Services made to citizens in each of the core services:

PROVIDE LIBRARY SERVICES

Design and Features

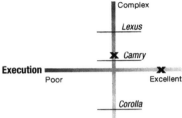

CURRENT LEVEL OF SERVICE

Design and Features: Our level of service is above a Camry. We are a Lexus in staffing and service, Corolla in size of collection (books and other materials). We are open 71 hours a week, 7 days a week, with staff hours at .67/capita.

Execution: Our quality of execution is excellent in customer service and good-excellent in quality of collection based on in-house surveys.

Cost:	Year 1 $2.2M	Year 10 $4.6M

	Year 1	Year 10
Lexus: Open 71 hours (current), 2nd branch in 2015, greater INCREASE in materials budget to grow to 4 items per capita	$2.6M	$6.8M
Camry: Open 60 hours, closed 1 day and 2 evenings, staff hours at .61/capita, one branch by 2010, slight INCREASE in materials budget to grow to 3 items per capita over the long term	$2.2M	$4.6M
Corolla: Open 50 hours, closed 2 days, staff hours at .57/capita, limits on children's programming and Internet access	$2.0M	$2.8M

FIGURE 3.6

KEY ISSUES

- Cannot house growing collection. Max out in 3 years.
- Storytimes and programs are full. No growth over past 3 years.
- Parking is becoming a barrier. On peak days, people park 2–3 blocks away, garage full.

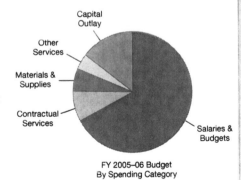

FY 2005–06 Budget
By Spending Category

COST DRIVERS

- Population growth, especially families
- Economic swings—libraries busier during downturns
- Costs for materials increase, pegged at Consumer Price Index
- Salaries based on market
- Branch at Camry level: $5.7 million in capital costs not reflected

COST CONTROLLERS

- Personal access to computers at work/home
- Growth in typical non-library using populations (single adults, baby-boom senior citizens)
- Library too small to serve growing population

FIGURE 3.7

PER CAPITA SPENDING

• College Station*	$11
• Tyler	$14
• Pflugerville	$18
• Longview	$19
• Frisco	$20
• San Marcos	$23
• Cedar Park	$24
• McKinney	$25
• Austin	$27
• Georgetown	$27
• Bryan*	$31
• Denton	$43
• **Average**	**$24**
• **Round Rock**	**$25**

*Bryan administers the College Station program

To follow state standards to the letter, there would need to be an increase in funding for materials to meet the Camry level of 3 items per capita, hence an increase from where we are today.

If we met the Camry level in collection size, we'd have to have a branch—we don't have room to store that much material.

If we go to a Corolla level, over the next 5 years all remaining meeting rooms will need to be programmed for library only use. After 2010, the library will be static, with no room for changes or growth.

FIGURE 3.8

After receiving the briefing at each of the core service areas, citizens were asked to register their views on an advice scorecard as to what to do in that service area: reduce services to the "Corolla" level (and reduce property taxes), keep services at the "Camry" level (and keep taxes as is or raise taxes modestly), or raise the service level to the "Lexus" level (and raise taxes modestly to significantly). After completing this part of the advice scorecard on a computer workstation at the meeting site, citizens were asked to enter their street address, which told them the valuation of their residences. They were then given real-time feedback on the effect of their advice on

- the city tax rate—if it raised or lowered the rate and by how much
- the cost or savings to the city budget
- the change in their current and future tax bills. This is the aspect of the process that was truly "leading practice"—it connected each citizen's personal tax impact to the service levels they preferred.

The last part of the advice scorecard asked the following questions (among others):

1. Are you willing to raise taxes?
2. Are you willing to raise user fees?
3. Are you willing to cut services?

The results were clear: Most people—60 percent—wanted to maintain the Camry level of service. Only 15 percent recommended lowering service levels to the Corolla level, while 25 percent recommended raising them to the Lexus level. This pattern varied by service area, but the basic pattern was true across all core service areas:

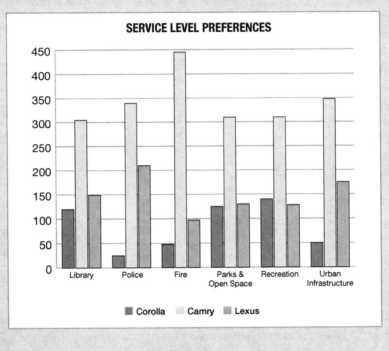

FIGURE 3.9

Residents were also clear on how to fund these service levels: 65 percent were willing to raise taxes, 82 percent were willing to raise user fees, but only 39 percent were willing to cut services. All this work was covered extensively by the media, so when the council followed much of the Round Rock citizens' advice over the course of the nine-month process and in the budget decisions that followed, there was little adverse citizen reaction or negative press.

Both of the case studies in this chapter deal with design and features quality. In the Prince William County plans review case study, we saw the unit realize that their conception of the services was misaligned and that the customers at the counter were displeased with the value they received. They had to revise the design and features of their services. In Round Rock, the city sought direct feedback and reacted to the customers' views of the appropriate levels of products and services.

In this analysis, we want to ask ourselves two summary questions:

1. Are we doing the **right stuff** (i.e., the right key products and services at the right design and features quality level)?
2. Is it for the **right people** (i.e., the right customers/stakeholders)?

If we can answer these questions in the affirmative, are we high performing? The answer: partially, but not definitively. We can say that we are being effective—the customers are getting what they want, need, and expect on time, on budget, and with good customer value. But we may still be doing too much rework, requiring too many reviews, or using an otherwise inefficient process—in these cases, we would not be high performing. We'll take up this aspect of strategic thinking later, in the theory of the business, when we discuss execution quality.

First, we must perform an analysis to determine the extent to which we are satisfying our stakeholders' expectations and to explore overlaps and conflicts that may exist between what one beneficiary customer or funding source wants, needs, and expects and the desires of others. In addition, we must interact with the customers to understand future desires so we develop the capability and capacity to satisfy them then as well.

Strategic Stakeholder Value Analysis (SSVA), in combination with the DFQ (and, later, execution quality) analysis, is how we assess customer value and how we answer KDQ 3 (According to whom are we high performing?). In Chapter 2, we discussed the variety of stakeholders that we must work with and serve and whose expectations we must meet. We identified them as beneficiary chain customers (those who use the products and services we produce), food chain customers (those who provide us with funding and/or policy direction), partners (people and entities inside and outside our unit/ organization with whom we must work with very closely to produce value for our beneficiaries), competitors (those with whom we can or do compete), and other stakeholders (those not in the preceding categories but who can influence us in sometimes positive, but more often, potentially negative ways).

KDQ 3: ACCORDING TO WHOM ARE WE HIGH PERFORMING?

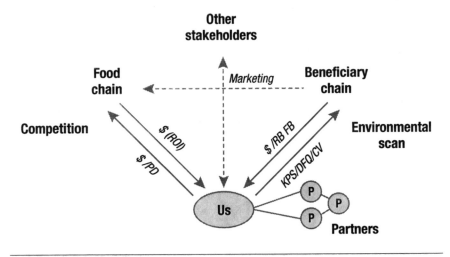

Key: $ = Money; PD = Policy direction; ROI = Return on investment; RB = Repeat business; FB = Feedback; KPS = Key products and services; DFQ = Design and features quality; CV = Customer value; P = Partners

FIGURE 3.10

The SSVA begins with clarifying who "we" are by including our business partners with whom we must work effectively to deliver value in the customers' eyes. Then, at a minimum, we want to examine our stakeholders' views from the perspectives of the **Pick 3** indicators:

- **Quality of our products and services:** Are we delivering the appropriate level of design and features quality, and how good are we at what we do? Are we delivering leading practices in process design and implementation (i.e., execution quality)?
- **Customer value:** Are we seen as responsive and dependable? Is working with us convenient? Are we easy to access? Are our cycle times and speed of delivery the best in the business? Do customers see us as effectively meeting their requirements?
- **Financial performance:** Can we demonstrate that we are effectively driving our cost down, correctly sizing and meeting our revenue/budget, and are a low-cost, high-quality producer?

In addition, do we know what other performance criteria our stakeholders apply, and are we certain of our superiority in each of them? We can examine what the relationships—positive and negative—among these stakeholders are. Is there a political component to their actions? How do we mitigate or manage these interactions? Are we seen as "good" by the beneficiary chain and the food chain? Are there, or should there be, links between the food chain and the beneficiary chain, and do we need an effective marketing strategy to improve influence and perception? We can also explore who our stakeholders could/should be in the future.

In the Prince William County case, this interrelationship was clear. A good number of the beneficiary customers were very unhappy with the design and features quality and customer value they were receiving. Not only did they let the fire marshal's unit know it, but they involved the food chain quite loudly, often by complaining to the board of county supervisors and the county executive—neither of whom was bashful about letting the fire department know that their expectations were not being met. This is probably not the preferred way to hear that you have a big problem! So they undertook focused action to understand the voice of the customer to be sure that their wants, needs, and expectations were clearly understood. Then they had to determine how to meet them and how to do so both effectively and efficiently. We'll discuss efficiency more later.

In the Round Rock case, engaging the community's stakeholders in defining the design and features quality of the city's core services was the primary aim. Through a variety of means, the city reached out to discern the level of goods and services its citizens desired. Further, because of the involvement of the mayor and city council in the process and the fact that the council received direct feedback from the process, the connection between the beneficiary chain and the food chain became easier to assure.

In examining our stakeholders' views, it is important to identify any conflicting desires among them, for we can deliver on only one set of expectations. If the beneficiary chain wants "it" fast, and the food chain wants "it" cheap, we need to define what we will do so that all parties understand when and how much we are going to deliver. It is this expectation that we will then deliver and measure; only then can we expect satisfied customers. Often, it is the violation of expectations that causes negative views of our performance.

It is helpful to do a **benchmarking** or **leading practices review** that compares what we do to others who perform similar functions. The focus for us when dealing with DFQ is what kinds of products and services are being provided by other public, nonprofit, or private sector organizations that could meet the wants, needs, and expectations of our stakeholders. Are we keeping up with new research findings on whether our programs and services are evidence-based and whether there are other innovations in methods to achieve the results we want that are more effective? In the following discussion of execution quality, it will be clear that benchmarking and leading practices review should also extend to questions about the efficiency of our administrative systems and work processes. What is the norm in our field in terms of key products and services, design and features quality, and customer value (and execution quality) against which we need to compare?

At this point in the strategic thinking process, it is helpful to do an environmental scan—both internal and external to the organization. The acronym SWOC/T stands for strengths, weaknesses, opportunities, and constraints/threats. Strengths and weaknesses refer to our organization (they are internal) in its current state—our strengths right now; what we excel at; the core competencies, facilities, systems, alliances, resources, and technologies that provide us with a competitive advantage; and the things we can capitalize on in the short term. This is important to know because we can use these advantages to leverage our strategies and make rapid improvements, rather than having to create new capabilities.

Current weaknesses are the opposite. What are we not very good at? What are the skills, talents, core competencies, facilities, systems, alliances, resources, and technologies that leave us at a disadvantage? What are we unable to take advantage of in the short term, and what should we consider developing in the future? Note that this analysis does not suggest that the weaknesses must be turned around. That may be necessary, but we will make that determination later as a result of the strategies we decide we need to employ. At this point, we just want to identify them.

Opportunities and constraints/threats are fundamentally different from strengths and weaknesses. They are an assessment of the external environment—outside the unit or organization—and things over which we appear to have little control but may want to take advantage of or avoid should they occur. In addition to being external, they are future-focused—they may happen. Opportunities, therefore, answer this question: What are the things that we believe may develop in the environment that have the potential to present us with prospects in the future?

Constraints/threats, on the other hand, may have the potential to limit our ability to achieve our goals. As with opportunities, these are hypothetical and are used to focus our attention but not to limit our thinking. For critical issues and dramatic shifts, we may develop a variety of scenarios regarding our strategic direction so that it can be changed quickly should the need arise.

Once we have a good idea of our current state regarding performance as well as our potential, a **gap analysis** is often a helpful way to think about our desired future state and our strategic direction. We analyze the difference between our current performance and our stakeholders' wants, needs, and expectations and prioritize items from the customers' view and their importance in accomplishing our vision. This provides a list of issues to be dealt with, either tactically or strategically. If the requirement is tactical—that is, shorter term, more specific, and well defined, then it should be moved into our current management problem-solving process rather than becoming part of strategic planning. If the requirement is strategic, we move along to the second part of strategic thinking: theory of the business.

STRATEGIC THINKING: PART 2—THEORY OF THE BUSINESS

This is where we evaluate our current ability to deliver on future performance. We engage KDQ 6 (How good are we at delivering our products and services?). We also examine Change Levers 4 through 6 (strategy, structure, and systems) to see what will require modification to get us to our vision. It is unlikely that everything needs to be changed, but it is equally unlikely that nothing needs to be improved. Here, we sort out where changes are required and what should be left as is.

We begin with a series of questions on the soundness of our service delivery approaches and whether they support us in accomplishing our vision and mission effectively and efficiently.

- Are we clear about our key business assumptions and our logic (causal) model for getting results? Have we examined the service delivery mechanisms we use to be sure they actually accomplish what we intend? Are we sure that they encompass the leading practices available to achieve the results we seek?

- Do we have a sound approach to strategic outsourcing decisions? How do we handle "surge" demand and surplus production capacity?

The next factor for examination is **organizational structure**. We evaluate our current structure and change it if there is a better way to support our vision and strategy. Most organizations have inherited a "stove-piped" structure from their Industrial Model past that emphasizes suboptimization—that is, focusing on performance of the part of the organization that *you* are in, even if it's at the expense of other parts and the achievement of the overall vision and mission. This is where leadership function 3, suprasystems integration and stewardship, comes into play. We need to glue the parts back together to accomplish the organization's vision and to integrate and align the parts to form a whole. Seeking the integration of the parts of the organization into a seamless higher-level whole, we ask

- In our current structure, do we perform our work very well without friction among the parts, or should we explore other models, like matrices, business centers/lines of business, process- or product-focused structures?
- Does our service delivery work really get done within the formal units shown on our organization chart, or is it the product of cross-unit networks or microbusinesses (including support functions like finance, human resources, etc.)? If the latter, have we organized so that leadership work gets done appropriately for those networks or microbusinesses?
- Do cross-cutting projects and processes have a clearly accountable process/project owner, with roles/responsibilities clearly delineated among all players? (See the Bellevue Development Services case study in Chapter 2 for an illustration of a governance process for a cross-functional microbusiness).

Finally, we review each of our administrative/business support systems and technical work processes. In the second dimension of quality, execution quality, we assess which systems and processes aid us in improving our performance and which constrain us. While often considered a "given," with a belief that little can be done to improve them, these are often the areas of most waste in organizations. In local governments, this area of investment in improving our performance is often overlooked, or we assume that we are already very good at our systems and process.

Execution quality (EQ) is independent of design and features quality. EQ is the ability to execute flawlessly a leading-practice process to deliver whatever we have defined as the required DFQ. Whatever we, along with our stakeholders, determine to be the appropriate place on the DFQ scale, Corolla or Lexus, we need an excellent execution process to produce it. We must also have excellent execution of our planning, design, engineering, production, procurement, facilities, workforce, and other support systems as well.

Looking back at the horizontal scale on Figure 3.3, the left side is labeled "poor" execution quality and the right side is "excellent." The two questions on this scale are

1. Do we have the **right process** (i.e., a best-practice process for delivering the design and features required)?
2. Is the process being **done right** (i.e., is it being executed flawlessly; is there a minimum of scrap, rework, warranty, and waste)?

If our work process is not a leading practice, we have a high cost in doing an inefficient process perfectly. If we can't execute our leading practice process as designed, we have a high cost in doing a perfect process poorly. When we deliver excellent execution quality over time, running the appropriate leading practice processes flawlessly, we are efficient. The more efficient we are, the lower our execution costs and the shorter the process time.

In the Prince William County fire plan review case, not only did they need to get the design and features quality right (right products and services delivered to the right customers), they also needed to work directly on dramatically improving their execution quality (right processes, done right). Everyone had a hand in reviewing the processes and improving them. Using Continuous Quality Improvement (CQI) tools, they tried different approaches, shifted to the processes that worked well, and learned from ones that didn't. The remarkable reduction in review times from more than twelve weeks to two weeks, and even one-day turnaround, could only come from understanding the DFQ their customers expected, revamping their business strategy and approach, and then creating the most efficient processes and doing them really well to produce the best EQ. Similarly, the Round Rock case also involved EQ: "Regardless of design and features [quality], the city strives to execute its service delivery as efficiently as possible. We measure execution [quality] through benchmarking, customer surveys, and industry best practices."

The systems and processes we want to assess are

- **Administrative support systems.** This includes human resources (i.e., do we have the right people with the right skills, competencies, attitudes, and behaviors being delivered to the right place at the right time? Are our systems leading practices for job design, recruitment, compensation, classification, retention, rewards, appraisal, and accountability?). How about our systems for financial management, procurement, contracting, information technology, facilities and equipment, communication, legal, vehicle maintenance, etc.? Improvements to these support systems speak louder than any other actions an organization can take in convincing employees that management is "walking the walk" and that real change is happening.
- **Work processes.** Do we have best-practice work processes tailored to the appropriate design and features level and delivered flawlessly? Are we continuously improving? If necessary, can we reengineer a process from the ground up?
- **Work management and control processes.** Does every member at every level of the organization have the systems and skills to monitor and take appropriate corrective actions on our key success factors?
- **Continuous process improvement processes.** Do we have the tools/ discipline for continuous process improvement (e.g., Lean/Six Sigma evaluation and reengineering, business process redesign, activity-based costing) widely distributed throughout the organization and within each individual? Is continuous learning and improvement part of our organizational DNA?

In an example of strategic thinking, the city of Dublin, Ohio, examined the capabilities in its human resources system. They were concerned about their hiring, promotion, and employee development systems. They understood that if they wanted better performance results, they needed to concentrate on how employees were selected and supported once hired. They also decided that they wanted to use CCHPO's Networked Talent Model approach to define position responsibilities, so they revamped their entire human resources process to implement it. They then translated their strategic thinking into strategic planning and implementation, the concepts of which will follow the next two examples.

CASE STUDY

The Use of Core Competencies in Dublin, Ohio

—*Michelle Crandall, deputy city manager of Dublin, Ohio*

INTRODUCTION

In 2005, the city of Dublin, Ohio (population 43,000), began exploring best-practice methods for the professional development of existing employees and the hiring of new employees. At the time, we realized that current hiring and promotional practices did not always result in employees with the desired values, traits, behaviors, and competencies needed to be successful in various positions. Furthermore, the city had no formalized processes in place to help employees develop competencies for each type of position. In particular, like many local governments, Dublin had promoted several employees to supervisory roles based on technical skills, and these employees were struggling with their new management and leadership responsibilities.

SELECTION OF A CORE COMPETENCIES TOOL

To address these hiring and development challenges, we began using the Lominger Leadership Architect[4] in 2006. The Lominger system is based on sixty-seven positive management and leadership "core competencies" and nineteen negative behaviors that are considered "career stallers and stoppers." The core competencies range from high-level skills such as strategic agility and learning on the fly to more basic skills such as customer focus and time management. Competencies are divided into six areas: strategic skills, operating skills, courage, energy and drive, organizational positioning skills, and personal/interpersonal skills. Very few of these deal with technical competencies of a position; the assumption is that the organization knows the technical competencies it needs in a particular position (e.g., a building official or engineer).

These competencies and behaviors are provided in the form of a deck of 86 four-by-six-inch cards. The front of each card describes, from a behavioral aspect, what the competency looks like when it is done well. The back describes what the competency looks like when the skill is overused as well as if it's not done well. The cards are used to determine, through a team sorting process, the critical competencies desired for individual positions or groups of positions.

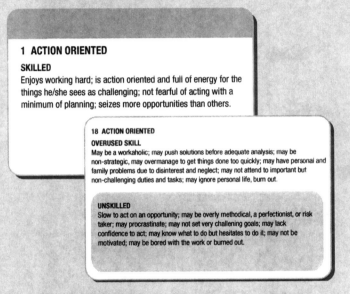

1 ACTION ORIENTED

SKILLED
Enjoys working hard; is action oriented and full of energy for the things he/she sees as challenging; not fearful of acting with a minimum of planning; seizes more opportunities than others.

18 ACTION ORIENTED

OVERUSED SKILL
May be a workaholic; may push solutions before adequate analysis; may be non-strategic, may overmanage to get things done too quickly; may have personal and family problems due to disinterest and neglect; may not attend to important but non-challenging duties and tasks; may ignore personal life, burn out.

UNSKILLED
Slow to act on an opportunity; may be overly methodical, a perfectionist, or risk taker; may procrastinate; may not set very challenging goals; may lack confidence to act; may know what to do but hesitates to do it; may not be motivated; may be bored with the work or burned out.

FIGURE 3.11 Sample Competency Card, Front and Back

IMPLEMENTATION

We began implementing core competencies by training a group of facilitators in how to conduct "card sorts" that would result in a list of ten to twelve key competencies needed for individual positions and, in some instances, groups of positions. Each sorting exercise involved bringing together a select set of employees who were familiar with the position being examined (e.g., the appropriate department director, the supervisor of the position, high performers already in the position, individuals who work closely with the position). On occasion, someone from outside the organization would be included. For example, for the city's network administrator card sort, an information technology director from a neighboring community was invited to lend his insight and expertise.

The sorts began with the group discussing the key functions, goals, and expectations of the position. The participants also discussed what barriers may exist that a successful incumbent in the position might need to overcome and what has differentiated high performers in this position in the past. These preliminary questions were meant to ensure the entire group had a common understanding of the expectations and challenges associated with the job functions. Following this discussion, participants were asked to place each core competency card in one of three stacks: (1) highest or most desirable traits, (2) moderate or somewhat desirable traits, and (3) lowest of the desirable traits. Participants were given approximately thirty minutes to complete this sort. A total of twenty-two cards could be placed in the "highest" and "lowest" stacks; twenty-three cards could be placed in the "moderate" stack. This was the most challenging part of the process, as participants usually ended up with far more cards in the "highest" stack and were then forced to place some in one of the other two stacks.

FIGURES 3.12, 3.13, AND 3.14 Flat Three-Way Card Sort

Once this step was complete, a large tally sheet with all sixty-seven core competencies was used to capture cumulative group sort results. Participants placed a green dot beside each competency contained in their "highest" stack and a red dot beside each competency contained in their "lowest" stack. Results were reviewed by the facilitator, and the competencies that received the highest number of green dots were marked. Depending on the tallied results, the group then discussed the merits of each marked competency and the need to add or remove any from a final list of core competencies for the position.

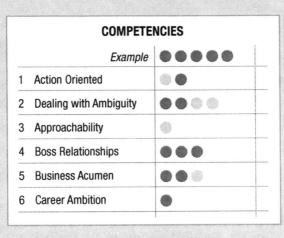

FIGURE 3.15 Example Portion of a Group Tally Sheet

ESTABLISHING CORE COMPETENCIES AND INTEGRATION

The first two competency sorts we completed were for the executive team members and all other managerial (supervisory) positions. These were followed by sorts for individual professional positions, such as planner, engineer, landscape architect, and building inspector. Finally, a sort was performed for the city's clerical support positions. After several months, nearly every position in the city had a list of critical competencies needed for successful performance.

With the goal of integrating competencies into job descriptions, performance evaluations, development plans, and hiring and promotional processes, the next critical step was to ensure that supervisors gained a deeper understanding of the competencies and how they could be used effectively to help employees develop the necessary competencies. While most supervisors had been involved in at least one card sort and had a basic understanding of the "why" behind the competencies, they did not have a good understanding of the "how" of using the Lominger tools. One-day workshops were held with all supervisors to build their coaching and development skills and to demonstrate how core competencies would be incorporated into performance evaluations. That year, everyone who participated in the workshop had core competencies included in their performance review process. The following year, core competencies were included in all employee performance evaluations.

Each year, as part of the evaluation process, employees are required to work with their supervisor to determine one or two core competencies that are in need of improvement. The evaluation form must list the competencies that will be focused on and what activities or assignments the employee will pursue in order to improve. Research conducted by Lominger found that only 10 percent of learning and development is the result of reading or coursework, 20 percent is the result of learning from others, and 70 percent is the result of hands-on learning and challenging job assignments. When people are asked to think about their typical development plans, they quickly realize that the opposite is true, in that traditional plans identify mostly reading or coursework. Based on this knowledge, supervisors and employees are asked to focus on specific "stretch" assignments that will help the employee develop. For example, if an employee struggles with comfort around higher management, his development assignment might be to work on a project that requires him to present final recommendations to a group of department directors.

Beyond performance evaluations, we also used the Lominger competencies to develop performance improvement plans for individuals who exhibit traits and behaviors that result in below-par performance. In these cases, the improvement plan identifies competencies that are in need of improvement with specific examples of when the skill was not used or was overused. Typically, the career staller and stopper behaviors are included. For example, the improvement plan might identify that the employee has a "lack of composure." Examples of behavior related to this staller would be included, along with the expectation of future behavior.

An excellent Lominger resource that we made available to all supervisors was *FYI—For Your Improvement: A Guide for Development and Coaching*,[5] by Michael M. Lombardo and Robert W. Eichinger. The book contains a section for each core competency and provides examples of development assignments that help to develop each. It has been a wonderful resource for supervisors who are trying to help employees improve their performance.

HIRING AND PROMOTIONAL PROCESSES

Lominger also provides a competency-based tool for behavioral interviews that we have used almost exclusively for our hiring and promotional processes. For each of the sixty-seven competencies, the tool has a list of potential questions that help interviewers determine if the candidate possesses that particular behavior/competency. In first-round interviews, the city generally focuses on basic technical skills that may be needed for the job. This allows us to determine those who meet (or exceed) the basic background and skills needed for the job, which could make them eligible to move on to the next phase. Second- and, if needed, third-round interviews focus on position-specific competency-based questions. For example, if one of the critical competencies for a position is "giving and receiving feedback," we might ask the candidate, "Have you ever had to give an employee negative feedback? What were the specific circumstances, and how did you approach this discussion?" The beauty of behavioral interview questions is that a candidate cannot respond with a theoretical or general answer; they have to refer to a specific instance. This also allows for follow-up questions to better understand how the candidate handled a certain situation.

There is a skill, almost an art, to excellent behavior-based interviewing. For this type of interviewing to be successful, you or your human resources representative needs to be comfortable with silence, know what to ask as follow-up questions (and how), and not be willing to let a candidate off the hook by answering with generalities instead of specific situations. These are not easy questions to answer; candidates typically need time to think and may need to skip a question or come back to it later. For members of the interview team who are not comfortable with silence or tend to want to help the candidate with an answer, this method will not be high on their list of fun things to do. But the results will be well worth the effort. After all, past behavior does predict future behavior, and if you can extract behaviors from your interviews, you will ultimately end up with a preferred candidate whose competencies closely match those required for the job. We have conducted several interview processes where, after the first round focusing on technical skills, we thought we knew who the top candidate would be, only to have that change later during the behavioral interviews.

ONGOING INTEGRATION

Seven years later, the city of Dublin is still using the Lominger leadership architect competency system. We have seen increased success among employees hired and promoted based on the Lominger competencies, and more employees actively engaging in their ongoing development. It has become part of our organization's language when discussing employee hiring, promotion, and development. While many processes, programs, and flavor-of-the-week management programs have come and gone over the years, the city's core competency tools have held strong. It is not uncommon to hear a front-line employee mention a core competency by name, which is a sure sign that the process of integration has been a success.

In another case study, the city of Rockville, Maryland, concluded that in order to see the Networked Talent Model fully employed, it would need to change some of the city's human resources systems. They would have to create more formal expectations for performance of leadership, management, task/technical skills, and team skills. They refined a system to evaluate and recognize employees that creates accountability for these at all levels of the organization.

CASE STUDY

Performance Evaluation and Recognition System in Rockville, Maryland[6]

—Michelle Poche Flaherty, served as the internal change consultant for the city of Rockville, Maryland

Rockville, Maryland, located 34 miles north of Washington, D.C., boasts more than 60,000 residents, a culturally diverse population, and nearly 80,000 jobs within the city. The city of Rockville integrated the Networked Talent Model into the way its employees think about work collectively, both as an organization and as individuals, when introducing new city employees in their orientation, in all job descriptions (see an example in the Appendix), in their performance evaluation system, in their rewards and recognition programs, and when measuring progress in their biennial employee survey.

PERFORMANCE EVALUATION: USING THE NETWORKED TALENT MODEL AS A FOUNDATION

The city uses interdepartmental employee committees to design and maintain its performance evaluation system and to administer recognition programs. The commitment of large, diverse groups of employees—together with support from an executive champion, like the city manager—has enabled the city to take on prized benefits and protected performance evaluation systems to bring dramatic change and improvements embraced by all.

In the early 2000s, the city's human resources staff formed the Performance Planning and Appraisal Team, an interdepartmental committee of employees, to rewrite the criteria used to evaluate employee performance. The group included representatives from every department, level of authority, and union or bargaining group.

The committee crafted new evaluation criteria based on the four skill categories in the Networked Talent Model: leadership, management, teamwork, and task/technical skills. The evaluation criteria were heavily weighted for leadership, management, and team skills. They created focused performance criteria for each of three roles: administrative employees, union workers, and police officers. All standards used descriptive language that detailed what performance looked like when an employee was highly successful, successful, acceptable, or unsatisfactory in each criterion. Once the new criteria were established, each employee and supervisor in the organization participated in important discussions about performance expectations and detailed information about the evaluation process. The evaluation criteria were refined in 2010 to make them more objective and to add different expectation levels for supervisors and managers (see the Appendix).

Since Rockville's performance expectations are heavily weighted toward leadership, management, and team skills for all employees, only three of eleven evaluated competencies are for task/technical work for non-supervisory employees. Three elements are for leadership skills, two are for management skills, and three are for team skills (see table 3.2). This weighting reflects the emphasis the organization places on leadership at all levels. At the same time, a rating system with negative consequences for low performance in any single category ensures accountability for every expectation, including those related to task/technical performance.

Employee	Task	Leadership	Management	Team Skills	Total
Non-Super	3	3	2	3	11
Supervisor	2	4	3	3	12
Manager	2	5	4	3	14

TABLE 3.2 Rockville Evaluation Elements

PAY FOR PERFORMANCE, NOT JUST SENIORITY

In the mid-2000s, Rockville's city manager, Scott Ullery, proposed that the city change its pay system to include rewarding performance in addition to seniority and longevity. Rockville had a well-established system of pay grades and classifications that it did not want to change. Each pay grade is characterized by a compensation range, where employees in good standing receive a merit increase each year until they reach the maximum. As a result, employees with longevity tend to be compensated at the top of their pay ranges and newer employees at the lower end, often regardless of the quality of their performance.

A new pay-for-performance system was implemented; it initially applied only to administrative employees. It was designed to retain the traditional merit increase for fully satisfactory performance in leadership, management, task/technical, and teamwork skill areas but reduced the merit increase for lower performers. The city also could withhold cost of living allowances for unsatisfactory performance.

A lump sum payment was added for exceptionally high performers. During the economic downturn in 2010, Rockville could not afford merit increases or lump sum payments but maintained the pay-for-performance system by rewarding high performers with additional time off. Over time, the employees in other bargaining units began to view the administrative employees' pay-for-performance system as attractive and have requested a similar pay structure as part of their contract negotiations.

In addition to amending the formal compensation system, the city manager also changed the traditional employee awards ceremony, where employees are recognized for milestone years of service. He introduced the City Manager's HPO Awards, which recognize employees who have demonstrated exceptional leadership, management, teamwork, or task/technical expertise in their work. Every October, all employees are invited to nominate individual employees and/or teams of coworkers for this honor. Nominations are reviewed by the HPO Committee, an interdepartmental team of employees, who make recommendations to the city manager for final review and approval. The city manager presents the awards at an annual ceremony with the mayor and council present. These awards allow us to celebrate our victories and reinforce our values around the HPO Model as an integral part of what we call "The Rockville Way."

WHEN INTRODUCING CHANGES, HONOR WHAT CAME BEFORE

Each change toward aligning our performance evaluation system was met with skepticism, complaints, and concerns from a handful of employees in the organization. But over time, these changes have been embraced—and even preferred—to previous practices. Rockville has found that the old practices don't have to be discarded in order to introduce new ones. Where performance was incorporated into the compensation or rewards system, the historically popular benefits and established processes were not discarded. Rather, we modified the established systems. This incremental evolution made a smoother transition for Rockville to continue its journey toward becoming a higher-performing organization.

EMPLOYEE SURVEY RESULTS

Every two years, Rockville conducts an internal survey to measure the quality of internal customer service experienced by employees and the level of implementation and satisfaction with HPO-related values in the workplace. Survey questions incorporate quality of participatory decision making, vertical and horizontal communication, leadership work and philosophy, and other desirable characteristics. Survey results are communicated throughout the city organization. Every work group participates in a facilitated discussion about what the results mean to them and establishes goals to leverage strengths and address opportunities for improvement identified from the survey data. Our goal is to move the organization along the continuum from Likert System 2 results to System 3 results (see Chapter 4).

Since using the Networked Talent Model as a standard for our work, the city's most recent employee survey indicates favorable improvements in most of our measured elements. This trend exists despite the downturn in the economy that has led to reduced levels of satisfaction in many nationwide employee surveys.

In both of the preceding case studies, the cities took a hard look, over time, at aspects of their human resources systems. They didn't change everything at once. Rather, they saw this work of leadership as an ongoing strategic responsibility with changes implemented, assessed, and refined as experience grew. Let's look at how this strategic planning and then implementation happens.

STRATEGIC PLANNING

We next move a level down in the Vision to Performance Cycle to **strategic planning**, which is a closing activity. We need to freeze the opening-up, analytical thinking process and decide what we are going to commit to do in the next three to five years. The two parts of strategic planning are to **set direction** and **capacity building**.

- **Set direction**. We establish the key focus areas, goals, and strategies to achieve our vision and mission. They are the higher-level targets around which we organize our programs and services and which guide the efforts of our department and agencies. The unifying direction is what helps units like the Prince William County fire marshal's office keep focused on what they must achieve.
- **Capacity building**. We focus on our strategic thinking assessment of our current capabilities in all the areas discussed above and our gap analysis that defines how they must change. We lay out the strategic priorities and schedule for capacity improvements that will enable us to accomplish the direction we set. This is a frequently neglected strategic planning element; most organizations just assume that they will have what is necessary to get the direction done. They wind up investing in organizational infrastructure and systems on a haphazard and opportunistic basis rather than thinking through where their investments will have the most positive impact. Both Dublin and Rockville saw their human resources system changes as essential to deliver the substantive strategic goals to reach their visions.

A good place to start strategic planning is with a modified brainstorming process. In the process of answering the following set of questions, it is essential to consider the strategic thinking we have done. To generate ideas, ask "What are all the things we could do; systems and processes we could address; changes to our business model/strategy, structure, strategies, and programs we could develop or refine; competencies we could obtain; equipment we could procure, etc. that will positively influence our outcome measures and get us to our vision?" Given the wide range of responsibilities in many local governments, it sometimes helps to break this question down into segments (for instance, concentrating on the strategies for elements of the vision). Another question that's often overlooked, but critical to the ability to implement new ideas and new processes: "What are the things we should *stop* doing?"

We must also introduce the product of the Values to Work Culture Cycle (see Chapter 4), the organization's adopted leadership philosophy, behavioral values, and operating systems values and ask, "What could we do to ensure our behaviors, systems, and processes are aligned and consistent with our leadership philosophy and values?"

If any part of this process could be considered art, it is the synthesis of the various ideas for improvement into well-articulated strategies. A strategy ought to answer two questions:

- Why is this strategy necessary to achieve our vision?
- What do we want this strategy to accomplish in our three-to-five-year strategic planning horizon?

Notice that "why" and "what" differ from "how"—mostly in the level of specificity and time frame. Strategic, by definition, is more general (see Figures 3.16 and 3.17). The specifics will be defined as part of tactical planning—it will allow for subordinate units to find their own appropriate methods to achieve the organizational strategies goals.

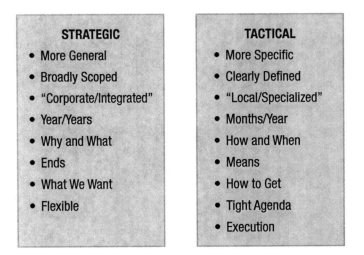

STRATEGIC	TACTICAL
• More General	• More Specific
• Broadly Scoped	• Clearly Defined
• "Corporate/Integrated"	• "Local/Specialized"
• Year/Years	• Months/Year
• Why and What	• How and When
• Ends	• Means
• What We Want	• How to Get
• Flexible	• Tight Agenda
	• Execution

FIGURES 3.16 AND 3.17 Strategic vs. Tactical

Once strategies are defined, it is time for more measurement work by revisiting KDQ 2 (How would we know?). This helps validate the logic of our strategy development and identify tactics going forward. At the strategic planning level, the measures will be a combination of both leading and lagging indicators: They will be leading indicators of whether the outcomes/impacts of our vision will be achieved and lagging indicators of the work we have to do to achieve them. Robert Kaplan and David Norton's **balanced scorecard**[7] approach to strategic measurement is a valuable tool. The balanced scorecard approach typically has four measurement perspectives: customer (vision/mission), financial, internal process, and learning and growth. The sequence in the public sector is usually expressed in this way:

Mission, Customer, and Stakeholder Perspective—How must we appear to our customers? Are we defining what customers and stakeholders want, need, and expect—will we, both now and in the future?

Financial Perspective—To succeed, how we will look financially? Are we making the best possible use of our resources? Are we good stewards of the public funds?

Internal Processes—To satisfy our customers (and achieve our mission) at what processes must we excel?

Learning & Growth—In order to acheive our vision/strategy, how must our organization learn, change and improve? ... both the individual and the organization? ... future value creation.

FIGURES 3.18

The causal reasoning is clear: In order to accomplish our vision/mission and have satisfied customers and stakeholders, we must make good use of our financial resources; in order to make good use of our financial resources, we must have efficient and effective internal process; and in order to have efficient and effective internal processes, we must have the right people, with the right skills, in the right place, doing the right things, including improving their processes and the work culture. Therefore, the things that would reside at the bottom are causal to those higher up.

One or more objectives is defined for each of the strategies and then analyzed in the context of the strategy map. We can point with arrows from the action to the anticipated effect and easily determine if the logic of our strategies makes sense. For example, missing or erroneous objectives in any perspective indicate a gap in our logic, calling for additional or alternate objectives and strategies.

To continue the measurement process for each objective, one or more measures, or metrics, should be defined. For each metric, a goal should be established that represents required or desired results. Tactical plans will specifically be developed to address *how* to move the metric in the direction of the goal. These measures will become leading indicators of our vision level outcome/impact performance measures and lagging indicators to our tactical measures. The objectives, measures, goals, and tactics comprise the balanced scorecard and become the basis for **monitoring and corrective action**.

The case study below summarizes how the balanced scorecard approach works in Charlotte, North Carolina. In it, we can see a fair amount of the Vision Cycle play out through strategic planning, starting with the community vision, through focus areas and corporate objectives, down to the individual performer level. A strategy map shows the causal sequence aimed at achieving the vision, measures, and targets for performance in the four perspectives of a balanced scorecard and the review of actual performance to keep on track or make adjustments.

CASE STUDY

Implementing the Balanced Scorecard in Charlotte, North Carolina

The city of Charlotte serves more than 731,000 residents across 180 square miles and is the country's second largest banking center. The city has a long tradition of performance measurement, having first instituted Management by Objectives (MBO) in 1972. It was the city's first step toward a system of performance management. In 1994, the city began its implementation of the balanced scorecard (BSC). As a result of the decades-long focus on performance management, the move to the balanced scorecard was a significant change, but not incredibly difficult. A great deal of communication through facilitated sessions with employees explained why the city was changing approaches with a focus on the benefits associated with the new system; as a result, resistance was minimal. The timing turned out to be significant, as the 1990-91 recession and subsequent restructuring lent credence to the need to become more "lean," to better define the highest priorities, and to align objectives and focus areas. The council adopted focus areas with the strategies, budgets, and highest-priority programs. Since then, the city of Charlotte has become recognized as the first and longest continuous government user of the BSC model in the world.

The BSC is a part of a well-integrated performance management and strategic planning approach reflective of the Vision to Performance Cycle, as it begins with the city vision, which is reviewed on a periodic basis. Each year, the council committees—structured around the city's five focus areas of transportation, environment, economic development, community safety, and housing and neighborhood development—review each focus area's vision statement and develop or refine key initiatives, measures, and performance targets. Changes and updates to the focus areas are presented by the committees to the full council at its annual retreat. During the annual retreat, the council also considers any wholesale changes to any of the focus areas. If none, a reaffirmation of the existing focus areas occurs. The focus areas and strategies are informed by ideas proposed by the staff and the committees.

Charlotte uses the BSC Strategy Map to describe much of the process, to validate the logic, and to communicate the relationships among the hierarchy of thought and action from the vision to specific actions and initiatives (see Figure 3.19). That logic goes like this:

The overarching vision is "Community of choice for living, working, and leisure." The vision is represented in the five city council focus areas. In turn, "comprehensive citizen service" is the strategic principle to guide the organization in service delivery. Comprehensive citizen service elements stipulate that we will

- Collaborate to provide a unified organizational response.
- Create a seamless infrastructure.
- Ensure data and information, processes, and services meet the corporate accessibility standard for structure, availability, and interoperability.
- Deliver responsive solutions to meet customers' expectation for current and future service.

In other words, comprehensive citizen service embodies the notion that our organizational components will behave as one business, thus improving the service experience for our citizens.

The focus area vision statements are

- "Charlotte will be America's safest community."
- "Charlotte will be the most prosperous and livable city for all citizens through quality economic development."

- "Charlotte will become a national leader in environmental and energy sustainability, preserving our natural resources while balancing growth with sound fiscal policy."
- "Charlotte will create and sustain communities of choice for living, working, and recreation."
- "Charlotte will be the premier city in the country for integrating land use and transportation choices."

For each of the council's focus areas, a plan is developed that includes initiatives, measures, and targets. The corporate scorecard (and strategy map) summarizes the broader strategies through the identification of corporate objectives and measures.

The BSC shows that in order to achieve our vision, we must "serve the customer"— at this point, we are at the mission and vision or outcome level in our thinking. The corporate perspective of "serve the customer" includes objectives for the council's six focus areas: reduce crime, increase perception of safety, strengthen neighborhoods, provide transportation choices, safeguard the environment, and promote economic opportunity. Each of these is described in detail in other charts and has a measure and a target associated with it. These would be considered lagging or trailing indicators, as they are mostly closely associated with outcomes.

The logic goes on: In order to serve the customer, we must run the business— meaning, at what processes must we excel to achieve the mission and the vision? And in order to serve the customer and run the business, we must manage resources— meaning, how do we ensure value in achieving the mission and vision?

Finally, the bottom of the strategy map is the "develop employees" perspective. The assumption here, of course, is that without empowered, motivated, and productive employees, we are not able to manage resources very well. This means we will have difficulty running the business effectively, and therefore will be unable to serve the customer and achieve the mission and vision. As you can see, the measures and targets established at the lower three levels are leading indicators for ultimate outcome performance. If we improve in these lower-level perspectives, our logic says we should achieve our desired result: vision and mission.

For each of the perspectives, there are specific objectives. The strategies are kept broad at this point, so that ultimately each of the key business units (KBUs) and support units through their departmental leadership teams will translate the council's guidance, defining what that means for us, what our strategies and measures are, and what we are going to commit to do tactically in the short term. Each KBU selects which corporate objectives it can influence. No KBU selects all sixteen corporate objectives. Once a KBU selects its corporate objectives, it then creates initiatives, performance measures, and targets.

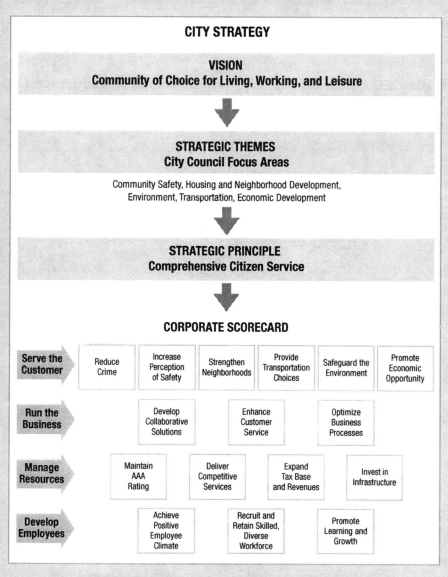

FIGURE 3.19 The Charlotte Balanced Scorecard Strategy Map

The product of this effort is a nested annual departmental operating plan and scorecard that specifically identifies unit-level performance measures and targets and the actions that will be taken to achieve these goals (see Figure 3.20 for an example of the fire department's BSC).

KBU-Balanced Scorecard Report

Reporting Period: July 1, 2011   to   June 30, 2012

Corporate Objective	KBU Initiative (* indicates Focus Area Initiative)	Measure ($ indicates incentive pay measure)	Prior Year Actual	Lead or Lag	Target	YTD	Status	Comments/Explanation (To be completed at mid-year and year-end reporting)
Serve the Customer — C1. Strengthen Neighborhoods	Strengthen and prepare the community	Percent of CMS 3rd grade classrooms that receive fire education programs $	85.3%	Lag	80%			
C2. Increase Perception of Safety	Provide emergency services (fire suppression, hazmat, etc.)	Percent of Telecommunicators answering phone within 10 seconds	99.3%	Lag	90%			
		Percent of alarms first fire company will be on scene within 6 minutes of telephone call*	83.2%	Lag	80%			
		Percent of first alarm fires to which an effective firefighting force will be on scene within 9 minutes	83.8%	Lag	80%			
	Provide effective public safety services (code enforcement)	Percent of fire code inspections conducted within state-mandated frequencies*	100%	Lag	95%			
	Provide effective public safety services (fire investigation)	Percent of arson cases investigators will clear*	45.7%	Lag	36%			
	Provide training opportunities	Number of All Hazards Incident Command System Training Courses offered in Charlotte UASI Region*	N/A	Lag	5			
Run the Business — B1. Optimize Business Processes	Provide up-to-date systems to support emergency and essential public safety service delivery	Consolidate the Fire and Police Computer Aided Dispatch (CAD) Systems by June 30, 2012*	N/A	Lag	100%			
Manage Resources — R1. Deliver Competitive Service	Monitor budget expenditures to ensure they are within budget appropriations	Percent of discretionary funds spent with certified SBEs	18.6%	Lag	10%			
	Maintain optimal staffing requirements	Percent of time minimum staff of 255 on fire companies will be maintained $	97.1%	Lag	95%			
	Maintain resource availability	Percent of fire companies in service during daylight hours Monday-Friday $	90.9%	Lag	80%			
Develop Employees — E1. Recruit and Retain Skilled, Diverse Workforce	Maintain certifications	Number of active firefighters that will maintain EMT certification	100%	Lag	98%			
	Promote a diverse workforce	Percent of women and minorities in firefighter applicant pool*	N/A	Lag	25%			
E2. Achieve Positive Employee Climate	Support physical fitness	Number of firefighters who participate in annual fitness evaluations $	97.9%	Lag	95%			
		Distribute wellness message in department newsletter $	N/A	Lag	100%			

FIGURE 3.20

Simply stated, the units replicate the activity that has been done at higher levels with the higher-level products as guidance. These are shared with the workforce and form the basis of the performance management system and, at the individual level, performance review and development discussions and individual development plans (see Figure 3.21).

City Council
Focus Areas

Corporate Balanced
Scorecard

Key Business Unit and
Support Unit Scorecards

Employee and Performance
Review and Development

Employee Developement Plan

FIGURE 3.21 How Council Focus Areas Translate
Into Operationalized Actions at Lower Levels

Specifically for each of these objectives (in all four perspectives), there may be corporate initiatives or actions planned, and there will certainly be key business unit and support unit operating plans identifying specific actions, including the responsibility of individuals in the organization to take action that ties to their unit's overall performance. (See Figure 3.22 for an example of how this flows from a broad policy framework to an individual mechanic working on the fleet.)

It should be noted that the employee in this case who is clearly responsible for obtaining the ASE certification is also responsible for unit performance. This is significant because in this process, the individual cannot be successful unless the unit of which he is a part is successful. It is this type of mechanism that causes people to look upward at the organization, seeing themselves as stewards of the whole rather than owners of the piece. Some of the parallel organizations (to be discussed in Chapter 5) at the work group levels have developed their own scorecards to ensure that the group is supporting the city's overall strategy.

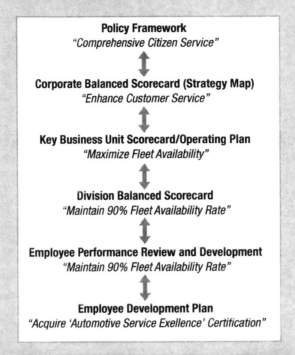

FIGURE 3.22 The Cascading Nature of the Operationalized Strategy

Having developed the scorecards to ensure alignment by nesting each within the vision, mission, focus areas, and objectives from the city council on down, the performance management process works in a variety of ways. Perhaps the most important parts of the entire process are the review of performance, assessment of progress, identification of gaps or issues, analysis of root causes, and corrective action to get back on track. In this way, the BSC is also the driver for investment and process improvement.

This is done through a variety of forums and at a variety of times. For example, the leadership team from the police department meets weekly to address the changing crime statistics and to be able to tactically redeploy based on evolving needs. In economic development, where the lead time between execution of tactical actions and visibility in the outcomes indicators is longer, the team meets less frequently. Other groups may review performance on a monthly or quarterly basis, depending on the quality of the indicators during various periods of time. No group meets less frequently than yearly, to coincide with the strategic planning cycle. Where measures are influenced by multiple key business units, the organization forms a focus area cabinet (or a macrobusiness). All units (or microbusinesses) involved in affecting these measures participate so that their efforts can be integrated and synergies can be identified.

For example, for the goal statement "Charlotte will be the premier city in the country for integrating land use and transportation choices," the cabinet consists of representatives from transportation, planning, transit, police, engineering, and the city manager's office. In addition, it is not unusual for Charlotte to bring in others with no direct line responsibility for any of these functions but who can offer different perspectives—a fresh set of eyes.

Charlotte visibly displays its performance measures that track trends and compares the data to benchmark performance, which in itself is motivating—the city as a whole and units in particular issue annual reports to share the data with the entire organization and the community, including posting them on the city's website. In addition, the city has set up a City Manager's Strategy Award, which recognizes a key business unit or team that has made significant progress in a key area. Recipient types, disciplines, service areas, and categories vary from year to year. In 2010, the award was presented for impact on overall comprehensive citizen service; in 2009, it was for delivering competitive services; and in 2008, it was for enhanced customer service.

Part of what has made Charlotte so successful in this endeavor is their participation in the University of North Carolina School of Government's North Carolina Local Government Performance Measurement Project, more commonly known as the North Carolina Benchmarking Project. From its website, here is what has been learned from the project:

1. Local governments can produce accurate, reliable, and comparable performance and cost data, which can be used for service improvement.
2. Specific service definitions are vital to performance measurement and benchmarking, including explanatory information.
3. Data availability and data quality are very important to performance measurement.
4. Auditing or verifying the accuracy of performance data is a necessary component of performance measurement and benchmarking.

Performance measurement and cost accounting are time consuming. However, performance measures provide valuable information in the quest to provide quality services at reasonable cost. Find more at http://www.sog.unc.edu/node/909.

Tactical/Operational/Project Planning

As we reach the lower levels of the Vision to Performance Cycle and engage the **tactical/operational/project planning** level, the work shifts from being leadership work to near-term, task- or management-focused implementation work. This is the point at which many organizations fail. They either neglect the development of the tactical actions required or, having identified them, fail to execute well. Too often, the top part of the Vision Cycle has been considered the work of top management, acting alone. As a result, when the strategic plan shows up at the unit or microbusiness level, it has not yet been engaged by this "new" level. Lack of participation in the strategic planning process by units at all levels often results in either direct opposition or passive-aggressive behavior at the unit level. This is precisely why units and microbusinesses need to "run the cycle" at their level and then participate in a top-down, bottoms-up, horizontal-integration nesting process to align the plans at each level. If the people at the service delivery level (or front line) of the organization continue to do what they've always done, no performance improvement can be expected.

The two parts of tactical/operational/project planning are **action planning** and **resource planning**.

- **Action planning.** If we are dealing with an actual project at this level, then this step creates the project plan. Usually, it will include a work breakdown structure (identification of the individual tasks that need to be performed to accomplish the work) and will use other project management techniques, such as sequencing, scheduling, resource estimation, and variance analysis. Responsibility and accountability for the actions should be clearly identified. As will be discussed in Chapter 5, change management (for the "people part" of any project) should be incorporated into the project management plan from the outset of the project. The fundamental concepts underpinning project management are critical to execution success: The focus is on a causal sequence aimed at delivering outputs and making estimates of the expected schedule all along that sequence. The accomplishment of activities as predicted by our project plan serves as one of the first leading indicators to let us know if we're in trouble (Did the activities occur when we said they would?).

- **Resource Planning.** In addition to detailing the actions, events, and activities that need to occur, the organization must create a matching resource plan that covers personnel, equipment, facilities, training, technology, and other costs. Once the resource plan matches the action plan, we can track the accomplishment of the scheduled activities against the estimated resources to be utilized.

In the measurement area, we are now ready to establish our tactical leading indicators: measures that will predict whether we will achieve our outputs (and, thereby, our goals and objectives and outcomes/impacts). The two most common are input measures (Did we get the personnel, facilities, equipment, data, information technology, etc., we estimated for each activity?) and throughput measures (Were the milestones accomplished when we said they would be?). To summarize the measurement hierarchy, it would look like the following:

1. **Vision Level:** Outcome or Impact Measures
   - Timeframe: 5 or more years out
   - Type of Indicator: Trailing/Lagging

2. **Strategic Planning Level:** Strategic Goals and Objectives Measures (e.g., Balanced Scorecard)
   - Timeframe: 3 to 5 years out
   - Type of Indicator: Leading to the Outcome/Impact Measures; Trailing/Lagging to the Tactical Measures

3. **Tactical/Operational/Project Planning Level:** Input, Throughput, Output Measures
   - Timeframe: now to 18 months out
   - Type of Indicator: Leading to the Vision and Strategic Planning levels; Output Measures are Trailing/Lagging to Input/Throughput

Monitoring and Corrective Action

The last phase of the Vision to Performance Cycle, **monitoring and corrective action**, is the actual implementation/execution level in the V2P Cycle. The first key question here is "Are we on budget and on schedule (with the required design and features quality, execution quality, and customer value also being delivered)?" If we are not executing according to our estimates, then recovery planning and remedial actions are required immediately, and these two questions must be asked: "How much of the original plan can we still achieve, and what changes will we need to make in our projected outputs?" and "Whom do we need to notify that we will be missing our output estimates (and presumably our strategic plan level and vision level objectives, as well)?"

If we are on target, however, we proceed and continue monitoring. A formal review of project and service performance must be established in the organization at every level to look at trends of measured performance compared to the tactical implementation plan. A well-integrated, disciplined approach to V2P management at all levels is required to ensure that all of this leadership effort results in higher performance.

1   Tichy, Noel M. "The Teachable Point of View: A Primer." *Harvard Business Review,* Volume 77, Number 2, 1999. pp. 82-83.
2   Bossidy, Larry and Charan, Ram, *Execution: The Discipline of Getting Things Done.* Crown Publishing Group (NY) (June 2002). p. 103.
3   Information on the Leadership Architect can be found on www.kornferry.com.
4   Lombardo, Michael M. and Eichinger, Robert W. *FYI—For Your Improvement: A Guide for Development and Coaching,* Lominger Ltd Inc.; 4th edition (January 2004).
5   Michelle Poche Flaherty is currently President of City on a Hill Consulting.
6   Kaplan, Robert S. and Norton, David P. *The Balanced Scorecard: Translating Strategy into Action,* Harvard Business Review Press, 1996.

Engagement through Values to Work Culture

Many in local government will relate to parts of the **Vision Cycle** in Chapter 3, especially those whose councils or boards are known to set specific staff goals and even production timetables. As this information is relayed to departments and key staff, line managers determine how to best implement the goals, keep track of the deadlines and progress, and report when the work is done. Often the employees on the line have little involvement in the overall picture and are not actively engaged in accomplishing anything beyond a given task. They simply follow the boss's directions to get the work done. This brings "pretty good" task/technical/production results, at least in meeting the council's or board's routine, near-term priorities. Unfortunately, though, this approach neglects the longer-term strategic work of leadership, including the less familiar Values to Work Culture (V2WC) Cycle. This leadership function is less tangible, harder to quantify, and frequently of little direct interest to elected governing bodies—see Figure 4.1.

This "softer" leadership work often takes a backseat to the more task-focused Vision Cycle work of delivering services, building projects, and directly serving the public's most immediate needs. But the Values Cycle and the Vision Cycle work in concert. If the work culture is inherently distrustful, expect poor employee engagement and underutilized talents, skills, and abilities within the workforce. Typically a high-vision, low-values mind-set leaves employees pigeonholed in jobs that limit their contributions, creativity, and energy. The resulting negative impact on human capital alone reduces the likelihood that the government can perform at the level our communities deserve.

As the Wikipedia definition points out, engagement is a key issue for achieving success:

> *An engaged employee is one who is fully involved in, and enthusiastic about, his or her work, and thus will act in a way that furthers their organization's interests . . . [It] is the extent to which workforce commitment, both emotional and intellectual, exists relative to accomplishing the work, mission, and vision of the organization. Engagement can be seen as a heightened level of ownership where each employee wants to do whatever they can for the benefit of their internal and external customers, and for the success of the organization as a whole.*[1]

The Values Cycle takes on this issue of employee engagement. As noted earlier, the level of employee engagement in US organizations is very low compared to world-class organizations. Relatively consistent data show that less than a third of US workers are engaged in their work, while more than half are disengaged, and the rest are actively disengaged. Several studies point to the connection between such low levels of engagement and merely average organizational performance. The Gallup survey organization has been examining this connection for several decades. Their findings show that average-performing organizations have just below two engaged workers for each actively disengaged worker, while world-class organizations have almost ten engaged workers for every actively disengaged worker.[2]

It is not surprising that greater employee engagement results in a higher-functioning organization. It may, however, be surprising that the level of employee engagement is less about the attitude the employees themselves bring to the job than it is about the organizational work culture created in the place in which they work. Managers and supervisors sometimes say that the workforce is not as good as it once was, that employees are not motivated to do a good job, and that their personal values don't support loyalty, hard work, and dedication.

In this section, we aim to shift a good measure of the responsibility to those same managers and supervisors to create a work culture and climate where most employees choose to become engaged in their work, care about their organization's vision and mission, and deliver high performance. The concern is about releasing **discretionary effort**: how much of their talents, skills, and abilities employees choose to utilize at work as a direct contributor to organizational performance. Every day, some employees choose to give their very best to achieve their responsibilities, some choose to do just enough to satisfy their supervisors' minimal requirements, and others actively resist performing their responsibilities. High-performing organizations support employees in delivering all they can bring to their work. Doing this is more natural than restricting employee contributions.

In recent years, much has been written about what leads to an engaged workforce. Consistently, the following types of factors emerge as important:

- having a personal connection with the purpose of the organization and its work
- being able to take responsibility with autonomy for your part of the work connected to the purpose
- having work that is interesting, with variety and challenge
- having the ability to achieve results in something that is important
- being valued by those you respect and having your work recognized and appreciated
- having a trusting relationship with your supervisor and senior management
- having clear expectations about what is required at work
- having your opinion sought and valued on important items
- being able to grow and advance in your skills and abilities
- being able to rely on others to do their part

How do organizations decide that they want these factors to be part of their work culture? Many, of course, don't stop to think about them at all; they just carry on as things have been in the past, the way the traditional

Industrial Model has evolved. Those organizations that are purposeful about ensuring that these factors exist turn to the work in the HPO Model's Values Cycle. They create shared value sets, spelling out the relationships between managers/supervisors and employees; what they expect will motivate and energize all employees; what level of autonomy and empowerment people should have; how decisions should be made; and what standards they want to guide all employee behaviors (including managers/supervisors). They identify how their operating and support systems should serve both the purposes for which they were created and the needs of internal line business partners in trusting and respectful ways. Further, they spell out expectations about these values, strategically committing to align actual behaviors and systems to the stated values, coaching people on acting in accordance with the values, giving feedback on how well they do, and taking corrective action to resolve any discordance.

The Values Cycle is designed to produce a statement of values and a plan to implement and enforce them. Although the cycle looks primarily at one key diagnostic question—KDQ 7 (How do we treat each other, our partners, our beneficiaries, our food chain, and our other stakeholders?)—it also directs attention to KDQ 2 (How would we know if we were high performing?). Many technically oriented organizations are challenged by these questions, since they tend to focus on technical performance rather than also considering the effect of personal behaviors on performance. The work contained in the Values Cycle is critical to building trusting relationships among the people within an organization and between the organization and the external world; in this sense, the cycle is all about building trust. Like the Vision Cycle, it proceeds from high-level, conceptual work (imagine a marble accelerating down a funnel) and moves down the cycle, with each lower level being more near-term focused and specific. We begin the values work by addressing the three values sets, introduced in Chapter 2, that are the building blocks of a high-performing organization's work culture:

- **Leadership Philosophy:** A statement of philosophy explaining the assumptions upon which management and supervisory actions and behaviors are based and judged.
- **Individual Behavioral Values:** A shared values set that helps establish the human side of the organization's work culture, provides a standard

for judging interpersonal behavior, and defines how we treat each other and our stakeholders.

- **Operating Systems Values:** Values that define the technical side of the organization's culture; provide a standard for judging the organization's strategies, structures, and systems/processes; and guide our business/administrative operating systems and our technical work processes.

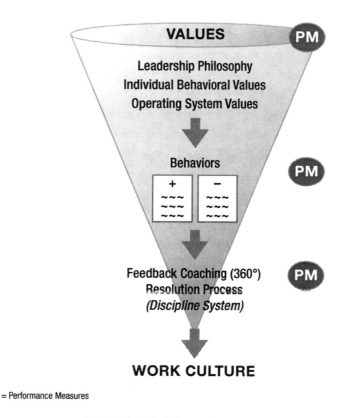

FIGURE 4.1 The Values to Work Culture Cycle

Let's take a look at each of these three value sets that make up the Values to Work Culture (V2WC) Cycle. "Pulling apart" the values work into these three sets helps us to think about and reflect upon them. Any final values statement that is adopted for implementation may state them separately or may integrate them together.

1. LEADERSHIP PHILOSOPHY

Leadership philosophy is the major determinant of the trust level that will exist between the workforce and management. Patrick Lencioni writes in *The Five Dysfunctions of a Team*[3] that "Trust lies at the heart of a functioning, cohesive team. Without it, teamwork is all but impossible." Well-formed teams, operating as microbusinesses, are a primary source of high-performance in twenty-first-century organizations. Since trust is essential to how teams operate, it is imperative for the organization to create an environment that stimulates trusting relationships throughout. This is so critical to high-performance that in the HPO Model, leadership philosophy is in the "number one" change lever position. See Figure 2.2 in Chapter 2.

The approach to examining leadership philosophy is based on a theoretical base developed by a number of authors[4] to view, discuss, diagnose, and finally articulate an organization's leadership philosophy. How organizations answer the following questions (and translate them into action through their systems and processes) determines their actual leadership philosophy:

- What is the nature of people and their attitudes toward work?
- What is the primary source of motivation for most people?
- What is the distribution of knowledge and creativity and, therefore, how should decisions be made?
- What is the "nature of work"?

The range of possible answers to these questions is displayed in Figure 4.2. On the left half of the figure are organizations that see most people as not liking to work hard; not being ambitious or wanting responsibility; not doing a good job unless directly and closely supervised; motivated by coercion, threats, and punishment; and operating with limited knowledge, talent, and creativity. Contemporary organizations reflecting these views are likely to have control-oriented, multilayered hierarchies, dictating exactly what workers must do most of the time. Line employees are rarely consulted or involved in the managerial function of designing work processes. *Work* is a set of discrete tasks that workers perform as directed by the supervisor. Line workers are not asked to think creatively about how to improve their work or the systems and processes they use, and suggestions they make are often not taken seriously. Even today, these notions still permeate many parts of public and private sector organizations. A substantial body of evidence shows that if an organization is characterized by these beliefs in practice, it is highly likely that its performance suffers dramatically.

On the right half of the figure are organizations that see most people as wanting to do a good job because it is a core human need and as wanting to be part of something meaningful; being motivated (once basic needs are satisfied) by challenge, responsibility, achievement, recognition, personal growth, and advancement to more challenging work; and being knowledgeable and having creative capability. Such organizations expect good problem solving, continuous study and improvement of work processes, and innovation requiring consultation with and involvement of a wide range of knowledgeable employees. Under these beliefs, work is seen as integrated processes larger than any single individual and needing knowledgeable, broadly skilled, and talented workers who collaborate to ensure that jointly held objectives are accomplished. In his book *Drive*[5], Daniel Pink singled out, from decades of research on employee engagement, three similar key motivational factors: autonomy (having a "say" on what and how work gets done), mastery (getting better and better at something valued), and purpose (contributing to something meaningful and important).

The work of Rensis Likert provides a "lens" for helping organizations diagnose their leadership philosophy. In his research, Likert found that organizations' "outputs," (or performance) when compared to others in their same sectors, varied with their sets of behaviors and beliefs.[6] Poor/mediocre performers had a belief set named System 1 (S1): Exploitative autocratic-mediocre, System 2 (S2): Benevolent autocratic-fair to good, System 3 (S3): Consultative-good to excellent, and System 4 (S4): Participative-excellent. Under Likert's approach, a shift from one position on the continuum to its nearest neighbor results in both a mind-set shift on the part of management and a corresponding behavior shift. Despite the implication that System 4 results in the best performance, however, few organizations in the local government sector can easily embrace a pure System 4 culture due to the unavoidable external demands and expectations in the political context. Instead, a combination of Systems 3 and 4 is possible and is capable, if the other parts of the HPO Model are also successfully addressed, of supporting superior results.

From Likert's and similar empirical studies and from the authors' own applied experience, we believe that organizations seeking high performance

LIKERT'S FOUR LEADERSHIP PHILOSOPHIES

SYSTEM 1 (Exploitative Autocratic)	SYSTEM 2 (Benevolent Autocratic)	SYSTEM 3 (Consultative)	SYSTEM 4 (Participative)
• People are seen as basically lazy, selfish, dishonest, and inept; they will not work unless constantly threatened and closely supervised; workers are exploited and have little recourse.	• Not much shift from S1; people are still seen as self-centered and in need of close supervision; because management wants to prevent costly turnover, however, policies are more benevolent.	• A major shift from S1/S2; people are seen as wanting—even needing—to do a good job; if they know what needs doing and have the skills, they will do a good job without very much external control or direction.	• Very similar to S3; people are seen as wanting—even needing—to do a good job; if they know what needs doing and have the skills, they will do a good job without very much external control or direction.
• People are motivated by the fear of the loss of job, pay, or dignity; they will be terminated or punished if they do not comply with management's directions; "it's my way (the bosses) or the highway."	• In addition to fear/punishment, status is added as a motivator; if workers are mindlessly loyal and compliant, they are rewarded with the illusion of advancement; S2 organizations usually have many status layers with each layer having many pay "steps."	• Once the basic "hygiene" factors (pay, benefits, working conditions, safety, etc.) are taken care of in a "fair" way, then motivation is seen as coming from within the work; it must provide challenge, growth, recognition, and a sense of contribution.	• Once the basic "hygiene" factors (pay, benefits, working conditions, safety, etc.) are taken care of in a "fair" way, then motivation is seen as coming from within the work; it must provide challenge, growth, recognition, and a sense of contribution.
• Knowledge, ability, and creativity are seen as concentrated in management; workers are seen as largely incompetent; as a result, there is no need for management to consult, because labor has nothing useful to say.	• Knowledge, ability, and creativity are still seen as concentrated in management; some confidence is shown in the technical ability of workers; but organizational decisions are still made without consultation.	• Knowledge, ability, and creativity are seen as widely distributed; management does not know all the answers (or even all the questions); it needs help if the best decisions for the customer and the organization are to be found; consultation is the norm; less hierarchy is needed.	• People are seen as being so capable that many responsibilities seen in the past as being solely the work of managers can be transferred to self-directed work teams who perform these leadership/management functions as a natural part of getting the technical/task work done.
• To best control labor, work is divided into small ("dumber and dumber") pieces; there is a supervisor for every 6–8 workers, a manager for each 6–8 workers, to tightly control, direct, and punish; results in a steep, high hierarchy.	• Work is still broken into pieces with management responsible for the integration of work; "critical parent-child" relationship between management and labor (and between each layer in the steep hierarchy).	• Work is seen as complex processes involving networks or employees working together to reach goals; management's responsibility is to create a culture (values, strategies, structures, and systems) that allow for maximum consultation.	• Work is seen as complex processes involving collectives of employees working together to reach goals; teams are responsible for task/technical, managerial, and leadership functions.
• This is a "master-slave" style; it is clear that the worker is not important to the organization; "if you don't like this deal, there's a bus leaving every 5 minutes;" its only positive aspect is that it is honest about not caring about the worker; fear and mistrust characterize relationships.	• This style, while more benevolent, is manipulative; "masters" treat the "servants" better because "good help is hard to get," but there is still no say for the servants on "management" issues; mistrust often characterizes the relationships.	• This style is "adult-adult" in relationship; management is still accountable, but it recognizes that it must consult widely if good decisions are to be made.	• This style is "adult-adult" in relationship; management (and team leaders with delegated responsibility) is still accountable, but recognizes it must play a stewardship role in creating empowered work teams.

can use neither of the left side autocratic leadership philosophies (Systems 1 and 2). The "parent-to-child" (or worse) assumptions underpinning the two autocratic philosophies simply do not correctly match the nature, capability, personal expectations, and dedication of today's workforce, nor do they support the need of today's organizations for help from all levels of the workforce in adapting to rapidly changing conditions. Furthermore, these two autocratic philosophies do not provide for the workforce to effectively improve performance. Organizations that try to implement many of the current performance improvement initiatives (like LEAN quality improvement programs), without changing their leadership philosophies toward the more "adult-to-adult" Systems 3 and 4 philosophies are likely to fail in their efforts, because these initiatives assume that at least a System 3 (adult-adult, consultative) leadership philosophy is already in place. This also explains why many Total Quality Management efforts failed in the 1970s–1990s.

For many control-oriented managers, the idea of empowering the workforce and substituting a shared vision and set of operating values for personal control may sound threatening. In his book *The Empowered Manager*, Peter Block recognized how hard this shift can be for managers who are steeped in the control mind-set of the traditional Industrial Model when he wrote:

If managers have to choose between giving up control for the sake of higher performance and maintaining control knowing performance will be less, in most cases managers choose to maintain control.[7]

But creating a consultative/participative leadership philosophy does not mean creating a directionless organization with employees doing whatever they want. That would be *permissiveness* or *chaos*, not collaboration and participation. Rather, a consultative/participative philosophy means building a shared vision of where the organization needs to go, constructing an organizational work culture and climate with operating values that enable all employees to actively and creatively participate in pursuing the vision, and then removing excess bureaucratic controls and creating a sense of freedom—within the boundaries established by the vision and values—so that people can commit their full talents and energies to accomplishing their shared goals. A shared vision and values set, then, becomes the authority for action. Choices that are consistent with the shared vision/values require less and less review, control, and direction. The conjunction between the Vision Cycle (where the shared vision is created and the operating systems and work processes are developed and modified, as described in Chapter 3) and the Values Cycle (where the shared values are created) becomes apparent. Work needs to proceed and be interwoven in the two cycles for the organization to engage the entire workforce in achieving high performance.

Ultimately, however, managers remain accountable under both Systems 3 and 4 for all decisions and for timely performance. If a team cannot or will not reach a decision within the time frames required, it is the responsibility of the manager to take the information provided by team members and make an executive decision. A deadline should never be missed because the team can't reach a decision. Managers, using a System 3 (consultative) leadership philosophy, can, when necessary (e.g., when there is not enough time to consult, in emergency situations, when a timely decision for the team can't be made), be decisive, demanding, and even directive, relying on previous plans and consultation when available and appropriate. They just can't be abusive, demeaning, or condescending; it is never okay to treat employees as serfs, servants, or children (which would make the leadership philosophy a System 1 or 2). In cases like this, the manager would also be obligated to explain the reasoning behind her decision to the team. Subsequently, if the team sees a way she could have reached a better decision, she would expect them to discuss it with her because she is always trying to improve her decision-making competency—but that last decision is already made.

The power of undertaking the leadership work of the Values Cycle is seen clearly in the next case study, about the Social Services Department in Lynchburg, Virginia. You will also see the crucial role that leadership teams play in accomplishing an organization's leadership work, which we will be examining in Chapter 5.

CASE STUDY

The Department of Social Services in Lynchburg, Virginia[8]

—A. Tyler St.Clair and Mark C. Johnson. A. Tyler St.Clair was Lynchburg's Organizational Development staff person. She served as an internal consultant for the Lynchburg Department of Social Services from 1995–2000. Mark C. Johnson was

the Director of the Lynchburg Department of Social Services from January 1995 until December 2010.

The city of Lynchburg, Virginia, has about 75,000 residents. Its Department of Social Services currently comprises 130 staff members, with about 45 percent of them dedicated to social work, 45 percent to financial assistance, and 10 percent to administration and administrative support. The organizational structure includes a director, an assistant director, a chief of financial assistance, program supervisors, and 119 direct service staff members. But the setup wasn't always like this.

In January 1995, the Lynchburg Department of Social Services (LDSS) hired Mark C. Johnson to serve as director. He was new to social services, having been the administrator of a juvenile corrections facility for the previous ten years. He was familiar with the High-Performance Organization (HPO) Model and eager to apply its theories and principles to an organization that needed them. This case study covers a fifteen-year period that was initiated upon his hiring. By 2010, the organization's staff had grown from 96 to 130, primarily due to welfare reform initiatives.

Johnson's first step was to gain an understanding of the organization from the view of its employees. He conducted interviews with every staff member during his first two weeks on the job. His questions were the same: "What works well here? What is not working particularly well? What do we need to do differently?"

Staff members had little to say about what was going well, with the most positive response being that they liked their units. They didn't believe that the other units were doing a good job, although they believed their own units were slightly better. There was a tremendous lack of trust and little confidence that the administrators were competent enough to do their jobs. There was a great deal of segmentation and conflict within the organization.

As for what was not working well, the responses were varied: "The administration talks at us, but doesn't work with us." "Administrators are very arbitrary and punish us when we make mistakes." "Sometimes we are punished for things for which we didn't know we were responsible." "The administration has favorites." "Our compensation is inadequate, and no one is concerned about it." "The building in which we work [has] no security." "The vehicles we have to drive are in poor condition." "We need a new building, better computers, and better cars." "The administration doesn't seem to listen, there is no sense in complaining because nothing is done about the problems, and we may suffer negative consequences for sharing the concerns."

The interviews uncovered many agency problems at a very basic level to promote a safe work environment. Social Services was housed in a building constructed in 1907 as a general hospital, with a 1945 annex, in one of the city's high-crime areas, with open-air drug markets on a nearby street. One financial assistance staff member worked in the basement previously used as the morgue. The building had no security, and anyone could enter and subsequently accost his or her social worker, interrupt work, or access confidential records. During the new director's first week, a drug dealer entered the facility and stashed drugs in the drop ceiling of the bathroom. Little had been done to address these issues, thus communicating an attitude that worker safety was unimportant.

Administrators and financial assistance workers and social workers were in separate buildings, impairing communication among staff who served the same clients. Offices were very small, isolated, and lacked the capacity for confidential record storage. A host of maintenance issues remained unaddressed, creating very poor working conditions.

The staff concerns clearly revealed a functioning Likert System 1 style of management. Unaddressed safety needs reinforced the perception that employees were not valued, and there was significant potential for someone to get hurt, given the nature of the environment, clientele, and work culture. Social science regarding motivation offered powerful wisdom about how to address these issues. The first simple step was to communicate meaningful concern for the agency's staff members.

Johnson asked the city's police department for a security analysis of the building, prompting new lighting for the building, more secure locks on the doors, and new procedures to control access to the building. Now, caseworkers personally received each client and escorted him or her to their office. Thus, the receptionists knew where the workers were and had a clearer schedule, and there was more consistency in the agency's "reception persona."

Johnson also established a set of conduct standards for clients (called a "bar policy") that brought increased physical and emotional security to the organization. Clear expectations for behaviors in the building were communicated to clients and staff. When clients were verbally abusive or behaved in a threatening manner, the director warned them by letter that a reoccurrence of that behavior would result in their being barred from the social services building. No warning would be issued for aggravated cases. In either case, legally mandated service delivery would be provided to the client, often in a meeting room near the complaint desk of the police department. This simple step to make people safe was truly appreciated by the employees.

PERFORMANCE ISSUES IN THE ORGANIZATION

Once safety was addressed and employees began to feel that they were being heard and having their basic needs met, Johnson moved on to improving the department's many performance needs. When he asked about performance, supervisors of each service area were able to offer only cursory information. Supervisors said that their work was generally good but that there might be some timeliness issues. As it turned out, the agency had 4,000 active Medicaid cases, and roughly 40 percent of Medicaid reviews were overdue. Overdue reviews of spend-downs or incomes created cases in which clients might be approved for Medicaid but not receive their money or, conversely, others received money for which they were ineligible.

Actual measures reflected far worse performance, with timeliness an issue throughout the agency. In Medicaid, the agency was timely 60 percent of the time; for Temporary Assistance for Needy Families (TANF), 65 percent of the time. The agency was compliant with foster care policy mandates (e.g., plans, frequency of visits, going to court) 70 percent of the time.

Furthermore, there was an increasing number of adult clients in need of adult day care, companion care, and investigations of allegations of physical and emotional abuse and financial exploitation. There were no performance measures available for the 2.5 staff members providing adult care service delivery, but it was clear they were understaffed to meet the growing needs.

Another problem was structural, but manifesting itself in performance. Staff members who investigated complaints of child abuse and neglect and those who monitored cases were in different units. The workers did not work together, and as a result, children were not as safe as possible. After investigating a child abuse or neglect case, the investigator would file a report. Upon initiating work with the child and family, the ongoing unit workers often failed to talk to the investigators and provide information to each other as case status changed. These workers did not see themselves as part of an integrated microbusiness but rather as separate units with their own responsibilities. With significant animosity between the two units, this surfaced in performance. In 1994, 7.5 percent of children receiving ongoing services were maltreated again, even though Social Services was supporting the families.

In addition, there was no measurement of customer service quality within the agency; staff members were not responding to clients well. Receptionists were often abrupt and/or curt and did not listen to clients. Systems required frustrated clients to do the same things two or three times. Social workers seemed to make predetermined decisions about families based on the appearance of their house rather than asking questions and listening carefully. In many parts of the agency, the attitude seemed to be "These people are lucky that we are willing to help them." Staff commonly refused to return client phone calls—another pervasive attitude seemed to be "I'm too busy."

Staff conflict was prevalent between and within the units. Five of the eight units in the agency had a history of considerable unaddressed conflict. Staff members were jealous of coworkers whom they perceived were being held accountable to different standards.

Johnson concluded that LDSS was ripe for change, with many opportunities for intervention, explaining, "Staff members didn't know what was expected of them and there were no measures of performance, so they established their own measures or standards. People in a very confusing environment with very little information often felt they were not receiving what others were. There was no clarity of purpose or clear sense of direction; that created many kinds of conflict. The lack of measurable indicators for performance further increased interpersonal conflict."

INITIATING THE HIGH-PERFORMANCE ORGANIZATION WORK

With some basic health and safety issues addressed and a more receptive workforce, it was time to formalize a change mechanism. The agency needed a group to champion the change and a place to start. Johnson worked with the city's organization development consultant to plan a high-performance strategy that would work for LDSS's size, structure, and specific needs. The agency formed a leadership team, called the Facilitation Team, a representative group of twenty-four staff members drawn from every unit and level of the organization. With ninety-six total staff members, a relatively large number were directly involved in the initial leadership work. The team was comprised primarily of direct service staff members who wanted things to be better but did include all the supervisors and key administrators. When asked whether he chose "naysayers," Johnson responded, "Everyone was a naysayer at that point. I just wanted reasonable people on the team." The team generated excitement because a large number of people in the organization whose input had never before been sought were becoming part of a group that would influence what they did in their daily jobs.

The Facilitation Team met weekly for a half day from February through August 1995, first on site and then off site. The city's organization development consultant, who had an understanding of the HPO Model, designed and facilitated the sessions.

The facilitator lent expertise to the team's process, which was then reinforced on-the-job by Johnson, who had a clear personal inclination to lead in a facilitative style. Wanting to be "close to the process but not [to] spoon-feed or indoctrinate the team," he chose to be an equal member of the group. Initially, the team spent a lot of time talking about how they would be equal members and "wear the same hat." The director served as the between-meetings communicator, encouraging staff members and making connections between the work they were doing as a leadership group and the daily programs and tasks.

Early team-building activities for the Facilitation Team were critical in helping the members appreciate and work with its varied members. They took the Myers-Briggs Type Indicator (MBTI) and, for the first time, began to understand the impact of their differences on how the agency was functioning. They did values work using a simple leadership shield exercise to depict who they were as people. Team members left that meeting agreeing they would put their shields on their office doors so others would understand the values that drove them. At these early stages, the Facilitation Team could see the promise of their organization—which had been very diffused, segmented, and conflictive—coming together with a common purpose and could increasingly believe that they were contributing to becoming a healthier organization. They also began to understand themselves more, and the resulting energy was easily seen at Facilitation Team meetings. Unlikely individuals became some of the group's apostles for change. While some participants only complied, others were transformed by the work to build the agency's change mechanism.

The Facilitation Team first spent considerable time on creating an agency vision statement, and its focus was on individual responsibility:

> We encourage and support positive actions that families and individuals take toward the development of independence, self-worth, and responsible citizenship.

FIGURE 4.2

That doesn't sound like a typical social services vision—rather, a vision for society. The significance was heightened because federal and state welfare reform was becoming a reality. The agency's vision focused on client and staff independence and responsibility, themes that would be important for self-direction and self-sufficiency. Members of the Facilitation Team also began to see that if they could not influence their own and the organization's destiny through positive action, then they would be unlikely to influence the positive efforts of clients.

Addressing organizational work culture was critical, especially following the administration of an assessment of the Facilitation Team using Likert's Profile of Organizational Characteristics questionnaire, which can be seen in the Appendix. Members placed the agency squarely in System 1 (exploitative autocratic) and identified a goal to grow the organization into a System 3 (consultative). The leadership philosophy for the group unfolded into principles that became the foundation for both work culture and performance:

We believe that people are willing to accept collective responsibility and strongly desire to be a part of the decision-making process.

- We must create an organizational culture and environment which nurtures and develops all our talents and resources.
- Leadership is everyone's responsibility.
- All people are different and we should value those differences and grow from them.
- The sharing of knowledge and information is a right and a responsibility.
- People need interaction in order to identify with and communicate with others.
- Individuals are creative, responsible, make valued decisions, and take risks.
- Vision is shared by everyone: There is commitment to the vision.

FIGURE 4.3

The leadership principles became a useful tool for organizational reflection and change. While the agency's program supervisors met monthly to discuss management issues, a healthy exchange was activated by a discussion or activity on one of the leadership principles facilitated by a member. It also helped to present and discuss a leadership principle or a vision- or values-related component at each monthly meeting.

The leadership principles were also used in the recruitment and selection process. As usual, candidates for all jobs had to demonstrate technical qualities from the job description, but now they also had to demonstrate leadership competencies reflected in the agency's leadership principles. Last but not least, agency policies reviewed over time were modified based on the leadership principles.

The LDSS values work incorporated changes coming from welfare reform, increased client and staff diversity, and new research on healthy families and the concept of asset-based intervention. While the leadership principles focused on individual behavior and commitment, the values shaped how to think about and approach serving clients.

Lynchburg Social Services Values

- We believe in clear, honest communication with our clientele in order to encourage their personal growth.

- We believe that the recognition of diversity is important and must be respected in order to ensure the best service delivery.

- We believe that providing superior customer service consistently will guide our customers toward developing self-sufficiency and independence.

- We believe that it is important that the community be respectful and sensitive to individual differences and cultural diversity in order to create a community environment which utilizes all resources.

- We believe that it takes a coordinated community based effort to help individuals and families solve their problems.

- We believe individuals and families have the ability to solve their own problems and families are a tremendous resource in our community.

- We believe in mutual cooperation and individual responsibility in order to successfully accomplish goals and better manage one's future.

- We believe that the community's understanding of the agency vision, through education and public awareness, will ensure high-quality and cost-effective services.

FIGURE 4.4

While the Facilitation Team members had been sharing the progress made in weekly meetings with their respective units, they felt that reporting on the change levers to the full staff would crystallize the effort for the entire organization. There had never been an all-staff retreat for the organization, and the idea was greeted with great enthusiasm. The full-staff retreat was a huge success; everyone attended as Johnson arranged for staff members from other agencies to maintain routine operations during the event. Kicking things off with a discussion about the new vision statement, the director talked about being called to a higher purpose and helped the group see that the vision applied to the people in the agency as well as the clients and the work of the agency. Other members talked about the values, and skits demonstrated the leadership principles. Circumstances had been so bad that the hope of something better got people moving.

The message had been sent and received. This was no longer the concern of just twenty-four people; the circle of invested staff members had been expanded to all ninety-six. The whole organization was about to move in the same direction.

RESOLUTION BEGINS

While the Facilitation Team was initiating change and helping the organization join in the process, work was also being done on the facility. In nine short months, the agency occupied a different building, resulting in further improvements to the working conditions that had challenged the agency. Staff members were involved in planning the space they would occupy based on client services and workflow. After years of not being heard, the new organizational culture of involvement was being reflected in asking employees to help with new facility decision making.

In addition, the city was developing a system to enable better fleet management where operating agencies were on the newly formed fleet board to give direct input. The board soon sought more feedback from users, an entirely new practice.

After the full-staff retreat, the team went to monthly half-day meetings as it refined its work systems and processes. Guided by its vision, values, and leadership philosophy and principles, the team began to focus on how to improve the organization. It developed a policy on chartering work groups and decided to focus on four specific issues in the beginning and later continued to charter teams for specific purposes.

The four initial work groups, provided with charters to guide them, focused on these areas: (1) how to communicate better as a staff organization; (2) developing the agency's welfare reform program that was to be implemented in October 1995; (3) eliminating duplication across the agency; and (4) how to occupy the new office space as planned. In the end, three of the work teams were effective. The team focused on duplication was relatively unsuccessful because even though workers had to enter the same information multiple times on different forms, external requirements over which the agency had little control impeded consolidation of processes.

The work of the welfare reform work group, which began in March 1995, was solidified when the rest of the work groups were chartered. Since Virginia was one of the first three states to implement the employment requirement of welfare, little outside experience was available for guidance. By October 1995, the work group had developed the welfare reform program, its staffing, and costs. The state approved and funded the program for its initial year (including generous allocations in the following years), and Lynchburg became the first urban locality in Virginia to implement the state's welfare reform initiative.

The welfare reform work group agreed to serve as one of six experimental sites for the state for research purposes. The group carefully monitored success and provided statistics to enable conclusions about welfare reform. By February 1996, the experimental sites were telling the state what LDSS already knew: If you require people to work, they will do so. But if you do not require people to work, they won't. By that spring, the state comprehensively enacted welfare reform to enhance the personal responsibility of welfare recipients to move away from dependence on government support toward self-sufficiency. As the benefits of the program crystallized, employment rates for Lynchburg's recipients grew. By the end of 1997, 75 percent of the agency's recipients were engaged in work activities, compared to the previous employment rate of 36 percent.

The communications work group did a great job. In the previous Likert System 1 leadership philosophy of the agency, communication had been downward, inadequate, and often punitive. The work group defined a communications policy still in effect today so that communication is consistent with the organization's values.

The policy mandated monthly unit meetings, required higher-level administrators to attend them twice a year, and defined what constituted a full staff meeting and its purpose. It provided for interunit staff meetings so that staff members were aware of what was going on in other units. It created a quarterly newsletter, still issued today.

Of course, some strategies ultimately proved ineffective. For instance, an early strategy that created an agency-wide bulletin board for units to share what they were doing and the big issues that they were facing proved less helpful and was discontinued. The communications work group's initial report made significant changes in the quality of the agency's communication and it continued to recommend improvements over time.

The group charged with relocating to another building was also highly successful. Members determined where to place offices so that people could work together in clusters, advised about the telephone system and voicemail response, addressed common meeting space use and reservation, and helped make decisions about office furniture purchase and placement.

Finally, the agency had found a way to simultaneously move out of its punitive, command-and-control style and enhance the work culture and performance of the agency. The use of work teams to address change issues for the agency proved to be a viable strategy over time.

WORK GROUPS CONTINUE TO PLAY A ROLE

The agency had a second major relocation for which it reconstituted the work group in 2002 as the "environmental work group." They were challenged with a move to a historic warehouse located in the heart of downtown. The group dealt with the geography of unit positioning, moving from closed offices to work cubicles, handling conference space and break areas, and creating and managing confidential interview spaces for intermittent use. New issues emerged, like how to keep individual work areas quiet within the more open warehouse environment. The work group addressed security concerns, such as when workers entering the building on weekends to catch up with caseloads triggered the new alarm systems. The requirements to ensure good work in LDSS were made clear to the project manager, ultimately resulting in a building that was functional, used creatively, and "owned" by the staff who contributed to its planning.

Four very important teams chartered in 2000 and 2001 focused on improving business processes dealing with customer service, child protective services among intake/investigation/ongoing services, lack of adequate adult protective services staff, and financial assistance.

The customer service work group produced an agency customer service plan that outlined requirements, targets, and measures. The plan defined specific behaviors to be used with clients, such as staff returning all phone calls within 24 business hours and personal voicemail greetings being updated daily and identifying who could assist in a staff member's absence. The work group set an agency target of overall 95 percent client satisfaction and developed a survey instrument to measure it. The survey's first reporting year, 2002, showed an overall satisfaction rate of 86 percent, and the satisfaction rate has increased each year. The survey has since been used as a model for social service departments in the state.

The two work groups looking at business processes supporting adult services client work and child protective services (CPS) ultimately merged to address concerns. They determined that the needs of adults should be addressed by a self-contained unit, and that the CPS ongoing staff members should merge with the CPS investigators, creating a new CPS unit, including intake, investigations, and ongoing services functions. The work group used resources in a local college to identify the evolving needs of senior adults in Central Virginia which led to adding three new positions and reallocating three vacancies to the unit.

The financial assistance work group tackled even greater segmentation in order to move to a "one-stop shop" model. The agency had focused individual groups of workers on Medicaid, TANF, food stamps, and intake—a complex service structure that could give each client four different caseworkers. Typically, a host of operational issues impaired service delivery outcomes among the different groups involved. The work group that studied this problem suggested a generic delivery model. Rather than four sections, each dealing with an individual program, there would be two sections: one serving adults and the other serving families and children. Any staff member in either unit would be able to handle any type of policy issue for their group of clients. The change required staff members to understand the relationships among the programs. Individuals who were traditionally policy experts in one area (e.g., food stamps) were now required to become policy generalists, thus expanding the purpose and the scope of every staff member's job to take a more broadened view of success in the organization. While staff members recognized that they needed to change, it was still very difficult and sometimes overwhelming for them to understand three very complicated programs. In addition, many had to change the unit in which they worked and thus physically move. The work group worked with all unit members to explain the need for the new system, hear and respond to their concerns, keep them informed about the changes, and facilitate problem solving in the units. High performance is about changing the way you do business, aligning resources to meet the service needs, and making sure that staff members are right in the middle of these alignment processes.

There were two other significant work groups to profile in the agency's move to higher performance. Recognizing that controlling "who was coming in the gate" was an important part of high performance, a recruitment and selection work group was chartered. This group made sweeping, long-lasting changes by integrating the leadership philosophy/principles and values into agency recruitment and selection processes. Each selection first required panels to do a behavioral interview with an assessment center based on the leadership philosophy and values as a second step. The panels, representing the units themselves including direct service providers, the supervisor, and a representative from any unit affected by the work of the unit, were recertified in the skill of behavioral interviewing on an annual basis. The assessment centers were required to be relevant to the type of work for which the candidates were applying (versus an "off the shelf" approach).

The work group updated the processes in 2006 and 2008 with improved standardized methods for reference checks and communication with candidates during the selection process. It soon became clear that individuals who invested to be on the panels tended to be better candidates in subsequent promotional selection processes. The internal messaging began to permeate the organization that good candidates had to be more than just technicians in their current jobs and that leadership qualities were important. Performance indicators in LDSS consistently reflect that they recruit and select people who act in accordance with the vision, values, and leadership philosophy of the agency.

Another group focused on upwards assessment was to develop ways for staff members to give supervisors objective, confidential feedback. The work group developed an "upward assessment" that gives each worker the chance to offer feedback to his or her supervisor as well as to those positions that serve everyone—the director, assistant director, and facility manager. In an online process completed annually in the fall, individuals who are assessed get a confidential report that includes all input, but they cannot see who gives specific feedback. They then develop performance improvement plans for further developing their strengths and addressing problem areas, which they post on their doors and discuss with unit members.

Upward assessment remains in use within the agency and has been an effective developmental tool, providing a formal venue to give supervisors feedback to improve their leadership skills. It has given the organization a greater sense of cohesiveness because feedback is open, honest, and actionable.

LOOKING AT HIGH-PERFORMANCE RESULTS

While the department was required to use a citywide performance evaluation instrument to measure individual performance, LDSS developed individual performance contracts specifying how each person would be measured. The performance expectations incorporated the leadership principles, vision, and values; identified specific requirements from the customer service plan; and addressed the manner in which people led, collaborated, and communicated. Each unit met to define standards for exceeding, meeting, or not meeting expectations for technical work; those standards were also incorporated into performance expectations. After many years of arbitrary performance evaluation, employees understood from the outset how they would be evaluated in terms of both technical competence and leadership.

LDSS identified a number of helpful measures to monitor organizational performance and workplace culture. Monthly performance for 178 indicators were posted on boards and demonstrated vast improvements between 1995 and 2010, including

- The 1,400 overdue Medicaid reviews seen in 1995 were reduced to 36 by 1997. In the years since, the highest number of overdue reviews has been 75.
- The 1995 timeliness rate of 60 percent on Medicaid applications increased to 93 percent in 2010.
- A 65 percent timeliness rate for TANF applications in 1995 was increased to 95 percent in 2010.
- Compliance with foster care policy was 75 percent in 1995 and had improved to 95 percent in 2010.
- Recurrence of child abuse in ongoing child protective services was at 7.5 percent in 1995 and was down to 2 percent in five years; in 2010, it was down to 0 percent.
- The agency had no measures of customer service in 1995 but did not appear to be in a good place. By 2002, there was 86 percent overall satisfaction in customer service as measured by survey; by 2010, there was a 96 percent overall satisfaction rate.
- In 1995, the Likert Profile of Organizational Characteristics questionnaire reflected a System 1. The assessment was administered again in 1998 and reflected a System 2. Within five years, the assessment had moved to System 3, with a solid clustering of the responses. A 2010 assessment again reflected a high System 3.

What can you conclude from this case study? Investing in people works. HPO is about getting people to believe in themselves, ensuring that they have authority and influence, and then setting up the systems, structures, and strategies so that they can perform.

The Lynchburg Department of Social Services represents a sustained effort to become a high-performing organization. The first fifteen years of its change journey are described here, but the work continues. Though there is a different director today, there is still a Facilitation Team, there are still work groups, and the vision, values, and leadership philosophy and principles are still a force for change in the organization.

Mark Johnson's actions to transform Lynchburg Social Services demonstrate that, while there is no single way to implement High-Performance Organization methodologies, it is wise to address early on the kinds of safety and security issues he found upon entering this shockingly wounded organization. They represented what Frederick Herzberg termed "hygiene" factors: the kinds of issues that, while they will never motivate employees to do great work, will *de*-motivate them when significant. Safety and security are basic needs that have to be addressed before higher-level concerns can be solved.

Johnson began by asking employees for their advice, setting up a values discussion climate, and establishing a glimmer of hope for the organization's future. Careful not to overpromise and to take on only as much as the resources and work culture would permit, he worked over fifteen years on a transition that even today is not yet "done." He empowered a carefully selected, cross-representational Facilitation Team that quickly tackled vision, mission, and strategic customer issues. The team broadened the organization's internal/external stakeholder inclusiveness network. It practiced and reinforced empowerment with clear Systems 3 and 4 behavior and thinking. Knowing that results would require measurement and sound data, the Facilitation Team pushed for increases in accountability. The work was done incrementally, the answers to general questions informing actions that would lead to increasingly specific actions through smaller and finer circling down through both the Vision to Performance and Values to Work Culture Cycles. It is easy to understand that as the work in Lynchburg progressed, the level of employee engagement increased. When Systems 3 and 4 leadership philosophies become rooted in such an organization, employees feel like they make a valued contribution to a meaningful purpose, and they become more committed to bringing the discretionary effort to be higher performing.

In another case study, we look at how Sarasota County, Florida, turned to its employees to help cope with the difficulties springing from the recent recession. It built upon its long-term investment in developing its organizational culture and commissioned teams of volunteers to undertake a series of initiatives. Engaged employees, operating in Systems 3 and 4, delivered specific results that produced tangible cost reductions, efficiencies, system improvements, and employee development tools.

CASE STUDY

Challenges, Solutions, and Innovations Alliance
in Sarasota County, Florida[8]

—Mary Sassi Furtado writes about events that occurred when she worked in Sarasota County, Florida.

Sarasota County, located on the southwest coast of Florida, has a population of about 390,000, operates with an annual total budget of $870 million, and has 3,257 full-time employees.

The recent unprecedented and difficult economic times have had a dramatic impact on local governments, including the struggle to balance the service demands of citizens against budgetary realities. As challenges escalate, crucial conversations with employees become increasingly important. While most government leaders understand the need for courageous discussions, understanding how to best engage employees on emotion-laden topics is another matter altogether.

To help weather the storm, the Sarasota County Government (SCG) deliberately turned to its philosophical commitment to the Networked Talent Model, where all levels of an informed and engaged workforce participate in solution generating and decision making in pursuit of a common goal.

Over the years, SCG employees have taken advantage of opportunities to learn together, offer feedback, share ideas, and recognize performance. Award and recognition programs, team assessments, etc., have created an environment conducive to and supportive of positive cultural change. In addition, the investment in initiatives like the Leadership Development Program (LDP), Academy of Leadership Excellence (ALE), and the Building High-Performance Organizations (HPO) seminar have created further capacity by reinforcing the expectation for leadership to exist at all levels of the organization.

The success of these past efforts set the stage in January 2009 for the emergence of the Challenges, Solutions, and Innovations (CSI) Alliance to actively engage a large, cross-functional group of employees to address enterprise-wide challenges through innovative thinking and low-cost solutions.

PROGRAM OVERVIEW

The CSI Alliance created a standing cadre of employees who could jump in as needed to provide county-wide solutions that balanced the perspectives and expectations of multiple stakeholders (including citizen/taxpayer, commissioner, manager, and employee) in pursuit of the best community solution. The county saw tremendous value in the ability to rapidly convene small groups of high-performing employees for change initiatives that could yield tangible solutions with wide buy-in and support. The desire to achieve a shared understanding among all employees of the drivers of change and to optimize opportunities to share responsibility for employer/employee communication provided additional support for the concept, as did the notion of building on existing efforts to instill leadership capacity at all levels with a propensity toward action.

The alliance consisted of a network of about 150 to 200 employees from all levels of the organization who volunteered to participate in conversations about the future of SCG. The initial invitation went to graduates of the LDP, ALE, and HPO programs: solution-oriented, future-focused team players who could consider issues from multiple perspectives and synthesize this information to form a well-rounded, informed, and realistic stance.

CSI Alliance members signed up for initiatives in which they had the strongest interest, choosing from a list of topics generated with input from the organization at large. Anyone in the organization could suggest potential CSI Alliance discussion topics, regardless of rank or work unit affiliation. Executive sponsors worked with organizational development staff to delineate the scope of each initiative, creating a clear, concise, and measurable call to action while managing expectations around what each initiative set out to accomplish.

Typically, each initiative was composed of one facilitator, two executive sponsors, and twelve to fifteen primary participants (with designated backups) from across the enterprise. Each initiative had a predetermined duration to ensure continual forward progress toward stated outcomes and avoid an endless series of meetings yielding no tangible deliverable. Expected time commitments were communicated up front. Subject-matter experts, such as support staff from risk, information technology, or human resources, joined each initiative according to the topic's requisite competencies.

Building upon shared learning was a fundamental tenet of the initiative's success. Each CSI Alliance participant received an orientation to the alliance and an overview of the current challenges the county faced. The first meeting of each initiative focused on "learning before doing," to build a common understanding of the current state and relevant contexts among all participants. Solid data about the issues and problems within the scope of the initiative, discussion about levels of freedom that the participants had in approaching their work, and succinct goals and associated evaluation metrics for each initiative were shared early on. This allowed members to identify potential solutions, hone them over a short time, and rapidly move toward an implementation plan. While it wasn't explicitly acknowledged as such, the members of each initiative strove to operate in Likert Systems 3 and 4 consultative/participative leadership philosophies. The process of formulating and evaluating potential solutions was highly Likert System 4 (adult-adult, participative), and group members "checked their titles at the door" so as to not stymie the free flow of ideas or impede group creativity. The groups worked to consensus and made formal recommendations to each initiative's executive sponsors, who had the formal authority to accept or reject these recommendations or propose modifications. In effect, once recommendations were forwarded, a Likert System 3 (adult-adult, consultative) leadership philosophy was employed. Early on, SCG had established a ground rule where executive sponsors had to explain the rationale behind their decisions on each recommendation, sharing the reasons why a particular recommendation would be rejected. This was done to reinforce the organizational values of transparency and adult-to-adult communication, foundational elements of the entire CSI Alliance experience.

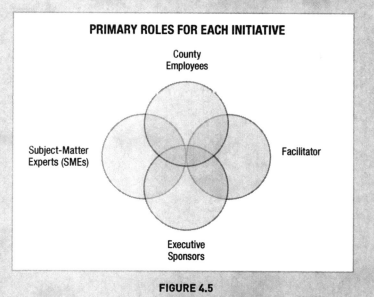

FIGURE 4.5

As with many new initiatives, employees were skeptical at first. While the outcomes achieved through collaboration are often superior to those derived by individuals working alone, this takes a lot more work at the front end of the process. It is harder to collaborate than it is to work in isolation, but the benefits are significant at the back end, where recommendations have widespread support. In the end, the up-front investment in team startup proved to be worth it. The most significant cost of each initiative was staff time. Expenditures for hard costs beyond staff time were minimal. The use of quality improvement tools helped generate creative ideas and expedite team decision making.

Here are some highlights of the collaboration between employees and managers regarding solutions to some of Sarasota County's most challenging issues.

CSI Alliance Initiative	Call to Action	Deliverables/Results
Employee Wellness/ Benefits	Control health insurance costs through • Healthy lifestyle practices • Wise cost-of-care decisions • Informed, engaged workforce How will we know if we've been successful? Hold increases >2% below national trend for 2011 (9% national average increase projected for 2010)	A comprehensive 2010 implementation plan designed to engage people in behaviors that improve individual health and control collective costs Increased levels of participation in HRAs and fitness screenings (supported by hard data) Premiums were actually reduced in 2011 from 2010 levels, and the 2012 premiums remain lower than in 2010
Employee Pay	Review compensation options that can generate $7 to $12 million in savings	Interactive data models offering employees the ability to see how various scenarios (e.g., pay cuts, furloughs, fewer hours) impact various budget scenarios Employee readiness (transparency, no secrets)
Rightsizing Process (Includes Layoff Process)	Identify ways to reduce FTEs through alternative work practices by June 1, 2009 Hiring freezes/vacancy elimination Job sharing Part-time Early retirement Adapt layoff process by July 1 Communication process Support for impacted employees Support for remaining employees	Employee-driven processes to ensure respectful separation practices (now available online) Smaller government

TABLE 4.1

CSI Alliance Initiative	Call to Action	Deliverables/Results
Internal Communications	Determine how to capitalize on existing technologies to improve communication Explore additional methods not currently being used Determine how to communicate with employees with no regular computer access Identify methods to encourage two-way communications	Blend of consistent, candid, and well-aligned messaging tools • Synchronized, all-hands, quarterly staff meetings across core services • Employee net • County administrator messages • FAQs • E-town hall meetings • Brown bag lunches with county administrator
Workforce Redesign	Evaluate a draft Workforce Redesign electronic book for clarity and understanding on topics such as matrix business model; position alignment, career paths; pay bands; and competitive analysis. Recommend methods to promote and implement the Workforce Redesign program.	Electronic book that incorporates voice, photos, models, etc., to reinforce both big-picture and detailed explanations of new business models, flatter organizational structure, broad banding practices, stewardship expectations, etc.
Performance Management	Improve the current employee performance management process by • Evaluating the performance management tool itself and proposing revisions aimed at increasing its utility and ease of use • Drafting a revised performance rating scale to replace the existing forced bell-curve ranking system	Revamped the individual performance management process, simplifying it as an online tool for both supervisors and employees providing 360-degree feedback. The group recommended not changing the overall rating scale of 1 to 5 but deleting the requirement for forced ranking. Addition of a section on adherence to county values and commitment to customer service
Mobile Workforce	Create the foundation for a successful mobile workforce by • Supporting a cultural understanding • Defining metrics of performance • Drafting a framework for effective guidelines • Establishing competencies and capacities for qualified employees	Comprehensive eWork pilot program focused on minimizing employee space, increasing staff productivity, improving disaster preparedness, reducing mileage, and enhancing work-life balance

TABLE 4.1, cont.

CSI Alliance Initiative	Call to Action	Deliverables/Results
Internal Space Planning and Parking	Use innovative practices to address parking challenges by • Modifying existing parking infrastructure • Establishing new off-site parking alternatives • Identifying flexible work programs (e.g., eWork) • Suggesting alternative commute programs	Creation of approximately 100 extra parking spaces at the Administration Building; development of continuous feedback loop to monitor progress of internal building consolidation activities
Small Stuff Matters	Weave together several seemingly unrelated initiatives all aimed at increasing efficiency and reducing costs, and assist with gaining broad buy-in and resolving implementation-related issues • Provide feedback on planned office consolidations and contribute to crafting communications plan and implementation strategy • Clarify objectives of print consolidation project and develop strategies to ensure acceptance among employees • Draw renewed focus to energy management activities, such as limiting in-office appliances and powering down computers	Closed and demolished an entire campus facility, which allowed the repurposing of the land for a new Emergency Operations Center Print consolidation program with new network printers forecast to save about $3 million
Enterprise Transition Monitoring Team (ETMT)	Provide a venue for identifying and addressing transition issues across the enterprise by • Serving as liaisons with core service peers • Using peer feedback to identify current, emerging, and ongoing transition issues • Creating an action plan of recommended solutions • Providing ongoing feedback on status of transitions	Continuous connection to employee issues accompanied by employee-driven solutions Success with the ETMT has unexpectedly spawned multiple transition teams (by employee request)

TABLE 4.1, cont.

Of particular note is the electronic book that the workforce redesign initiative team developed. It is an innovative method of describing to the county's workforce the transition in business models, work culture, performance expectations, and other human resources changes. The emphasis of this product was to ensure consistency of communication throughout the organization to avoid misinterpretation or misinformation from persisting.

More significant than the specific accomplishments of the individual initiative teams, though, was the magnitude of the impact on the county organization as a whole. The operation of the CSI Alliance demonstrated SCG's commitment to the principles it had begun to espouse—that demonstrating leadership was everyone's job, that empowerment leads to the best solutions, that transparency and authenticity were base expectations of the organization as a whole, and that community stewardship and commitment to the public service ethic was the driving force behind everything that happens in local government. This initiative formalized a community of employees with demonstrated capacity to step forward and quickly address emergent issues and enhanced response readiness and resiliency; it also has strong benefits over the long term. Engagement in the process by executives, managers, and facilitators was encouraging and reinforced authenticity. The dialogue was broadened; conversations slowly began to involve those employees beyond "the usual suspects," and Alliance participants would often speak up on behalf of those who weren't willing to speak up for themselves. Participants felt that they were getting information "from the horse's mouth." Rumors were reduced, because more people heard information firsthand rather than through the grapevine, and this rumor control function was deliberately woven into initiative design.

In times of rapid change, the CSI Alliance provided an employee-centric vehicle that formed renewed commitments to action, catalyzed shared ownership of the future, and institutionalized the sharing of honest and accurate information based on data. The effort succeeded in building new alliances, deepening employees' understanding of ongoing economic challenges, and increasing accurate information transfer between employees, departments, and the enterprise

Of course, the level of employee engagement has not risen to new heights across the board. Yet there appears to be dramatic change in engagement among a very large portion of the CSI Alliance participants. They have come to realize that they already have had a significant positive effect through the Alliance, that their efforts have truly been valued, and that they each have a leader within themselves that has a key organizational role to play in the future.

Most governmental organizations have actual leadership philosophies that do not neatly fit with any one of the four specified systems. Much more often, they are "all of the above." Based on administering the Profile of Organizational Characteristics survey instrument (derived from Likert's larger Survey of Organizations and available in the Appendix), most organizations are a combination of all four systems—called **System Zero** or **laissez-faire**. Another way to interpret these results is to conclude that top managers in System Zero organizations are not doing part of their leadership work. Specifically, in failing to define the leadership philosophy to be used by their organizations, they are, by inaction, letting each manager/team leader use any of the four systems, even though the two "left side" systems (Systems 1 and 2) are associated with lower performance. Most organizations with a significant number of technically trained professionals who have moved up into management—including most local governments—are System Zeros. When they learn the differences between these philosophical approaches and write their own leadership philosophy statements, nearly every local government selects a combination System 3 (consultative)/System 4 (participative) leadership philosophy.

As an example, the city of Brooklyn Park, Minnesota, drafted a leadership philosophy. Members of the Executive Leadership Team (ELT) asked a group of employees who had studied the HPO Model to prepare a draft leadership philosophy statement for review. That group had a lively discussion about their beliefs and their answers to the four fundamental questions that form the basis of a leadership philosophy: (1) the nature of people and their attitudes toward work; (2) what motivates people; (3) the distribution of knowledge and creativity in the organization and how we should make decisions as a result; and (4) the nature of work. They then prepared a statement that seemed to fit that city's style so that others could review it. The ELT reviewed the statement and asked other employees to review and comment on it. From this consultative process, the city developed and adopted its leadership philosophy:

We, the employees of Brooklyn Park, believe

- People are the most valuable asset [heart] of our organization.
- An empowered workforce takes pride in providing exceptional service.
- Our organizational culture promotes continuous learning, self-improvement, and professional growth.

- Employees are motivated by interesting and challenging work that provides opportunities for achievement.
- Sharing information and contributing our knowledge and creativity
in a mutually respectful and trusting environment strengthens our
organization.
- The best decisions are made using consultation or team-based participation.
- We are stronger and wiser as a whole and together achieve results unat-
tainable by individuals.

When reviewing a first draft of a leadership philosophy, there is often a
natural tendency to be critical of the individual words. It is helpful to remember that this first draft from a team will be subjected to testing in the organization, often requiring several more drafts. What's important is that there is
now a shared set of beliefs. Even while the draft goes through its evolution to
a final form, senior managers of the organization need to commit themselves
to behaving according to the beliefs expressed in the draft. Once an organization defines its leadership philosophy in conceptual terms, it is ready to
implement it by taking it down the rest of the Values Cycle. Suppose an organization has drafted a very clear, strong leadership philosophy statement and
posted it on the wall. And then it gets violated every day. What, exactly, has
been accomplished? Some people might say "nothing," but it's really worse
than that. It's one thing to suspect that values we *might* share are being violated in the organization; it's another to be able to see it clearly because the
statement on the wall identifies them explicitly. What develops is a serious
increase in cynicism and resistance to whatever improvement efforts follow.
If an organization doesn't intend to take the effort all the way to the bottom of the Values Cycle—implementation, including feedback, coaching, and
resolution—it shouldn't begin doing the values work, especially composing a
leadership philosophy.

The next level of the Values Cycle begins the implementation process. Leadership philosophy statements (and the other values defined) tend to be written in general terms. Without further clarification, the leadership philosophy
might generate a variety of interpretations about how people should actually
behave in a given situation, even if they are trying to live up to the philosophy!
If we are less clear about the real behaviors that would be consistent with the

leadership philosophy, seeing varied behaviors might lead to the perception that the values are constantly being violated.

At the Behaviors level of the Values Cycle, organizations specify which positive behaviors will support the leadership philosophy (and other values) and which negative behaviors need to be eliminated because they violate the values. Behaviors are different from attitudes and beliefs. Attitudes and beliefs are, like values, internal to an individual and therefore not easily seen by others. What really matters for an organization are the actual behaviors exhibited in the workplace. Behaviors are clear when two or more people can observe the actions of another and agree that it is either compatible or incompatible with the values. A federal regulatory agency went through this process and identified behaviors that were productive and counter-productive. The following example looks at one of the eight leadership philosophy values they articulated: open communication and credibility—being believable and honest. Here are a few of the behaviors they developed to define and illustrate this value:

A. Productive Behaviors

- sharing information up, down, and across (e.g., information should be shared with necessary individuals/teams, especially with people whose performance will be affected; informing people of the reliability of the information)
- telling the truth—using qualifiers (e.g., "As far as I know") when information is uncertain because things may change; saying when you can't say; informing people if the situation changes and why
- actively listening (e.g., making eye contact, not interrupting, giving undivided attention) even when you don't want to
- acknowledging/admitting lack of information/knowledge (e.g., saying when you don't know or don't understand)
- avoiding use of offensive language; knowing your audience/individual (e.g., no racial slurs, off-color jokes, religious/ethnic jokes, or religious profanity).
- giving and soliciting frequent, polite, and constructive feedback (e.g., being specific, suggesting how to improve, giving positive feedback)

B. Counter-productive Behaviors

- making vindictive or malicious comments
- being overly critical
- using a condescending tone or attitude or belittling employees
- using an aggressive/threatening voice, tone, and/or body language
- having hidden agendas
- manipulating for personal or professional gain

Leadership philosophy and the examples of the desired behaviors are aspirational statements. They rarely describe what is happening right now across the organization. Making those aspirations a reality requires implementation strategies to inform, coach, and evaluate individuals at every level about desired behaviors and to revise organizational systems and processes to align with the values. These strategies are then matched with tactics and resources to achieve them. This work of leadership is done in the Vision Cycle (aligning the human resources and other systems). Further, each level of the organization has to identify how the leadership philosophy applies in its specific work environment. Since police officers and sewer crews, for instance, have differing work circumstances, each group has to figure out how the behavioral elements apply in realistic terms to the situations its members encounter.

The final steps in the Values Cycle—feedback, coaching, and resolution—are the key to changing the work culture. Executives, unit managers, and other employees must develop a collective understanding of expected behaviors and how they will align their own behaviors with their shared values. They have to create mechanisms for everyone to make positive changes, hear from others about how well they are progressing, and, if needed, get help in shifting the way they operate. Finally, there must be effective ways to hold everyone at every level accountable for living the values.

A number of organizations have turned their Behaviors-level work into 360-degree feedback instruments, where managers, team leaders, peers, direct reports, and sometimes customers/stakeholders give feedback confidentially to the person being assessed. These are often used initially in a developmental way to help improve performance and behavior, but eventually they need to feed into the appraisal process. Coaching is frequently offered to assist individuals in understanding how they are seen by others and exploring how they might bring their behavior into alignment with the values. Resolution requires the organization to deal with those who can't or won't exhibit the shared values. Without this step, an organization doesn't really "live" the values that define how its members are to operate. You may have to ask violators—whether managers or employees—to either change their behavior in a reasonable time frame or "make a contribution to some other organization." Following through to resolve situations in which members are unwilling to live within the established values is the ultimate test of whether an organization is committed to a high-performance work culture.

One US Navy unit felt so strongly about the importance of leadership philosophy that it undertook a significant effort to assist its senior managers and selected supervisors to ensure that their behaviors modeled its philosophy. It employed a process using an online tool developed by CCHPO called the Leadership Philosophy Questionnaire[9] and outside coaches from CCHPO over an eighteen-month period. Here is its story.

CASE STUDY

Fleet Readiness Center Southwest in the US Navy[11]

—Timothy J. Hoffmann was the Lead Change Agent for Fleet Readiness Center Southwest from March 2007 until September 2010.

The Fleet Readiness Center Southwest (FRCSW) is a US Navy organization of approximately 4,000 people who repair, recondition, and rebuild US Navy aircrafts, located on Coronado Island near San Diego, California. Captain Fred Cleveland and Captain Mike Kelly—the Center's commanding officers during this case study—and their staffs were utilizing a number of quality improvement strategies. They began using the HPO Model to engage workers throughout the facility in accomplishing the leadership, management, and technical work in this improvement effort.

An important item in this effort was the establishment of an FRCSW leadership philosophy:

The members of Fleet Readiness Center Southwest are committed to transforming our workplace culture in a significant and dramatic way to facilitate progressive leadership based on the following:

- The FRCSW Team is committed to excellence—leadership characteristics exist at all levels of the organization.

- We are highly motivated and share a common vision to obtain a clear understanding of our collective goals and objectives.

- We value every team member's participation and unique capabilities, and consideration is given to all in the decision-making process.

- Our collective success is larger than any individual. Collaboration is valued and recognized.

- We are all committed to high performance and hold each other accountable.

- We treat each other in a professional and compassionate manner, even when demands are great.

- We are honored to be a part of the FRCSW Team. Our contributions to the defense of our nation are valued, and our mission is noble. We are a world-class maintenance, repair, and manufacturing organization.

FIGURE 4.6

As an older, industrial-type facility, FRCSW had many of the characteristics of a System 2 (parent-child, benevolent autocratic) style as described by Rensis Likert. To make effective strides in execution quality using Lean/Six Sigma and other process improvement tools, it was clear that the leadership philosophy had to change to a Systems 3 and 4 (adult-to-adult, consultative/participative) philosophy. Most managers and a number of front-line employees were introduced to the concepts of the HPO seminar materials and the resulting FRCSW leadership philosophy; the target was set. But as some senior managers changed and others did not, mixed messages were being sent. Transitioning to the more adult-to-adult system that involved line employees in many aspects of the work previously done primarily by managers did not go as smoothly as hoped. FRCSW asked for assistance in transitioning a group of its senior managers.

One tool that proved helpful is the CCHPO Leadership Philosophy Questionnaire (LPQ), which was developed collaboratively between the principals of Commonwealth

Centers for High-Performance Organizations Network and Dr. Bruce Brown, chair of the Psychology Department at Brigham Young University. The LPQ is a 360-degree feedback instrument designed to assess how managers in an organization behave relative to the standards of a Systems 3 and 4 leadership philosophy. It is coupled with a debriefing and coaching process aimed at assisting managers in aligning their behaviors with the highly desirable Systems 3 and 4 leadership philosophy.

The LPQ instrument itself is an online questionnaire in which designated individuals receive feedback from those to whom they report, their peers, their direct reports, and selected others. The anonymity of those offering feedback is protected, and they can complete numerical ratings as well as textual comments and examples of behaviors.

The questions were developed to probe perceptions of four groups—superiors, peers, direct reports, and selected others—about how the behaviors of the person being rated compare to the articulated leadership philosophy of the organization. The questions focus on four sections: the nature of people; motivation; the distribution of knowledge and creativity and how decisions are made; and the nature of work.

At FRCSW, sixty-five managers, divided into six cohort groups, received 360-degree feedback and coaching. The participants were from six groups in the hierarchy: senior managers, project managers, competency managers, mid-level managers, uniformed officers, and front-line managers. For each cohort, managers/ team leaders were rated by approximately fifteen to twenty individuals in three rounds at six-month intervals. After each round, those rated received coaching from the CCHPO Network to ensure independence from the organization.

The LPQ consists of four sections related to one of the four questions that make up the leadership philosophy. In answering specific questions in each section, the rater chooses from descriptions that fit one of Likert's five management systems (including Systems 1-4 and System Zero). At the end of each section, two performance questions call for textual responses to the open-ended questions:

1. "How could this team leader/manager improve in the area of motivating co-workers?"
2. "How does this team leader/manager excel in the area of motivating co-workers?"

After all the sections are finished, two additional textual questions wrap it up:

1. Describe the three most important specific ways this person could improve his or her leadership effectiveness—things this person should stop doing, do differently, or start doing.

2. If you were to identify the two or three most important ways this person demonstrates effective leadership, what would they be?

This exercise produces a lot of data when there are fifteen to twenty raters. The information is presented to the participant in an interactive, online report, which shows the rated person's results graphically. Quantitative data are arrayed in a diagram that shows scores for questions having to do with people versus a focus on tasks.

After each round of ratings, the executive coach had face-to-face feedback sessions to explain the results, assist with interpretation of the data, develop action plans, and provide an additional level of accountability within the program. Coaching sessions ranged in duration from one to two hours and could be face-to-face or via telephone and email. Coaches could also deliver competency-based mentoring using the Lominger Leadership Competencies and specific developmental tips from the *For Your Improvement*[10] book. Coaches and participants jointly determined the need for any additional sessions. At the completion of the three rounds of assessment and coaching, participants had to discuss their third-round results with their managers, for both accountability and reinforcement. The process used by the organization is illustrated in Figure 4.5.

The results of this feedback and coaching process had significant success but did not change everyone overnight. Four groups of managers showed significant progress over the eighteen-month feedback period in moving toward Systems 3 and 4 behaviors.

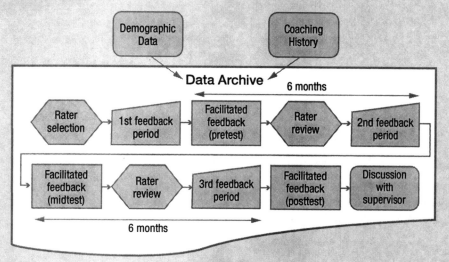

FIGURE 4.7

In addition to changing personal behavior, an organization's actual leadership philosophy is also shaped by the way its systems and processes interact with employees. For instance, if an organization's leadership philosophy and values state that it trusts knowledgeable employees to make independent decisions within their work environment, but their operational practices require multiple layers of reviews and signoffs, how can the leadership philosophy come alive? Within the Vision Cycle, the administrative systems and work processes have to be examined to see if they support the realization of the leadership philosophy—and, if not, they must be scheduled for revision. (See the following discussion of operating systems values for more on this topic.)

Finally, just as we asked KDQ 2 (How would we know?) at every level of the Vision Cycle, we must ask it again during the Values Cycle. At the top of the cycle, for example, we might use Likert's Profile of Organizational Characteristics survey to assess an organization's leadership philosophy. Further down the cycle, we could use the LPQ to give 360-degree feedback to individual managers and team leaders on the level at which they are living the organization's leadership philosophy. We could also design our own customized instruments to deliver 360-degree feedback or use less formal methods of face-to-face feedback. In addition, assessments are available for organizational work culture, such as the KEYS instrument from the Center for Creative Leadership, the US Office of Personnel Management's Employee Viewpoint Survey or Organizational Assessment Survey (OAS), and CCH-PO's Performance Diagnostic Questionnaire (PDQ). The next two values sets, individual behavioral values and operating systems values, also need to be taken through the Values Cycle from conceptual definition to implementation, although these are sometimes collapsed into an integrated values statement.

2. INDIVIDUAL BEHAVIORAL VALUES

This second set of values in the HPO model is the most common in local governments. Often called core values or guiding principles, they spell out important employee behaviors necessary to achieve a desirable work culture. Sometimes, though, organizations simply list their core values on posters or the back of a business card and assume people will understand and follow them. In such situations, the stated values are of little day-to-day relevance.

Little attempt is made to bring these values to life in actual governmental operations or to square them with the operating guidelines people use to manage within the organization. In short, organizations rarely *implement* their values.

Prince William County, Virginia, uses the **RICTER Scale** to explain and implement individual behavioral values. It became a fundamental expectation of how everyone should guide their own behavior. To make this happen, the county defined what their values concepts meant and launched a comprehensive campaign to assure that everyone knew and understood their meaning. They integrated their values into their business flow at all levels of the organization—for instance, they became the core of the county's budget congress, described in Chapter 5. Further, they were incorporated into the newly designed system of employee evaluation and compensation. The case study below describes the individual behavioral values that Prince William County established as well as the way they connected them to the Vision Cycle to develop a system to support the behaviors throughout the organization.

CASE STUDY

Values and Performance Management System in Prince William County, Virginia

In the late 1990s, a group of Prince William County employees met to discuss what the organization needed to do to improve its performance. They had been appointed by the county executive's office to be the steering team, or guiding coalition, for an organizational change and development initiative. They were to achieve the county's strategic plan goal for effective government: to continuously inform and educate staff as a means to achieve an accountable, responsive government with effectiveness and efficiency. The group chose the name Training, Leadership, and Customer Satisfaction, or TLC.

The conversation soon turned to organizational vision and values—or rather the lack of them. It seemed that they had been waiting for a relatively new county executive to tell the organization what they would be and then promulgate them to the staff. This was how most group members had previously experienced the establishment of vision and values elsewhere: They arrive from a leader whose responsibility it is to determine them.

Finally, the budget director mused, "If these are to be the organization's vision and values, why are we waiting for the county executive to tell us what they should be? Shouldn't the organization be figuring them out and creating a culture that becomes the organization's culture, irrespective of the coming and going of county executives?" This shift in attitude launched the group on its arduous but successful effort to draft an internal vision to guide the staff in accomplishing the strategic vision established by the board of county supervisors.

VISION

Prince William County Government is an organization where elected leaders, staff, and citizens work together to make our community the best.

We, as employees, pledge to do the right thing for the customer and the community every time.

We, as a learning organization, commit to provide the necessary support and opportunities for each employee to honor this pledge.

FIGURE 4.8

Once this vision was in place, TLC turned its attention to the organization's values, or individual behavioral values. It focused on primary drivers of a culture that would help achieve the substantive goals in the strategic plan and the customer satisfaction level the county sought. After settling on six values to propose to the organization, it sought feedback from the county's management team; it then broadened its effort to understand people's reactions to them. Next, it developed a way for the values to become memorable to everyone in the organization: a graphic to picture and link the values and an acronym that people could refer to and that would actually guide behavior.

TLC knew that simply naming the values would not be enough. They developed a short definition of each value so that it would be more clearly understood and serve as a benchmark of expected behaviors. Having developed these values and measures, the group recognized a need for wider engagement and launched a process to gather feedback from employees. This process was intended not only to clarify the definitions of the values but also to engage employees in sharpening the behaviors corresponding to the values and the actions that would help the county achieve a culture that reflected the values. The handout that was used for this effort is shown below.

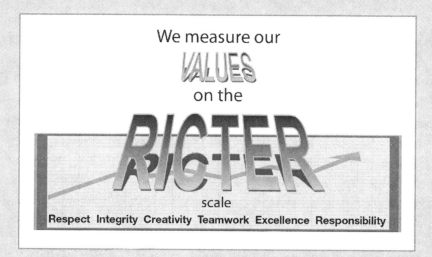

We measure our **VALUES** on the **RICTER** scale

Respect Integrity Creativity Teamwork Excellence Responsibility

FIGURE 4.9

RICTER ORGANIZATIONAL VALUES DEFINITIONS

Respect: We believe all people have value and we show consideration for all persons with whom we have contact—our customers and fellow employees.

Integrity: We have the courage to consistently do what is right, honest, and fair.

Creativity: We find better ways to do things. We are innovative in achieving excellence.

Teamwork: We support and encourage others as we work toward our common goals.

Excellence: We exceed expectations for the results we produce, the quality of our services, and the interactions with our customers.

Responsibility: We seize the opportunity to do the right thing in carrying out commitments and obligations.

DISCUSSION QUESTIONS FOR ENGAGING STAFF IN PROVIDING FEEDBACK ON DEFINITIONS

1. Are there other definitions for these values that you want to suggest?
2. What behaviors would you expect to see if people were operating/behaving in accordance with our values?
3. What would be the best way for PWC government to achieve a culture that reflects the adopted values?

Once the values were adopted in the Prince William County hierarchy, it undertook a major effort to be sure that each county employee could both identify and understand the expectations of each value. Information was sent to each employee on MyDesktop, the computer information system accessible to many employees. A new county executive, who had been a part of TLC, focused on the vision and values whenever he talked with employees. He also featured one value a month in the county executive's corner on the front page of the employee newsletter. In those articles, he delved into what the selected value meant in terms of the behaviors consistent with the value. (An example of these articles appears in the Appendix.) Further, a video showing employees telling personal stories of how the values were used and describing what the values mean to them was widely distributed. This video can be seen at the following link:

http://pwcgov.granicus.com/MediaPlayer.php?view_id=17&clip_id=1009

With the variety of ways employees were being confronted by the vision and values, the county executive and management staff hoped that they were understanding and starting to live the expectations. To get confirmation, in 2003, the county administered an organizational survey using the services of the Weldon Cooper Center's Survey Research Center at the University of Virginia. One important focus area of the confidential survey was determining the extent of employee familiarity with the vision and values and their perceptions of how extensively people practice them. The county was impressed by the employees' overall response rate and their favorability of findings. The analysis showed that Prince William County employees not only seemed to "own" the values but were adopting them in their everyday work, as the following figures show:

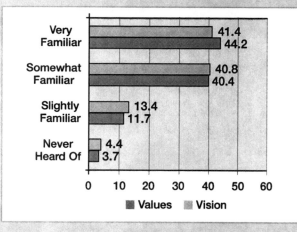

FIGURE 4.10

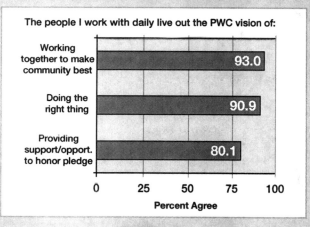

FIGURE 4.11

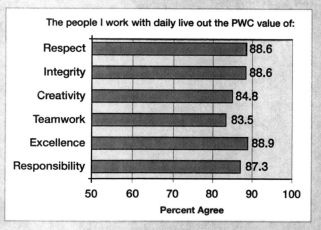

FIGURE 4.12

In subsequent years, the county made an extraordinary effort to create a performance management system that evaluated employee performance. The concept was to include factors not typically found in most such systems. The county wanted to weigh the employees' performance of their assigned responsibilities, of course, but they also wanted to make clear the connection between their work and its impact on the citizens and customers of the community. Further, they wanted to encourage application of the knowledge and skills that individuals have and how they lived the county's values. To accomplish this, the new system divided an employee's evaluation into two parts, each worth 50 percent. One focused on what the employees accomplished in terms of individual performance, how the department or division met its key goals and objectives, and how the county fared in its expected performance as measured by the annual citizen survey. The other 50 percent was based on the employee's knowledge, skills, and application of values.

To move from a more general description of the values to something that could be measured for every employee, the county needed specific measures of the behavioral performance under each value. To address this need, the employee committee that had designed and introduced the performance management system was asked to develop descriptors to evaluate compliance with the values. Below is an example of the descriptors for the "respect" value.

Employee Performance Management System
Value Descriptor

Measure: Respect

Descriptor:
We believe everyone has value and we show consideration for all customers and fellow employees

Description:
Individual Contributor
- Seeks to understand other points of view, listens without interrupting
- Participates openly and honestly, shares knowledge and opinions with others
- Provides constructive feedback; speaks about others in positive terms
- Handles interactions with sensitivity
- Speaks about others in positive terms
- Fosters a culture of sensitivity to diversity among employees and with customers

---

FIGURE 4.13

Similar descriptions were developed for all values and incorporated into the performance management system. This informed an evaluation of each employee in terms of the actual behaviors for all the values the organization believed would move the workforce toward higher performance.

In another case study, the city of Salisbury, North Carolina, zeroed in on one specific value that became the focus of an extensive citywide campaign to shift individual behavior and improve performance. This story, like the Prince William County case study, reinforces the way the leadership work of the Vision and Values Cycles combines to achieve results. Conceptually, identifying the values and desired behaviors is categorized as work of the Values Cycle, and the systems development that enables and supports behavioral change is categorized as work of the Vision Cycle.

CASE STUDY

The Value of Customer Service in Salisbury, North Carolina[13]

—Written by Evans Ballard, the budget and benchmarking analyst in the City of Salisbury, North Carolina and William C. Rivenbark of the University of North Carolina at Chapel Hill.

For Salisbury, North Carolina, with a population of about 30,000, the period before and during the recession was difficult in the city government workforce. The governor's effort to balance the state budget impacted every city department, and one of the consequences was a reduction in force. City Manager David Treme was growing increasingly aware that his departments were strapped for funding, armed with fewer staffing resources, and struggling to keep up with their production workloads and customer service obligations. He decided to provide internal technical assistance to help them with performance analysis and cost data. While this would add new costs to his reduced operating budget, he reasoned that the incremental cost of providing this help would be offset by the benefits.

While the performance measurement effort was progressing, the staff realized that a large missing component of their system was qualitative feedback from their customers. They sought a grant from the National Center for Civic Innovation and the Alfred P. Sloan Foundation-supported Government Trailblazer Program to increase communication with and feedback from the city's customers. One phase of the grant they received supported a mail survey that would collect qualitative customer feedback data; another funded three distinct focus groups the following year.

The results of the survey were a mixed bag. Salisbury's citizens believed the city did an exceptional job in police, fire, and solid waste departments. The condition of the city streets, however, received poor marks; this spurred additional funding for asphalt paving and repair. The survey feedback that generated the strongest reaction from the city manager and staff was the courtesy extended by the city's workforce in their dealings with customers. When asked if city employees were courteous, 57 percent of respondents either disagreed with the positive statement or expressed an indifferent response. Only 43 percent answered that city employees were courteous.

Having been introduced at UVA's Senior Executive Institute to Jim Collins' book, *Good to Great: Why Some Companies Make the Leap . . . and Others Don't*,[12] Treme asked his leadership team to read it and begin transitioning the organizational culture. The city started training its employees based on the book's concepts. Resulting discussions focused on the theme of customer service as Salisbury's lynchpin or, as Collins called it, the "hedgehog" principle: a clear, simple understanding of what the organization can do best. Building on the employee feedback and the grant-funded community focus groups, this principle emerged as a unifying foundational value essential for the work in every city department and service. Over the next several months, Treme repeated in individual conversations and in groups that customer service was critical for three reasons:

- Relationships with customers transcend all departments, no matter what their goals and objectives are.
- Relationships with customers are critical to service delivery, because they impact communication, expectations, attitudes, and the customer experience that drives opinions.
- The employees had come to view customer service as the defining success measure.

Treme and his leadership team's first task was to create awareness that customer service needed to be the most important performance measure for the city. Each employee would have to own this value at a personal level. He understood that having this value "come to life" in the organization would mean changing actual behaviors and introducing improved customer focus across the board, in every department, every team, and every individual job. To grow this competency in the whole workforce, Treme hired a new key staff member, a facilitator, with the skills and competencies that would support a broad strategic intervention. New hires, especially for positions that had not existed before Salisbury's reduction in force, were rare. New facilitator hires—or anyone not directly involved in production work—were unimaginable in such a period of financial austerity. Yet Treme supported the hire because he saw the value of customer service as a core step toward higher performance; he demonstrated his commitment with his budget priorities.

Treme asked the facilitator to work closely with the human resources staff. Together, they guided an organization-wide intervention to improve customer service. They created a cross-functional design team of front-line employees to build customer service engagement. They adopted a motto—"Salisbury is driven to serve"—and identified ten keys to customer service. They then created strategies to support the culture change they sought. The design team knew that after awareness and desire to improve customer service had been rooted in the workforce, knowledge on how to carry it out and the ability to put that knowledge into action would require training and additional on-the-job effort. So every employee, from bottom to top, attended customer service training. They also created a public communications strategy, with a campaign to further spotlight customer service and the value of feedback from the public in continuously improving service delivery. This included a formal customer feedback process to reinforce customer service importance and enable employees' ability to carry it out. A final and equally important piece of the intervention strategy required the continuous reinforcement from Treme and the immediate supervisors of the workforce. For instance, in the months that followed, public acknowledgment, customer service stories, and examples of employee customer focus initiative were shared citywide. Customer service impact became a factor that would be considered in all major organizational decisions. It became a key selection criterion in hiring decisions and was added as a vital element of performance evaluations for individual employees who are expected to exhibit this valued behavior in all their interactions.

After two years of implementation, a follow-up survey showed that while citizen satisfaction had improved in twelve of the thirteen discrete service areas, customer service had shown the most whopping increase. Now, 68 percent of respondents found that city employees were courteous, while the remainder disagreed or were ambivalent—a reversal of the original survey result. Five years after the original survey and after two years of focused intervention, positive response of Salisbury's customers on the level of city customer service went up 25 points—a 58 percent increase.

As this case study is being written, two years after the follow-up study, Salisbury managers and a majority of the employees see customer service as a continuous journey, more a part of the culture than a destination. They attribute this change to continued awareness, the desire to own customer service as a personal value, and organizational support in delivering good customer service every day. They cite continuous management reinforcement and support and enhanced communication systems and policies as examples of the culture change and as the reasons behind its sustained success. The fact that the ongoing commitment remains more than two years after the last survey indicates that a cultural intervention has taken hold and that customer focus, a core value of the city, is part of every job. In the last year recorded, the city received more customer service compliments than in the previous ten years combined!

3. OPERATING SYSTEMS VALUES

A sometimes harder concept to grasp is the idea that an organization's administrative/business/regulatory systems and technical work processes have values embedded within them. People are accustomed to think of processes as just technical constructs—an array of steps and actions that ultimately treat everyone neutrally. Yet most organizations experience a large number of complaints about how systems are hard to work with, are top-down, emphasize control, don't trust users, require a lot of permissions, don't respond in a timely way, keep people in the dark about where they stand, don't deliver what they need, etc.

Think of some purchasing, hiring, evaluating, or budgeting systems you have encountered in your career. Do any of those descriptions sound familiar? Making sure the cross-organizational systems contain the right values to be used effectively is a significant responsibility of the leadership team at the top of the organization. They represent the primary users of such systems and need to assure that organizational systems embody the correct operating systems values and still meet legal and accountability standards. So, they must work through the Values Cycle in identifying what those values are, what they would (and would not) look like in action, and so forth. Then the effort shifts to the Vision Cycle, where the existing systems and processes are evaluated to see how well they comply with the desired values. This leads to the priorities for inclusion in the capacity building strategy of the organization described in the Vision Cycle section. This same type of work cascades down, recurring at the department or unit level for those systems and processes that are within the boundaries of the units, and nesting further, even down to the line level.

Often, governments don't specifically set out a separate list of operating systems values and instead look to the relevant parts of their leadership philosophy and individual behavioral values to guide how their systems and processes operate. For instance, let's look at the leadership philosophy of the city of Bellevue, Washington:

We are One City, defined by a culture of quality, community value, and sustainable financial performance, and committed to continuously improving our workplace and culture:

- We value our customers and employees and consider their interests in everything we do.
- We trust and respect one another.
- We are driven to make a positive difference in our community.
- We embrace shared leadership throughout the organization.
- We support learning and innovating at all levels of the organization.
- We practice open communication and we share the rationale for our actions.
- Knowledge is widely distributed and creativity is nurtured throughout the organization.
- We strive for timely decisions made in a participative manner, consistent with our vision and core values, by the people closest to the matter.
- Our collective success is larger than any individual. Collaboration is vital, valued, and recognized. We hold ourselves mutually accountable for the health of the organization and each other's success.

A number of the items in this leadership philosophy have specific relevance for how they believe the systems and processes of the city should operate to support their performance. For example, applying the tenets of the philosophy, the systems and processes of the city would naturally have to consider the interests of both the city's customers and employees and exhibit trust in the employees in their operation; the reasons for actions in the various support systems would have to be clearly explained; and the various processes in the city would have to be efficient so that timely decisions would be made. The work under this value set is to identify the values that should apply to the organization's systems and processes, evaluate whether they currently reflect the values in their operations, and, if not, determine when their revision should be undertaken in competition with the other system and processes that need revision as well. This way, the organization creates a strategic plan to assure that its systems and processes demonstrate the values in a culture that supports higher performance in the long run. Creating a separate list of operating systems values, though, can make them clearer and focus attention on alignment of the organization's systems and values.

1 Wikipedia definition
2 Gallup, Inc. *State of the Global Workforce; Employee Engagement Insights for Business Leaders Worldwide,* 2013.
3 Lencioni, Patrick. 2002. *The Five Dysfunctions of a Team.* San Francisco, CA. Jossey-Bass
4 Including Rensis Likert, Marvin Weisbord and Douglas McGregor.
5 Pink, Daniel H. *Drive,* Riverhead Books, 2009.
6 Likert's work used the term *outputs* from systems thinking, as in "inputs, throughputs, outputs, feedback." It corresponds to our use of the word *performance.* Likert looked at an organization's reputation for product and service quality, customer responsiveness/dependability/satisfaction, and financial performance (what we called "Pick 3") to create his index scores to rate an organization's "output."
7 Block, Peter. 1991. *The Empowered Manager: Positive Political Skills at Work.* San Francisco: Jossey-Bass, p 46.
8 A. Tyler St.Clair is the Associate of the Commonwealth Center for High-Performance Organizations and a team member with the University of Virginia's Senior Executive Institute. Mark C. Johnson is the retired Director of the Lynchburg Department of Social Services.
9 Mary Sassi Furtado is currently the assistant county manager of Catawba County, North Carolina.
10 The Leadership Philosophy Questionnaire (LPQ) is available from the Commonwealth Center for High-Performance Organizations, Inc. Email: solutions@highperformanceorg.com
11 Dr. Timothy J. Hoffman is currently the Logistics Management Integration Department Head for Fleet Readiness Center Southwest.
12 Lombardo, Michael M. and Eichinger, Robert H. *FYI—For Your Improvement: A Guide for Development and Coaching,* Lominger Ltd Inc.; 4th Edition (January 2004).
13 Adapted from an article in *Public Management* by William C. Rivenbark and Evans Ballard, August 2010. Evans Ballard is the Budget and Benchmarking Analyst in the City of Salisbury, North Carolina and William C. Rivenbark is a Professor and the MPA Director at the University of North Carolina at Chapel Hill.
14 Collins, Jim. 2001. *Good to Great: Why Some Companies Make the Leap . . . and Others Don't.* New York, NY: Harper Business.

Creating Change Mechanisms to Accomplish the Work of Leadership

In the previous chapters, we reviewed the experiences of some organizations that explored the basics of the High-Performance Diagnostic/Change Model and various methods to improve performance. In their own ways, members of these organizations answered some of the seven key diagnostic questions to realize both Vision to Performance and Values to work Culture. In this chapter, we'll examine how some created change mechanisms—or parallel organizations—to help them accomplish this work of leadership and its five functions. We'll also share some basic approaches to managing change.

EXAMINING WHY THE WORK OF LEADERSHIP OFTEN DOESN'T OCCUR IN ORGANIZATIONS

Why do so few organizations perform the leadership functions if they are so important to sustained high performance? Typical responses include "We didn't know we had to," "We don't have the skills," and "We don't have time." The first two excuses are no longer valid: By now we know that we have to cause the work of leadership to occur and that the entire team must develop the skills both individually and collectively to do this work.

The lack of time issue, however, can be a problem for getting the work of leadership accomplished. Most traditional hierarchies focus almost entirely on pressing, near-term tasks, even if they're not very significant. Many organizations move from one crisis situation to the next without dealing with the significant but less pressing, longer-term issues, which—if handled proactively—might have prevented many of the crises in the first place. For example, if we don't take the time to engage citizens and other stakeholders to understand and meet their needs, or if we fail to create and articulate a clear vision of the future, we can't evaluate the impact of our current way of doing things and undertake any necessary work to realign the organization's strategies, organizational structures, management systems, and work processes to achieve our desired outcomes. If how we allocate our time keeps us from doing the longer-term work of leadership, we can use a figurative lens to examine it—see Figure 5.1.

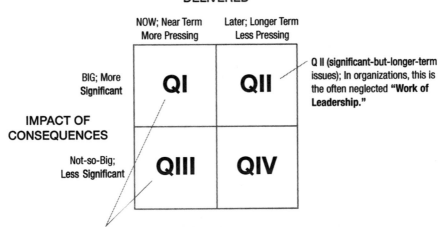

Q II (significant-but-longer-term issues); In organizations, this is the often neglected **"Work of Leadership."**

Q I ("crises" and other near-term, significant issues) and Q III (pressing, near-term routine task work); In organizations, these are **"the urgencies"**—they are made up of managment/task-focused work.

FIGURE 5.1

In both our professional and personal lives, we have to decide which of many competing issues, problems, and crises we will handle and which we will put off; we simply do not have the time to deal with them all. An internal lens helps us make judgments about the positive and/or negative consequences that logically or naturally follow from acting or not acting. We may not be aware of how we use this lens to choose, but it is operating nonetheless. In Figure 5.1, the horizontal axis on the diagram refers to *when* consequences will be delivered—now (near term) versus later (longer term)—and is sometimes called the "Urgent/Not Urgent"[1] axis. If we are facing two issues and both will deliver negative consequences, but the first issue's consequences will be experienced now while the other's will have impact later, which do most people address? *Now* usually wins over *later*.

The vertical axis of the lens is concerned with how significant the consequences will be—how big they are (how much the consequences will help or harm us)—and is sometimes called the "Important/Not Important" axis. If two issues, one big and one not-so-big, must both be dealt with within the same general time frame, which will most of us address first? Big wins over not-so-big most of the time.

In what order do most people handle the issues coming at them, then? Most people immediately identify Quadrant I (Now/Big) as the one they'd handle first—and that's appropriate. What do we handle next? Here it gets a bit depressing, because most people often say Quadrant III (Now/Not-so-big). Why pick that over Quadrant II? Because it's urgent, which frequently wins over importance. Even more depressing is what's picked to handle third: Quadrant IV (Late/Not-so-big). People describe their being exhausted from handling Quadrants I and III, so they do unimportant and mindless things to get some respite. So what gets handled last, if ever? Quadrant II (Big/Later)— and this is the work of leadership. This pattern is why most organizations don't get the leadership functions done at *any* level of the organization, let alone at every level.

Traditional hierarchical organizations, with their typical autocratic leadership philosophies, are designed to deal almost exclusively with Quadrants I and III, the task/management work. Such organizations ensure—through centralized, top-down control processes—that repetitive tasks get accomplished and that crises get handled reactively as they emerge using resource-intensive emergency problem-solving techniques. Indeed, many are so focused on Quadrant I and III issues that they often take measures to prevent members from working on critical Quadrant II issues: "If you have time, we have more 'real work' for you to do!" And since top managers are focused almost exclusively on Quadrant I crises, they often impose massive reporting requirements and status reporting meetings on everyone else, taking up what little time the lower levels might have had for Quadrant II thinking.

Ironically, in hierarchies hyperfocused on responding to Quadrants I and III issues, the management systems and work processes used for such task/management functions are often antiquated and inadequate—because doing the thinking to improve them is in Quadrant II. This traditional organizational approach may have worked better in the past, when workers were seen as unskilled or only technical, when the environment (including technology) changed slowly, and when the goal of most organizations was to move from poor to just-better-than-average performance. But not ensuring that the Quadrant II work of leadership gets accomplished at all levels locks many organizations into a cultural paradigm which, if not changed, leads to their inability to thrive in the longer term.

Clearly, to be successful in improving organizational performance, the work of leadership needs to become the focus of leadership teams at all levels of the organization, and the "urgencies" cannot be allowed to stifle this critical work. Furthermore, working in Quadrant II can help us understand why crises are occurring and we can begin the root-cause analysis to reduce them. We want to use process improvement tools to reduce systemic waste in organizations and help free up the time to do more Quadrant II work. Finally, we need to reduce most Quadrant III and IV work—by either delegating some of it to those who are more appropriate candidates for the work or simply eliminating that which is not necessary. Jack Welch, former CEO of General Electric, was famous for supporting "workout sessions" where frontline employees could identify waste in the organization's processes, policies, practices, and meetings and either improve or eliminate them—all within a hard-hitting, rough-and-tumble, two-day session.

Within these leadership teams, at all levels, individuals must begin seeing their jobs in three integrated parts—the task completion, management functions, and leadership functions—accompanied by team skills allowing them to function effectively in networks. The leadership philosophy used in the teams must be more consultative/participative, making it a high priority to abolish the use of autocratic management practices anywhere in the organization—even in the hierarchy.

DEVELOPING THE CHANGE MECHANISM: INTRODUCING THE PARALLEL ORGANIZATION

In her classic book, *The Change Masters*, respected researcher, author, and Harvard Professor Rosabeth Moss Kanter observed that the culture of traditionally run private sector organizations tended to kill off creative thinking at the very times they were desperate to get new products developed. She found that more innovative companies took another approach: They gathered people from all over the organization and moved them into a **parallel organization** with different rules from the production side (in the design world, this practice is sometimes called concurrent engineering). The people temporarily assigned to a parallel organization are able to work on new product development with few traditional constraints.

Expanding on Kanter's concept, parallel organizations can be very effective to accomplish all the leadership work: gather people together, move them out of the current hierarchy—even for only a few hours at a time—do some thinking together in a participative/consultative environment, develop ways to improve the hierarchy (like adopting and implementing a consultative leadership philosophy, instituting the Networked Talent Model of work, or beginning systematic process improvement), and *then* bring the results of the leadership thinking back into the hierarchy for implementation. That is the idea behind building parallel organizations at every level of the organization.

EXPLORING THE PARALLEL ORGANIZATION

To change the trappings of the traditional Industrial Model we must find an appropriate **leadership form**: the parallel organization. The parallel organization exists in addition to—not in place of—the hierarchy (management teams focused on near-term, task/management issues would still exist, but using a System 3 adult-adult, consultative leadership philosophy). The parallel organization is a permanent feature to ensure that all parts of the organization's "thinking work" is completed with the same rigor as the "doing work." By working in the parallel mode, the traditional hierarchy is transformed into a more open, transparent, flexible, engaged, and innovative one. The parallel organization is the reflective side of the organization, the "rehearsal studio" for learning and practicing new skills and behaviors and for doing the work of leadership. There must also be a smooth handoff between thinking and doing. To be effective, first-level technical team members need to spend at least 5 to 10 percent of their time in the parallel organization; significantly more if they're at the senior level.

The parallel organization is characterized by

- Disciplined and regular movement into Quadrant II (more significant, longer-term issues) to work on the five leadership functions.
- Within the Networked Talent Model, work is seen as holistic; leadership, management, task/technical, and team skills are seen as everyone's responsibility.
- A move to Likert's Systems 3 (adult-adult, consultative) and 4 (adult-adult, participative) leadership philosophies.
- The language reflects a stewardship mind-set—all levels rise above "turf" to serve and be responsible for the larger organization; there is linking with others to address cross-cutting issues; the word *our* is used more than the word *my*; and the perspective of team members is as "a board of joint owners."
- With a stewardship mind-set comes increased trust, more constructive conflict, honest commitment to shared values and goals, and joint accountability for results.
- Managers ultimately remain accountable under both Systems 3 and 4 for all decisions, whether made in the hierarchy or in the parallel organization. In the parallel organization, however, the goal is for the smart people who comprise the team to create smart answers for important issues. By definition, the parallel organization is focused on significant but less pressing matters, so there is more time for consensus building. In the rare case where no agreement can be reached, the decision process reverts to System 3.
- A culture of engagement and a feeling of commitment to purpose characterize the parallel organization and spread throughout the entire organization and to customers and partners.

The relationship of the hierarchy to the parallel organization is summarized in Figure 5.2.

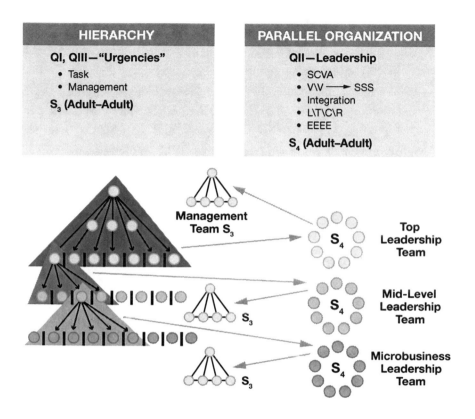

FIGURE 5.2 Leadership Form: The Parallel Organization

Teams need a minimum set of guidelines to follow. In the parallel organization, teams often start with the following guidelines, which embody many of the approaches described throughout the HPO materials (many groups also include additional procedural or behavioral guidelines).

1. **Normal hierarchical organization rules are suspended.**

   All team members are equal inside the parallel organization; decisions are made by consensus as much as possible, but note that decisions inside the parallel organization must also work in the hierarchy—a key role of team members is identifying, consulting with, and marketing to major stakeholders inside and outside of the hierarchy.

   In order to make decisions that work in the hierarchy while maintaining the integrity of the process, teams should not work in isolation and then surprise management with their solutions; rather, they need to consult frequently with management and other important stakeholders in the process. Bringing the hierarchy into the parallel organization enables the team to argue the facts, question judgments, and seek the best alternative in a setting where all are equals. Decisions in the parallel organization, which are longer range and for which we have the luxury of time, are deemed "made" when all team members believe

  a. They have been heard.
  b. Discussions have been frank and honest.
  c. All important views and information have been surfaced and thoroughly discussed.
  d. They "own" the decision as if they had made it alone and will actively support it.

2. **Focus is on reaching the best solutions possible for the whole.**
Team members must be committed to a shared vision and values for the organization; a member's worth is determined by his or her contributions (e.g., ideas, conflict resolution, consensus building, problem solving) to helping the team reach the best solution possible.

3. **Everyone gets a "promotion."**
To eliminate "turf" and reach solutions that are best for the whole, team members must "promote" themselves at least two levels in the organization so they can see themselves and their units as parts of a larger, integrated whole; members must view themselves as part of a "board of joint owners" of the whole.

4. **A "regenerative" culture is critical.**
There are three components here:
  a. **Trust-based relationships:** While operating in the parallel organization, all interactions must be based on complete trust.
  b. **Honesty:** Members are expected to level with each other and have no hidden agendas.
  c. **Mutual respect:** We can disagree without being disagreeable or making personal attacks; each team member must take personal responsibility for the success of every other team member.

5. **Confidentiality is key.**

   In order to achieve an open, innovative, and candid discussion of difficult or sensitive issues, it is often necessary for teams to establish a confidentiality rule (i.e., what is said and decided and why decisions are reached is on the record). Knowing *who* said what is not necessary.

6. **There is no retribution for following these guidelines.**

   Because a low-threat, high-trust climate is critical in getting candidness and promoting creative problem solving, no retribution for following these guidelines can be permitted; however, if members do *not* follow the guidelines, there must be consequences.

7. **Enforcing these guidelines is everyone's responsibility.**

   Because everyone is equal inside the parallel organization, everyone is responsible for making the process work.

One of the biggest challenges for local governments is sustaining a successful parallel organization. Local governments vary in scope and number of employees and are a diverse confederation of departments, professionals, and schedules. If the locality is large, it is sometimes difficult to develop across the organization a connection to the high-performance effort, much less ownership of it. If the locality is small, staff members often find themselves wearing multiple hats to cover basic functions and face significant challenges in managing the workload. Finding time for the work of leadership on an individual, team, and organizational basis is a testimony to one's seriousness about high performance. Finding the right formula for creating leadership teams and doing the leadership work while still doing the management and task work, though, *is* another daunting requirement of the effort.

Every organization must create a relevant structure that will operate parallel to the one focused on tasks/management implementation. One factor we know for sure: Teams that form to address the work of leadership and enhance organizational performance need a clear sense of purpose. In *The Wisdom of Teams*, Jon R. Katzenbach and Douglas K. Smith identify a key finding: "Significant performance challenges energize teams regardless of where they are in an organization."[2] It is critical to keep a meaningful parallel structure in which both teams and individuals believe that what they are accomplishing makes a difference. As soon as participants see that the task work has more rewards or that the products of their efforts are not seriously considered, energy wanes. Thus, a key task is to clearly focus parallel organization efforts and make them worth the effort in an ongoing way.

Another challenge is that the organization may enthusiastically begin to set up a parallel organization to serve across the government, neglecting application of high performance principles within departments, units, or microbusinesses. A primary leadership team may address the change levers of leadership philosophy, vision, and values and move on to the improvement of strategies/business models, structure, and systems/processes. There are laudable examples of organizations that address vision, values, communication, performance management, and organizational performance measurement on an organizational level. But they often fail to cause each network, department, and appropriate subunit to create a parallel organization for their own leadership work. Parallel structures that work to serve across the organization and within departments in an integrated way have the most potential for success because of their capability to affect the direct delivery of services.

The following case studies show how localities have developed various forms of parallel organization to accomplish the work of leadership. The first is a large county department that developed its senior-level Leadership Council and then engaged each of its lines of business in creating their own leadership teams. It also illustrates a long-term approach by a newly appointed department director on how to manage the changes that he foresaw being required to merge disparate agencies into an integrated, effective, high-performing department.

CASE STUDY

The Department of Public Works and Environmental Services in Fairfax, Virginia

—Carol Lamborn was the strategic initiatives manager, an original member of the Departmental Leadership Council

Fairfax County, Virginia, is large, diverse, urban and suburban, and Virginia's most populous jurisdiction, with a population of more than one million. With a complement of more than 10,000 employees, Fairfax provides all services typically found in cities and counties to its residents, businesses, and visitors.

A recent organizational change had merged three agencies with related, but separate, functions into a larger 1,500-person Department of Public Works and Environmental Services (DPWES). Each former agency had its own culture, had competed with the others for resources and influence—and had been quite satisfied with its own way of doing things. The deputy county executive, acting director for the first four months of the nominally merged agency, had kept only the essential operations moving, saving the most complex merger issues for the new permanent director. Consolidation and centralization/coordination of administrative functions were not addressed during this period, and conflicting or imperfectly aligned policies were placed on hold. Fairfax County had enjoyed a good reputation for its service delivery, and senior managers in the department were proficient at executing task and management functions, but substantial leadership focus had been diverted in favor of current production. Essentially, nothing had been done to implement the merger during the interim period. Other than maintaining essential operating functions, the work of leadership in the new organization was in cruise-control mode.

Thus, much was expected of John Wesley White the instant he was appointed permanent department director. Staff wanted a clear vision from him, direction on how things should be merged, and resolution of a number of outstanding conflicts. His charge from county executive Robert J. O'Neill was straightforward: Integrate the former parts into a smoothly functioning, high-performing department. Unfortunately, the task at hand was not simple. The newly merged agencies were focused almost exclusively on operations; little attention was paid to strategic work and the participative efforts required to build vision alignment in the subordinate units.

The easy approach for White would have been to come in, hear the staff's questions, and begin telling them what to do. In fact, as a former county executive and senior manager, he'd done this many times in the past. But he decided to begin differently. A graduate of the very first Senior Executive Institute at the University of Virginia and familiar with the HPO Model, he wanted to form cross-cutting groups to tackle the strategic questions of the purpose and vision of the new department, the appropriate culture for the new unit, and how to harness the best staff efforts in working together toward common goals. The challenge was to induce the employees of the newly merged agency to own the design of the agency's vision, mission, and values as well as its administrative structure, work rules, and all facets of building essentially a new entity. The director knew that guiding the staff in this unfamiliar territory would entail a new leadership approach. In particular, he needed to ensure that the senior staff would focus on leadership work in a cultural environment separate from their daily work. He also recognized the need to manage the change process without giving substantive answers about the design of the new agency.

White's first step was to establish a DPWES Management Council, made up of the twenty-five most senior managers in the department. The inaugural meeting of this new group demonstrated how stove-piped the previous organization had become, as the managers present—almost all of whom were engineers and most with more than twenty years in the county's service—were introduced to each other, largely for the first time. The majority of the Management Council members had never met face-to-face since interorganizational relationship building had never been a priority. What a challenge ahead for the new director!

The Management Council began as a forum in which managers could seek information on important issues or suggest that the director address them. At White's encouragement, the first several months were devoted to discussions about delegation of authority and empowerment, as well as creating more time for leadership work. The members of the Management Council tried to participate in the discussions, but were very skeptical. It took time for them to build up trust to collaborate across the previously well-established boundaries.

White decided that, in order to tackle tough organizational issues, the group had to be brought closer together. He asked Dr. Robert Matson at the University of Virginia's Senior Executive Institute to conduct a two-day team-building effort. Using the Myers-Briggs Type Indicator, supplemented by exercises to describe each member's personal background and work experiences, the group quickly became able to appreciate the constructive power of their differences and strengths and see their common humanity and the potential for relying on one another to navigate the challenges of designing a new agency. This proved to be an especially valuable change-management step.

While the team building produced a new spirit of collaboration, the members of the Management Council were still daunted by the challenge of unfamiliar leadership work. In order to equip them with the tools to do the work, White introduced the staff to the HPO Model through a three-day seminar called "Building High-Performance Organizations in the Twenty-First Century," conducted by Dr. John Pickering. The group seized upon the clarity and specificity of the model and almost immediately began to feel that they would be able to implement these steps together. They also decided that a smaller senior leadership team, eventually called the DPWES Leadership Council (DLC), should be formed from volunteer members of the Management Council.

TEAM START-UP

At the first meeting of this new leadership team, White asked, "What do you feel about the employees?" He was essentially opening up a conversation of values, but at the time, no one understood his question. The concept of organizational values had never been discussed by previous senior managers. The organizations had historically been traditional production-oriented, top-down operations.

A period of uncertainty characterized the start-up phase of the new leadership team. It was customary that everyone wait for instructions from the director and then carry out the tasks. This became apparent at the very first meeting when everyone waited for the director to tell them the answer to his question; they were also unable to have a conversation where all views counted equally. After the second meeting, they realized that they needed outside help in moving forward: Team members needed to open their minds and engage in conversation without the director taking the lead. White called upon CCHPO consultant Tony Gardner, a former Arlington County manager, to help with the team start-up and facilitation, which continued for several years.

White also ensured that he had representation from the various divisions on this team. He kept the ones who had volunteered originally and augmented them with others to get a cross-representation. The new members were still division directors but represented the major divisions/areas in the new organization. The team met offsite to focus on the work of leadership; this proved to be difficult in the beginning. All team members were task-oriented, not accustomed to collaboration, and struggled to understand the meaning of the work of leadership. For their entire careers, they had a blurred view of the distinction between leadership and management work. While the distinction between management and leadership work is fundamental to the concepts underlying the HPO Model, it was not a natural separation in the department's new organization, which is the case with most traditional organizations.

An alien concept to team members, the parallel organization was extremely difficult to embrace, in part because the organization continued to struggle with separating leadership and management work effectively. To many, it became a more mechanical approach—putting on the management hat versus the leadership hat—rather than intuitively understanding the differences. Struggling with this concept while attempting to do leadership work for the first time was extremely daunting and frustrating for many members. However, responsibility for carrying out directives was always a strong suit for this cohort, and they continued to labor through in hopes of seeing progress. At the facilitator's encouragement, the team grappled with this distinction through developing charters for a new DPWES Leadership Council and a Senior Management Team (SMT, see copies in the Appendix). The charters took several meetings to complete because of the members' struggle to understand what leadership work is and how management and leadership work were tied to each other. Many original team members still recall how relieved everyone was to sign the final charters.

During the discussions, it was determined that membership for both teams would be the same because of the natural transfer of leadership work into the hierarchy for implementation. The need for continuity and cohesiveness moved the team to bar substitutes for absent Leadership Council members. There were numerous discussions concerning the importance of allotting time for leadership work; a high expectation was set, and members were not to miss meetings for "in the moment" management work unless there were extenuating (Quadrant I) circumstances. Although the director received feedback from upper management and elected officials that they were not pleased with a group of key managers being "out of pocket" eventually for a whole day every two weeks (they also were struggling with understanding this new concept of leadership and management work), he defended the organization's need to develop managers into strong, well-balanced leaders. The DLC continued to meet off-site biweekly with a professional facilitator for more than five years.

The DLC established in its charter the expectations that it would operate under a Likert System 4 (participative) leadership philosophy, and in practice, almost every deliberation resulted in a consensus-based decision. Final decisions were transferred to the director or the SMT for implementation in the hierarchy. Since the membership was the same for the DLC and SMT, this transfer felt mechanical at times, but members gradually began to feel more comfortable with it.

The SMT worked under a Likert System 3 (consultative) leadership philosophy on task/management QI issues, with the director both facilitating and having the authority to make decisions. Early on, the director spent the additional time required to reach consensus in an effort to make the members become more comfortable with equal input and decision making. If no consensus was reached after discussion, the director made the decision, and on a few occasions, team members "punted" the decision to the director. By this point, the SMT was clearly striving for consensus whenever possible, working hard to create a new participative culture.

In the charter, the DLC adopted team behavioral practices similar to CCHPO-suggested guidelines, but in their own language. They started each meeting with a warm-up aimed at building a collaborative culture. Each member shared personal experiences, usually related to the day's agenda, thereby becoming more vulnerable and open to building trust. Patrick Lencioni has subsequently written about the importance of creating personal vulnerability as a way to overcome the distrust that abounds on many teams. As new or replacement members joined the team, an orientation was conducted to help bring them aboard into the team culture.[3]

GUIDING PRINCIPLES

One of first leadership responsibilities was to create a draft of guiding principles for the new department: vision, mission, values, and leadership philosophy. As they spent considerable time working on these, the process began to reorient the previously divergent cultures into a stronger, unified sense of how the new department could and should operate. Successfully working through some significantly different viewpoints encouraged and fostered more trust and collaboration. When the drafts were complete, the DLC developed a broad, inclusive process so each member of the 1,500-person department had a significant opportunity to hear directly from the DLC members what the guiding principles were about and how they were developed. Every employee had a chance to review and comment, both in a small group setting and online. Employee workshops were designed to further the direction of participative leadership, and each DLC member had a part of the agenda and actively participated in all of the workshops. Employees viewed this as quite different from their previous work experiences, where the department director would be the sole spokesperson at employee gatherings. In addition, employees realized that the DLC took their comments seriously and revised the principles based on what they heard (see a copy of the adopted guiding principles in the Appendix). One notable change was the addition of open communication as one of the values. The DLC assumed that communication was embedded in all of the other proposed values, but employees wanted it to stand on its own. Upon reflection, the DLC agreed that in order to advance the new department to be more participative and inclusive, an emphasis on communication and its meaning to gain a common understanding were critical.

ADDITIONAL PARALLEL TEAMS

The department reoriented itself into lines of business (LOB). The DLC decided that each LOB would establish a core team with a management team component and a leadership team component, mirroring the SMT and DLC parallel organization model. Since every line of business had significant leadership work to accomplish, the LOB leadership teams were chartered to focus on this work, thus beginning to assure that the work of leadership would take place in the organization at levels lower than the department's Leadership Council. Teams met monthly to focus on LOB work and provide opinions to the DPWES Leadership Council members as needed about DLC activities. This provided a substantial source of advice to the DLC members for the items on their DLC agenda. As the work of leadership expanded with various leadership teams in each line of business, the department invested its resources in an organizational development unit to support the various teams. Each LOB core team had access to these staffs to facilitate their meetings and develop the new teams. The work within the core teams increased performance in the direct services provided. A notable accomplishment from one of the core teams was conducting a Condition Assessment Survey for all county facilities. This resulted in enhanced funding of capital maintenance by providing a better understanding of the county's facilities investment and the funding required to properly preserve the investment. Other accomplishments in the first years were in the area of the new organizational values, including employee and supervisor leadership training and development, creation of issue-driven employee teams (which enhanced participation), and implementation of employee newsletters to improve communication and celebrate the department's successes.

Once the DLC had been operating for a stable period, team members felt the need to have a more formal way to get advice on the change process. This led to chartering a partners group, a larger, cross-cutting group of thirty to forty people at all levels across the organization who would help to further departmental change. The partners group was designed to create a dialogue with the DLC on proposed strategic initiatives being considered and to identify other areas where the DLC should be working to achieve the department's vision and values outcomes. It solicited employee feedback on the change process, presented new change strategies to the workforce, and served as a knowledge resource for the workforce on the model being used by the department. The partners group continued to be a valuable source of peer support for the initiatives sponsored by the Leadership Council.

Special-purpose cross-functional leadership teams were chartered to concentrate on specific QII issues, either time-limited or on an ongoing basis. For example

- **Department Apparel Team.** This seemingly less important subject was of significant interest to field workers. When the departments merged, distinctly different uniforms and attire remained in the various components, perpetuating feelings of separateness and fostering disharmony. People in some areas felt that others had more options and flexibility regarding field apparel. The Department Apparel Team tackled the subject with considerable consultation among the workforce.
- **Information Technology Team.** This self-formed group created a strategic technology plan and budget proposal. As its work developed, it became clear that DPWES needed an ongoing group to review major departmental technology initiatives, sort out priorities, and decide on the technological investments impacting the department's various functions. The Information Technology Team became a permanent special-purpose leadership team. It actually arose spontaneously from the spirit of the initial organizational changes to redesign the new department's website. Its success led to the department embracing a new concept of communities of interest and enabled members to continue as a valuable adjunct to the other means of leadership work.

In order to assist such parallel teams, the DLC assigned a liaison from its membership for each team with specific responsibilities spelled out in a charter (seen in the Appendix). The liaison prepared a membership roster, acquired a facilitator, attended the first meeting to clarify expectations, checked in on progress, communicated the information needed between the DLC and the team, helped determine when progress reports from the team to the DLC were appropriate, and performed a team evaluation when the project was completed. This new function created the need for additional discipline to ensure that the liaison role was not to give directions but to facilitate communications.

ANNUAL WORK PLAN

The DLC began to plan its own work for a year, mapping out key priorities for its agenda and scheduling them for the meetings. This timeline targeted and informed members' expectations. Often subgroups were created to prepare work for the larger team's consideration. Members were assigned homework between meetings to set the stage for in-depth content work at the sessions. Recognizing both the importance and the breadth of leadership work to be done, the DLC met regularly for two full Wednesdays each month. This was a major time commitment for a dozen top managers of a large and complex department, and members fretted from time to time about this. Several remedies were instituted to assuage concerns and allow members to keep their commitments. Most freed up the necessary time by ceasing things that ultimately did not require direct attention, delegating decisions to direct reports who enjoyed both the confidence this implied and the freedom to act independently. This allowed further expansion of the leadership work: Because each DPWES Leadership Council member was also a member of his or her respective core teams, monthly hours of leadership work increased even further—and rightly so, as leadership is where senior-level managers should spend most of their time.

STRATEGIC PLAN

Within the larger county organization, DPWES was the first to prepare a strategic plan. Some of the strategies that emerged were focused on building the department's internal capacities to deliver on the substantive work crucial to its mission. For example, one focused on creating a comprehensive and relevant employee development system that results in employees who exhibit teamwork, empowerment, and positive behaviors, and who possess current knowledge, skills, and abilities to enable individuals and teams to perform to their highest potential. Several tactical plans were then identified to achieve this goal, such as forming a Training Advisory Committee to create an employee development and training plan, and a Performance Feedback Team to develop a performance feedback system for departmental employees.

One of the department's strategies required an evaluation of organizational performance with staff and citizen input to improve service delivery, quality, and efficiency, thereby enhancing customer service and effectively meeting customer expectations. Pursuant to this, the DLC asked each LOB to review and evaluate processes during the year based upon practices such as benchmarking, performance measurements, customer and employee feedback mechanisms, the business's best management practices, and innovative technology. The results of these process reviews were reported to the DLC each year. Processes reviewed and improved in the first year included delegation of authority for construction contracting, establishment of annual/task order contracts for small capital projects, and the implementation of an e-permitting system for site and building inspections.

TEAM CHANGE

With time, the department sought to broaden the participation of all levels in the organization on the department's leadership and management teams. This permitted a wider sharing of views and perspectives, while the majority of members remained senior departmental managers. The DLC augmented its membership with several members from field and trades positions, technical or engineering jobs, and administrative roles, and included front-line supervisors and middle managers as well. The Core Teams followed this example by adding a cross-cutting representation of its respective line of business. The DPWES Management Council (MC) membership expanded to include all members of the augmented leadership teams, which resulted in an eighty-five-person council. The DPWES MC was an opportunity to network across lines of business and provide input into the decision-making process on departmental issues but also served as a forum for targeted training and awareness of topics relevant to the new guiding principles. One well-received topic was ethics. Small groups were asked to discuss what their actions would be for several scenarios that involved ethical dilemmas. Based on the wide range of responses, the session facilitated further discussions on the department's values and individual responsibilities to live out those values.

While the DLC was first facilitated by the CCHPO consultant facilitator, this changed over time. As the capabilities within the department grew and a pattern and practice of committed leadership work developed in the DLC over several years, the team moved to an internal facilitator from the organizational development unit. This required a clear agreement on expectations of the facilitator's role, responsibilities, confidentiality, and safety (freedom from retribution). The DLC and the facilitator spent time creating an agreement on how they would operate together. This model remained in effect through White's tenure as the department director.

Since White left the county, there have been two department directors. As with any significant shift, the DLC has undergone several changes throughout the years. The DLC, now known as the Executive Team and led by the department director, comprises the department's most senior managers, HR manager, and strategic initiatives manager when operating in management mode. The organizational development staff augment the team membership when it operates in leadership mode. The Executive Team continues to develop the departmental strategic plan and oversee its implementation through hands-on work and monitoring others' progress. As has been the practice, this team also has several permanent teams chartered for cross-cutting disciplines, such as communications, safety, emergency management, IT, and web development and support. Major strategic initiatives of the team include reinvestment of transportation and storm water infrastructure, the future direction of disposal of solid waste in the county, and further enhancements to the department's emergency management program—all of which are critical focuses for the department's operations. A new leadership and manager development program is also in the planning stages, as is a strategic plan for enhancing employee safety.

The "new" department is now fourteen years old. Through the years, the department has evolved as its leadership has changed and the organization as a whole has matured. However, the basic HPO principles and concepts that were introduced early on have stayed in place. While the term *HPO* is not mentioned as much as it was in the past, its concepts have been embedded in the department. Strategic planning—planning for the future—continues to be a priority. Organizational values and guiding principles continue to be a topic of discussion and focused action. Teams are very much a way of doing business at all levels of the organization—the days of direction without input or consultation from others are in the past.

This story describes an evolutionary journey that was not without growing pains or strife. The department has undertaken and endured remarkable growth and performance development since embarking on this effort. Many struggles and frustrations came with the enormity of moving age-old traditions and practices to a new place. John Wesley White is admired for taking on the challenge of a new department and being the lone ranger—setting a course that was both foreign and threatening to those around him. It takes a strong manager to stay the course in the midst of disruption, temporary loss of productivity, and pressure to not rock the boat. The county will always be grateful to him for taking this risk, both personally and professionally. Much credit also goes to the successive department directors who committed to stay the course. While their styles may have been different, their desire to continue has been evident. This journey has served the department well and will enhance their ability to meet future challenges with confidence.

One thing that emerges from this case is the importance of charters to the success of teams. Clarity of purpose and anticipated results, expectations about behaviors and operations, timetables, etc., are important agreements that guide a team. Furthermore, it illustrates the importance of the department director taking the long view. He understood that this would be a long-term process of change; he would have to both push and be patient. He didn't think he knew all the answers on precisely how things should go during the transition. And he enlisted his managers to help him define what they were after, what the problems were now and where they would emerge in the future, and the solutions that they should attempt in order to achieve their goals. He required that, as a part of their leadership responsibilities, they undertake this journey with him.

In another case study of a long-standing parallel team, Michelle Poche Flaherty describes how the Customer Service Action Team from the city of Rockville, Maryland, has shifted its roles as the needs changed over time. This self-directed team understood that its responsibilities were to support great customer service outcomes, and it had to encourage long-term expectations and interest in achieving this result.

CASE STUDY

The Customer Service Action Team in Rockville, Maryland[4]

—Michelle Poche Flaherty, then the internal change consultant for the City of Rockville, Maryland

Rockville, Maryland, is a suburban Washington, D.C., city of more than 60,000 residents. Known as "The Rockville Way," the organization's culture is centered on an expectation that employees go above and beyond the normal call of duty to provide exceptional customer service. This citywide focus caused the city to form the Customer Service Action Team, an interdepartmental committee of employee volunteers that has maintained its momentum for more than a decade. The team demonstrates leadership and teamwork as they motivate staff and produce results that strengthen Rockville's values and commitment to customer service.

BIRTH OF THE TEAM AND THE STANDARDS

In January 1999, a team of employees with representatives from each city department and all levels of authority kicked off the city manager's customer service initiative. This team's challenge was to develop a shared vision for the city's customer service standards that would be specific, measurable, and reasonable. This Customer Service Standards Task Force worked for six months to recommend standards to the senior staff. In February 2000, these citywide standards (which can be seen in the Appendix) were formally adopted. Since then, the task force has evolved into the ongoing inter-departmental Customer Service Action Team of employee volunteers committed to supporting customer service and charged with promoting the standards.

Today, the team is self-directed and operates as a participative parallel organization where members work on customer service improvements outside the normal hierarchy and without traditional constraints. It is currently co-chaired by a non-supervisory staff member and an internal change consultant. Although it began as a task force set up and directed by the city manager, the team demonstrated its ongoing value and became independent of direct oversight.

Because customer needs and expectations are continuously evolving, the team saw the need to review and update the standards regularly. Since they were adopted, the standards have been reviewed and updated three times: in 2003, 2007, and 2011. However, the team's stewardship of the standards far exceeds the adoption and revision of the standards themselves. They have institutionalized an organization-wide commitment to continuous improvement of customer service built on the foundation of the standards.

EMPLOYEE TRAINING AND CUSTOMER SERVICE MARKETING

Using a holistic approach, the team recognized the need for training and independently developed an in-house training program. Peer volunteers trained every employee to use courteous service techniques and to solve problems for even the most difficult circumstances or unhappy customers. The curriculum was then folded into the city's new employee orientation and training program to ensure that every new hire would continue to be introduced to the customer service standards and receive training in how to best provide a positive customer experience.

To reinforce customer service training, the team developed a marketing plan for ongoing support and communication. They continue to promote exceptional customer service and remind employees of standards by producing marketing materials such as posters, brochures, emails, and online videos. The ongoing campaign also promotes updated methods to strengthen knowledge and skills originally introduced in training.

REWARDS AND ACCOUNTABILITY

The team knew these initiatives could not be sustained over time without revising and aligning systems to support the customer service advances. The city integrated customer service into its accountability system as a specific criterion on each employee's performance evaluation. Representatives from the team participated in the citywide effort to design and revise performance evaluations, ensuring that customer service remains a measurable and reinforced expectation for all employees.

They also aligned the city's rewards and recognition system by independently creating and administering the city's Customer Service Employee of the Quarter award program. Four times a year, team members solicit nominations from employees throughout the city who wish to recognize their colleagues who have served internal or external customers exceptionally well. Each quarter, team members independently select one individual and one team to honor. Each is presented with a certificate at a reception held in their honor. Managers are invited to say a few words about the quality of the awardees' performance and contributions to the organization and the community. To promote the recognition, the team produces posters featuring photographs of the honorees and distributes them throughout the organization.

MEASURING PROGRESS AND OPPORTUNITIES FOR IMPROVEMENT

To maintain focus on and provide measures for customer service, the team designed and administered an organization-wide "secret shopper" program. Called "CSI: Rockville" ("CSI" stands for Customer Service Inquiry), it tests the quality of customer service in all Rockville city departments. They recruit employee volunteers to pose as city customers, train and supervise volunteers, and collect, analyze, and present the data to the senior staff of the organization. This labor-intensive program measures the success of the city in achieving customer service results. It has been extremely successful and is enthusiastically supported by city employees. Figure 5.3 shows the results of the most recent evaluation in comparison to several prior years.

Many organizations that conduct a secret shopper program contract with consultants to perform this service. Rockville does this important research and analysis in-house, coordinated by team members who do this work in addition to their regular job duties. Because this effort is undertaken by Rockville team members, we believe it is more likely to be supported by employees and bring about longer-lasting results.

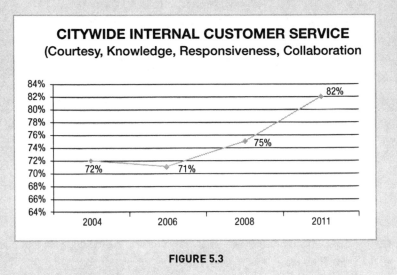

FIGURE 5.3

The next case study on parallel organization details how the Prince William County Budget Congress made a significant contribution to the county's successful navigation of the recent financial crisis.

CASE STUDY

Budget Congress in Prince William County, Virginia[5]

—Craig Gerhart was the retired county executive of Prince William County during the period of this case study.

As you have seen in earlier case studies in this book, Prince William County, Virginia, has invested heavily in developing, growing allegiance to, and putting its vision and values into practice. As this story opens, the county had seen a reassuring amount of progress. Employee surveys indicated broad acceptance of the county's guiding principles and reflected employees' beliefs that a large number of their colleagues demonstrated and lived by these guiding principles too. The county was riding high in the years preceding this case study. Its success was put to the test in a significant way when the recession hit. Prince William County was slammed first with a mid-year budget crisis in FY 2007 and then with several years of dramatic revenue reductions.

The crisis was costly. Housing growth was shut off quickly, the pattern of increasing real estate property values reversed, and other income streams were reduced.

That this occurred right in the middle of a fiscal year, after all operating plans were in place and running, only exacerbated the problem. The future looked worse, not better. It was clear that something needed to be done immediately to address the shortfall of millions of dollars in the current budget. And, an even larger problem was anticipated in the coming years.

Normally, to get out of this mess, county senior management would have turned to a crack team of seasoned, proficient budget staff that would squeeze the departments and agencies of short-term cost-saving "low-hanging fruit"—and, as they had been able to do in the past, eventually render up enough spending reductions to solve the problem. Sometimes more cross-cutting and brutal techniques were required in the past, when across-the-board budget reductions were administered. Here, the impacted departments were brought in to help administer the meat axe, facilitating the budget cuts in a participative way. These were historically unpleasant exercises, and some even requested to just move ahead this way and get it over with. The county's budget director was fully capable of leading these traditional responses to a budget crisis; however, the senior team recognized that the routine way of doing things would now clash with the county's leadership philosophy:

> We believe that valuable knowledge exists in all employees and recognize that improvements most often come from the people providing the service. We share information, consult with each other, and work in teams and groups to make the best decisions and produce excellent results.
>
> We are an organization of diverse, honest, and hardworking employees who trust each other to do the right thing and make the right decision every time. We are united around our commitment to the County's Vision and Values. To this end, we believe in maximizing talent, skills, and creativity. We encourage continuous learning, having fun, and recognizing achievements and contributions.
>
> We believe people are Prince William County's most valuable asset and are committed to sharing the leadership responsibility for making our county the best while creating a legacy of excellence.

This philosophy would not prescribe a draconian approach to handling the shortfall. Laying past practices aside, the county decided to leverage the crisis by enlisting people at the departmental and agency level in a budget task force to develop the solution. This team, comprising budget staff from the various departments and agencies, quickly analyzed and prioritized the options for meeting a nearly $20 million shortfall. Because projections in the coming years presented even tighter resources, the team's triage priority ranked all programs according to the following criteria: alignment with the strategic plan, mandates, organizational infrastructure, and community enhancement, which were subsequently ranked into high, medium, and low.

As the team members worked in a compressed time frame on a very important issue, they grew closer and more collaborative. They began challenging the "sacred cow" assumptions of the past, even those of their home departments, arguing respectfully about alternatives and coming to an understanding of the county's needs and priorities as a whole rather than by individual department. Their work was time-consuming, extremely detailed, and tedious at times. The team's recommendations and priority rankings produced several useful results, such as the "Budget by Post-It Notes" priority configuration you see in Figure 5.4. The budget director and county executive walked the Board of County Supervisors (BOCS) through the ranking results, enabling them to change placements/priorities by visually and physically grasping the enormity and complexity of the task. (This exercise also silenced some of the "cut the fat" challenges that derailed budget discussions when priority detail had not been so visually exposed.) The BOCS accepted every recommendation. The county staff had taken a risk in bringing to the board this much detail, all produced by the team of staff members. When it paid off, everyone breathed a sigh of relief.

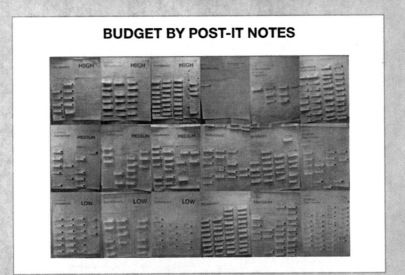

FIGURE 5.4

This had been a very successful one-time, emergency process. The county executive, Craig Gerhart, asked the team participants for feedback on the process and the outcomes. Many reported that they had felt empowered in their efforts and, for the first time, that they had a direct impact on the system for which they were responsible. They said previous practices had been autocratic, with decision justifications hidden from those who produced the budget details in the departments and agencies. Having experienced collaborative decision making on budgets at the macro level, the staff no longer wanted to work in departmental silos with negotiations hidden from those impacted. Even the local newspaper weighed in with a rare positive editorial[6]:

From Gerhart, some sensible ideas

"Government should be run like a business" is often asserted at budget time. And just as often, citizens get a list of reasons why it can't be run as a business. Gerhart's task is far more complicated and he wisely turns to the people spending the money to help find ways to cut. Now, you might think that asking the people who spend it to come up with ideas on how not to spend it is silly, but, in fact, many businesses do the same thing. Who better has an idea of the least used services or the impact of eliminating some? In his memo, Gerhart tells county employees, "…it is critical that we all believe and act upon our **Vision and Values**" as they examine what changes must be made—another proven successful business practice.

FIGURE 5.5

As the task force was completing its work, the county was already deep in developing the FY 2008 budget. Gerhart and the budget director considered the significant investment just made in helping departmental staff learn about budgets from a broader financial context and how collaborative energies had enabled them to work together for the greater good. Given such obvious success, why couldn't the process be applied in the FY 2008 budget cycle? But some of the recommendations from the team, while aligned with the task at hand and done through consensus, were not necessarily the most logical or prudent. The process, good as it was, would not withstand intense challenges, as it had produced some results that were admittedly still somewhat parochial and self-serving. Also, support for wholesale change in the annual budget and planning process was not strong among department and agency directors. And Gerhart was not certain of his readiness to cede his significant role, which he enjoyed and was used to. He deferred the decision on changing the FY 2008 process for a little while.

Gerhart consulted with several key department/agency directors and other trusted advisers. When he found that they were open to making a shift in the process, he had to confront his own reluctance. He was challenged by looking at the values, realizing the necessity of making a personal change if he really believed in those values. By this point, the county staff had worked hard to create alignment between their leadership philosophy and actions, systems, and processes. Now this last, largest, and most fundamental system—the budget process—was out of line with the philosophy that "Valuable knowledge exists in all employees," "Improvements most often come from the people providing the services," and "We work in teams and groups to make the best decisions and produce excellent results." In the end, Gerhart concluded that when faced with the vision and values he had been vigorously espousing, he could not turn back on this engaging and successful experiment that they had launched. The proof of its success went beyond the philosophy statements to the successes now documented and experienced by everyone in the county. All that remained was to "walk the walk" by officially launching the new budget development process. So the county charged midstream into the FY 2008 budget process, facing a challenging shortfall using the budget teams and Budget Congress.

It established a parallel organization Budget Congress process that ameliorated some of the nagging concerns raised by the original budget task force and implemented a revised process design that engendered significant employee engagement. At the initial level of the process were four functionally oriented teams: community development, general government, human services, and public safety. These comprised line and staff representatives of the departments. In turn, they selected two department/agency directors from each team area to form the Budget Congress to whom they would report their information and recommendations. The congress would then determine a set of recommendations to present to the county executive— who would have the final responsibility for the budget decisions that went to the BOCS. A healthy balance emerged between the role of the parallel organization and the hierarchy. Gerhart set out for the group the overall county situation, the very short time frame, and the desire to see them work within the context of our vision and values, and he conveyed his openness to hearing and acting on their recommendations.

When the four teams were set up, even though time was short (about two months), there was a significant amount of effort to establish a sound foundation for them to work together in a way that was different than many other teams. With the assistance of a county organizational development staff person, the budget director facilitated the teams' creation of a purpose and vision for their work. They articulated the Likert System 4 leadership philosophy they wanted to operate within, established that they

PWC Budget Process

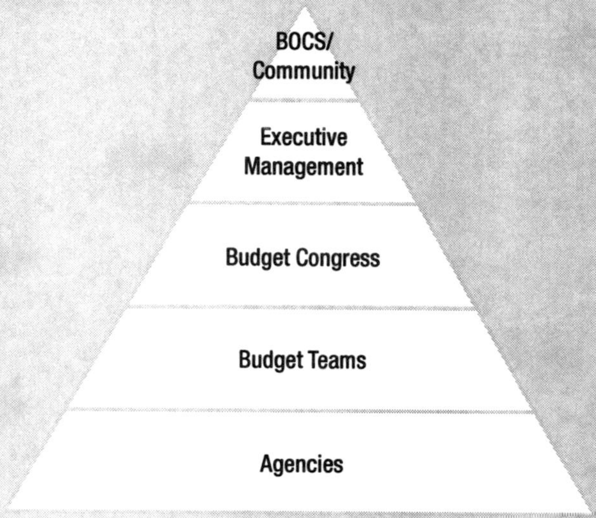

```
            BOCS/
          Community

          Executive
         Management

        Budget Congress

         Budget Teams

           Agencies
```

FIGURE 5.6

FOUR TEAMS

Public Safety
- Adult Detention Center
- Fire & Rescue
- Criminal Justice Services
- Juvenile Court Service Unit
- Police
- Public Safety Communications
- Sheriff

Human Services
- Area Agency on Aging
- At-Risk Youth & Family Services
- Community Services
- Cooperative Extension
- Public Health
- Social Services, Department of Youth, Office of

Community Development
- Development Services
- Economic Development
- Housing
- Park Authority
- Planning
- Public Works
- Transportation

General Government & Admin
- Executive Management, Office of
- County Attorney
- Finance
- General Registrar
- Human Rights
- Information Technology, Office of
- Library

FIGURE 5.7

would utilize the guidelines for operating in the parallel organization (see Figure 5.2), and elaborated on the RICTER Scale values (described in Chapter 4) to clarify them for each other (see Figure 4.7).

Using Our Values as a Congress

Respect
- For each other at all times
- For the process

Integrity
- Information we give to each other to make decisions
- Placement of activities

Creativity
- Budget Congress is a new idea for the County
- It requires new way of thinking—problem solving

FIGURE 5.8

Furthermore, they felt that to make the behaviors more tangible, they needed norms to explicitly state their expectations:

Team/Budget Congress Recommended Norms

- Begin and end meetings on time
- Remember you are now a member of a larger team, not just a department
- Focus on the greater good of the whole
- Be present to be heard
- Come prepared with your information, knowing the task and the intended goal of the meeting
- Listen
- Avoid sidebar conversations
- Raise questions, seek clarity, move on
- Seek compromise where appropriate, consensus on recommendations
- Participate—do not dominate
- Speak one at a time
- Work in the meetings—not in small huddles outside meetings
- Challenge appropriately
- Seek counsel of the budget office, OEM reps, and dept staff as needed

FIGURE 5.9

The teams' mission, set forth in Figure 5.11, would be difficult to achieve in a short time:

PWC Budget Congress

- **Identify Better Faster Cheaper ways of doing business**
  - Within departments
  - Across organization

- **Redefine Core Business**
  - Ranked priorities
  - Based on the criteria and risk
  - Answer the question: What if ⅓ smaller a year from now?

- **Share the answer to the ⅓ question with the Elected Board and community**

FIGURE 5.10

Budget Congress/Parallel Organization

- **Priorities come to Budget Congress**
- **All agencies on 1 of 4 teams**
- **Each team elects 2 members with 1 alternate to Budget Congress**
  - Alternate:
    - Liaison back to teams
    - Does not vote
    - Becomes member next year
- **County Executive and 2 Assistants consulted about recommendations**
- **Budget Congress makes final recommendations**
- **County Executive makes final decisions**

FIGURE 5.11

Members of the teams and the congress came to trust each other to a greater degree, but not perfectly. It would have been unrealistic to expect a complete transformation in such a short time after years of parochial thinking. Consistently, team and congress members said that learning the areas of government they did not have much contact with was incredibly valuable. The new system seemed to work well for FY 2008, producing the amount of reductions that were needed for the budget.

Using the same Budget Congress process for FY 2009 proved successful as well. As the members, now more familiar with each other, worked through the planning, review, and prioritizing, they grew closer and more honest in their collaborations. This was evident in the way disagreements were handled: more openly and focusing increasingly on facts and data. All the members' perspectives grew as they learned more about other agencies' issues, programs, and priorities. The financial situation had grown worse, and balancing the budget was a greater challenge. Nevertheless, the congress came up with a set of recommendations that met the constrained fiscal conditions and provided the BOCS with the ability to fund a major initiative that had broad public attention.

In contrast, the Budget Congress for FY 2010 had two years of practical experience to build upon, and it needed it. The magnitude of the previous budget's problem had grown dramatically. The county now faced a shortfall of more than $100 million between the county and the schools (for which the county provided a significant amount of funding). The sense of urgency among the budget teams and the congress was spurred on by the seriousness of the problem, but their experience from the prior years made them more comfortable in dealing with it. By now, trust among the team and congress members had grown significantly. All were able to see others' views during arguments for reductions in departments. Of course, a trace of "game playing" persisted among a few, but for the most part people gave and took feedback and changes in priorities based on the merits of the arguments became more the rule than the exception. Central budget office analysts became collaborators and staff support for the teams and congress rather than "judgers." During the process, the county executive and assistant county executives were consulted and were able to share their perspectives and pass on such information as reports from conversations with BOCS members so that the teams and congress participants got continuous information in the proper context. Rank did not mean that a member would rule. The most controlling of systems in most organizations, the budget process, had become far more open to people down the line as the members used an effective Likert System 4 to arrive at its budget proposals to the county executive.

In the end, the Budget Congress recommendations contained program reductions and changes as well as efficiencies, personnel cuts, and pay and benefit changes. Gerhart, the county executive, recalls:

> "As I reviewed their list, I said to myself at one point, 'This is the limit; we can go no further in reductions.' At that moment, I looked at the narrative of the Budget Congress and was amazed to see that it was the exact

point that they had said it recommended no further reductions. From their individual and collective work, their understanding of the county's overall situation and mine had aligned."

The process then changed to a Likert System 3 (consultative) leadership philosophy, because the county executive did have the responsibility to make the final decision on what to recommend to the BOCS. One important benefit of the Budget Congress process was that he was able to free himself from the usual series of intense budget reviews with each department and agency, plus all the preparation and follow-up for those meetings. Instead, he was able to begin a significant employee engagement process. Among other steps, he conducted a series of well-attended employee forums, which continued after the budget proposal. In the forums he defined the problems, discussed potential solutions, reported on the received recommendations, and sought employees' views on how to create the right budgetary balance for the community—including options for reductions to employee pay and benefits. To live up to the leadership philosophy, he tried his best to give every employee a chance to suggest how to approach this last issue. He discussed options, got a lot of feedback about alternatives to pay and benefit reductions, and shaped his recommendations based on that input.

The final budget recommendations so well mirrored those of the congress (and much of the employee feedback) that the product that went to the board was nearly identical to that which the county executive received. The proposed budget went forward with a 7.5 percent reduction from the prior year: services cutbacks and reductions in force, salary freezes and benefit reductions, and lower residential tax collections. When the board reviewed the budget, it found the community generally satisfied, employee groups publicly endorsing the budget (and their own pay and benefit reductions), and the departments and agencies defending the countywide budget proposals. The BOCS added back some small items, increased reserves, and moderated the tax rate appropriate to the economic times.

Gerhart explains:

"My experience with this parallel organization system convinces me that broader participation in this normally very controlling process produces better ideas, vision alignment, and commitment to the end result. Figures 5.12 and 5.13 represent my sense of how the traditional and Budget Congress methods differ. Key factors like a shared view of the whole, trust, and decentralization are strengthened in the new system. Further, as the county executive, I was able to shift my responsibilities to play a stronger leadership role in the organization, winding up with stronger relationships with both the employees and the board—in a volatile time when things could easily have gone the other way."

Traditional   vs.   Budget Congress

Traditional	Budget Congress
• Agencies work independently	• Agencies see full picture of county-wide needs
• Agencies as advocates	• Builds trust among directors
• Analysts as adversaries	• Peer pressure to do the right thing
• Centralized decision making	• Analyst as facilitator
• Agencies communication lacking	• Decentralized decision making
• **Information flows between agencies and analysts**	• Knowledge sharing
	• Time commitment by agencies

FIGURE 5.12

EXECUTIVE ROLE

TRADITIONAL

Task
- Meet with every agency director—some more than once
- Look over detailed spreadsheets for days with staff
- Finalize decisions
- Message to Board & Community

Mangement
- Message to Board & Community

Leadership
- None—No time

BUDGET CONGRESS

Task
- ½ day with teams finalizing decisions
- Message to Board & Community

Mangement
- Managing expectations
- Tactics
- Visual concepts that deliver message
- Message to Board & Community

Leadership
- Idea generation—e.g., employee survey
- More time with employees— multiple town hall meetings
- Tax Policy discussion with Board
- Meet with individual Board members
- Message to Board & Community

FIGURE 5.13

CHANGE MANAGEMENT

The work of leadership requires successful management of change. Great leaders see this as part of their responsibilities. Organizations that aggressively take on the pursuit of higher performance and build it into the organization's culture witness that the shift comes not serendipitously but from a disciplined change process over a substantial period of time.

Noel M. Tichy, author of *The Leadership Engine* and many other well-known books, worked with Jack Welch, former CEO of General Electric, to help him create his *teachable point of view*. Welch was asked to think through and write down fundamental questions about change, including what it would take for an organization to be successful, values he endorsed in supporting business goals, what it takes to motivate people in order to get emotional energy, and "edge," which he defined as a person's thought process for making difficult decisions.

Under Tichy's tutelage, Welch took his written teachable point of view and shared it with the managers who reported to him, where it was discussed, debated, and ultimately aligned. This generated an active discussion about what would make the organization more successful at its business. Tichy reports that he has used this strategy at Ford, AlliedSignal, PepsiCo, and hundreds of other organizations, where the conversations were cascaded down through the organizations.

Tichy's method of articulating the philosophy of change and using a teacher-learner strategy stimulates the thinking process and puts a change framework out into the organization with which people can identify. It is not a passive model, as individuals are required to think through what they have been taught and form their own ideas about philosophy and actions they should take.

What distinguishes those who enthusiastically take on change management is their willingness to shape a philosophy about successful change and pursue it thoughtfully and collectively with the other members of the organization. Local government personnel who take the time to think specifically about how change should be managed, develop principles to guide the process, and create a dynamic structure for the high-performance work to be shared by all are likely to be the most successful. In the following case study, we look at how developing a solid philosophy about why it is important to change, how people change, and what it takes to support that change can make the difference. In this example, one county administrator has taken the long view in developing his organization over more than a decade. He has employed the elements of successful change management and changed the culture of Campbell County, Virginia, by utilizing parallel organization teams to maintain a dynamic and responsive government—even in times of stress, scarce resources, and economic challenges.

CASE STUDY

Creating the Case for Change and Instituting a Parallel Organization[7]

—A. Tyler St. Clair, who has assisted with Campbell County's high-performance development efforts, and R. David Laurrell, then the county administrator of Campbell County, Virginia.

Campbell County, located in central Virginia, is a diverse county with a population of 55,000 and a local government staff of approximately 350. It operates with a Senior Leadership Team (SLT) comprising the county administrator and department and agency heads. In addition, elected officials such as the treasurer, clerk of the court, commissioner of revenue, commonwealth's attorney, and sheriff participate in the county's high-performance efforts on a variable basis.

County Administrator R. David Laurrell developed a philosophy of change that has enabled the county to create and sustain a high-performance effort for more than eleven years. It is remarkable how much organizational development has taken place in this quiet county in concert with an elected body easily described as "conservative." Courage, an ability to create a change mechanism that uniquely fits the organization, great timing, and political savvy have made this success story possible. The county has operated a vibrant, successful, change-oriented parallel organization for well over a decade through its Performance Improvement Teams (PITs).

Laurrell's natural orientation to change management has been to create a simple, yet comprehensive, approach that can be easily understood by diverse parties and to find ways to explain that appeal to common sense. Early in the change effort, he articulated five principles for successful high-performing local government to guide his own efforts, those of the county's Senior Leadership Team, and all employees. Over time, Laurrell has demonstrated how intrinsically these "mental models" affect the way he approaches organizational development.

In 2002, Laurrell wrote an article for *PM Magazine* entitled "Why Strive for High Performance?" based on his views and experiences in Campbell County up to that point. A portion of the article is included in the Appendix to provide a deeper understanding of the five principles that Laurrell believes should be implemented for high-performance success.

FIVE PRINCIPLES FOR SUCCESSFUL HIGH-PERFORMING LOCAL GOVERNMENT

1. **Embrace Change.** Localities working toward high performance will have to undergo fundamental cultural changes to move from technical thinking to adaptive thinking.
2. **Achieve Alignment.** In order for high performance to exist, there must be a shared vision between the democratic process, the political environment, and the organizational climate.
3. **Develop Your People Assets.** Focus on energizing the organization through developing personal, technical, management, and leadership skills in all members.
4. **Adapt Your Organizational Structures.** Enable your jurisdiction to accomplish great things by restructuring to allow people to be more creative and entrepreneurial.
5. **Support Experimentation and Renewal.** Understand and commit to the concept of creating a learning environment that enables change and adaptability. Foster out-of-the-box thinking, instill trust, and recognize the importance of failure in building a self-renewing, continuously improving organization.

Having articulated clear principles for successful high performance in local government, Laurrell's experience in Campbell County reflects his steady application of those beliefs and strategies over the past eleven years. The use of these principles by the county's Senior Leadership Team and employees earned Campbell County the Virginia Association of Counties' Best Achievement Award in 2010 for its sustained efforts in high performance. In this case study, we will describe some of the efforts since 1999 and the formation and operation of the PITs, then examine how Laurrell's principles guided these changes.

Before the establishment of the model described below, departments and employees had become relatively isolated from one another and duplication of services and resources persisted. Departmental yearly plans and budgets were based on current needs versus long-term priorities. This created an environment where departments, out of necessity, viewed the organization and service to citizens through a narrower perspective of immediate needs and limited fiscal and human resources. Processes implemented years before remained in place because that was the way it had always been done. No sustainable system existed to cultivate fresh ideas from the locality's most valuable resource pool: the employees themselves. Employees as a whole felt little connection between their individual tasks and a greater county purpose, and they did not feel they were an integral part of the larger county organization.

Laurrell prepared for the journey by formulating his principles for change and sharing them widely. He used the Venn diagram in Figure 5.15 to demonstrate how aligning the environments among citizens, the elected body, and the organization was critical.

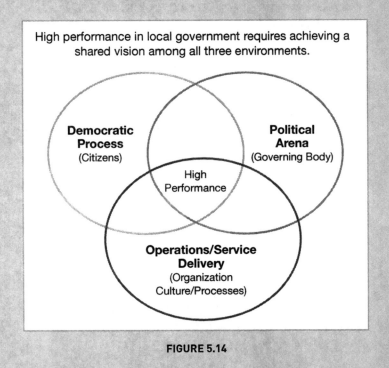

FIGURE 5.14

Before forming the county's Senior Leadership Team (SLT), Laurrell had developed a Senior Management Team (SMT) to coordinate county operations. The Senior Leadership Team has the same membership as the SMT; however, when they meet, they focus on different issues. The SLT became the first level of the parallel organization to develop in Campbell County.

The notion of serving as both a leadership team and a management team resonated with the Senior Management Team. The team determined that one of their four monthly management meetings would focus exclusively on leadership work. Early on, they began to share the responsibilities for facilitating the leadership team meetings so that each person had to think about what was required for a team to function successfully. They used simple definitions to distinguish between management and leadership: Management is focused on tasks and getting things done well today, and leadership is focused on making things work better for the future.

Laurrell worked with the SLT members on embracing change themselves and creating the opportunity for others in the organization to be involved in becoming a high-performance organization. The SLT members, in turn, began to discuss the need for change with their employees. The Senior Leadership Team established the county's second level of the parallel organization, comprising employee-driven Performance Improvement Teams (described later) that address common issues and improve services and procedures throughout the organization. Fundamentally rooted in the principles of democracy and energized with creative thinking, this parallel organization continues to be an avenue through which staff members at all levels of service collaborate equally to address the issues, problems, and future planning that affect county citizens, staff members, and stakeholders.

In 1999, even before exposure to the formal High-Performance Organization Model, Laurrell used a local university to deliver a program on quality improvement to county staff members. Learning concepts and strategies from the quality movement provided staff members with an initial framework for using teams to make improvements in the organization. The county also began to frame its change levers, undertaking a visioning session that involved both the elected body and staff members. For weeks, long sheets of white paper stretched along the walls of the courthouse conference room; anyone who wanted to add input to it was encouraged to do so. Simultaneous comprehensive planning efforts added citizen input to the process.

And an early vision statement emerged that continues to guide the county today. The vision has undergone some modification and expansion over time, but the alignment among citizens, elected officials, and staff has continued to be effective.

In 2002, Laurrell attended the University of Virginia's Senior Executive Institute (SEI). Two weeks at SEI gave Laurrell the opportunity to further crystallize his strategy for organizational development. How would he work with the team of county department heads to jointly own and further the work of leadership? How could he bring in development that would prepare all staff for the roles on the shoestring budget that had become the norm in Campbell County? How could he ensure that the five principles for high-performing local government were embedded in the organization for both new employees and long-time employees? Laurrell has implemented an organizational development model in Campbell County that includes his own elements, as well as those taken from his SEI experience and the HPO Model. One of the reasons for success in Campbell County has been his ability to tailor and continually refine a model that works for his jurisdiction. Over time, as department heads attended the University of Virginia's one-week LEAD program, the conversation and engagement among the team members about the work of leadership grew.

A challenge for many local governments is learning how to sustain the meaningful work of a leadership team over time. Teams often work busily on the initial change levers, producing a vision, values, and leadership philosophy. After that's done, they are not quite sure about their next tasks as a group. Campbell County's approach has been simple and highly structured. An annual set of topics is developed for each monthly Senior Leadership Team meeting, and members alternate responsibility for planning and facilitating the team's discussion. Sometimes the meeting is programmatic, and other times it is a lively discussion focused on a topic that stretches one's thinking. In this way, the Senior Leadership Team has continued to serve as an organizing component in helping the county embrace change over time.

PERFORMANCE IMPROVEMENT TEAMS

Beginning in 1999, the county embraced a philosophy that fosters employee leadership, encourages participation in collaborative, multi-departmental teams, and invites employee input into the long-term planning process. This innovative approach is based on the premise that all employees, regardless of full-time or part-time status, area of specialty, level of responsibility, or length of service, have valuable ideas and insight crucial to the organization's success. These beliefs are captured in the county's vision and leadership philosophy (see Table 5.1).

CAMPBELL COUNTY

Governing with Vision

To be the most collaborative, professional, value-driven locality in Virginia

Leadership Philosophy

We, the employees and leadership of Campbell County, are here by choice because we individually and collectively support the County's mission and values. We have a strong work ethic and share in a common goal of excellence.

We are accessible and accountable to the citizens of Campbell County in providing necessary and essential services.

We are open to change and the process of continual improvement. Together we are creating a workplace that values the unique talents and abilities of each person, provides an atmosphere of trust, communicates openly, and is motivated by the knowledge that what we do enhances the quality of life in our county.

TABLE 5.1

The Senior Leadership Team identifies issues and areas within the organization where improvements could be made and channels these issues to one of the Performance Improvement Teams. Employees throughout the organization can suggest items for inclusion, and the long-range planning process described later refers additional ideas. The names, number, and focus of the various teams have changed over the years to meet the growing needs of the organization. The original teams are shown in Figure 5.16. The Senior Leadership Team plays a foundational role in the parallel team process through the initial chartering of PITs on an annual basis, mentoring individual teams, and coordinating their work. It reviews the submissions and ideas of the PITs and provides constructive feedback or approval to proceed with recommended projects or processes. Projects are handed off to operating departments for implementation if they fall within their functional area or expertise, or they can be implemented by the PIT if deemed appropriate.

Employees from all departments are given the opportunity to volunteer for service on teams and to rate their team preferences. Employees have the option of participating; if they do so, their service time on a PIT is incorporated into regular work hours and individual work plans. They are assessed within the employee evaluation process and are recognized for leadership and active participation in the program.

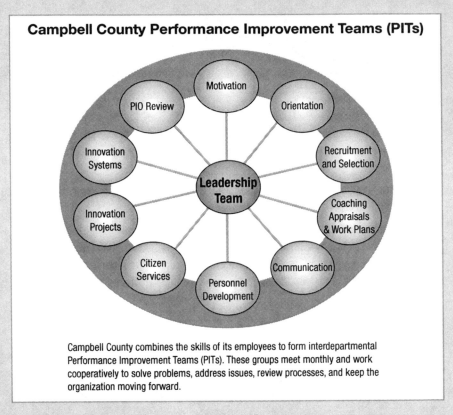

Campbell County Performance Improvement Teams (PITs)

Campbell County combines the skills of its employees to form interdepartmental Performance Improvement Teams (PITs). These groups meet monthly and work cooperatively to solve problems, address issues, review processes, and keep the organization moving forward.

FIGURE 5.15

The Senior Leadership Team members review employee team placement requests and make assignments. Factors they consider in making team assignments include

- representation from different departments
- different levels of supervisory responsibility
- different levels of experience
- racial and gender diversity
- a mix of complementary Myers-Briggs Type Indicator personalities

Once teams are created, they are given lists by the SLT of potential projects or areas that need attention or revision. Teams are then assigned a Senior Leadership Team mentor and an employee team leader. Team leaders set a regular meeting schedule to address key issues and cultivate ideas for improvement over the course of the year. The SLT mentor provides support and ensures that the team's work aligns with other projects and organizational change efforts in the county. Table 5.2 shows the "issues to consider" and "possible assignments" for the Citizen Services Performance Improvement Team.

CITIZEN SERVICES PERFORMANCE IMPROVEMENT TEAM

Team Leader: S. Harding

Mentor: N. Carmack

Mission: To review our customer/citizen services practices and identify areas for improvement or change and to examine the public's perception/opinion of how well we deliver services.

Issues to consider

- How do citizens feel about core services they receive from Campbell County?
- How do we best communicate our work to the public?
- How do we best get feedback from Campbell County residents?
- How do we define and address "quality of life" issues?
- What do we need to do in the area of e-government to improve electronic access in areas such as permits, payment of taxes, registering for activities, etc.?
- How do we use information from the "National Citizen Survey" to set benchmarks and identify areas for improvement?
- How do we continue to promote and reinforce the concept of "service excellence"?
- How do our practices reflect our HPO efforts?

Possible assignments

- Review results of "Citizen Survey"
- Review operational logistics (such as hours of operation, citizen access, etc.)
- Review and suggest improvements to our current customer service training program
- Review processes within the organization that involves citizens to see if they can be made less bureaucratic

TABLE 5.2

In this example, the development, execution, and review of the Citizen Survey were completed by the team, and the results and recommendations were reported to the Senior Leadership Team. To implement the recommendations, specific projects and tasks were assigned to staff members in operating departments that were most closely aligned with the initiative.

One purpose of the PITs is to cultivate interdepartmental collaboration and foster an environment where employees engage in activities impacting the broader organization and its mission—work that embraces a larger purpose outside of their daily tasks. Teams meet at least once a month. The experience allows employees from various departments to become acquainted with each other as well as the operations of other county offices and their staff's perspectives on common problems and issues.

These collaborations also promote communication conduits that cross many levels and areas of service and help staff members discover untapped internal and external resources. For instance, some departments now share equipment rather than purchasing it separately; other departments share employees with certain skill sets or materials to aid other departments with projects where that specific expertise or support is needed. In fact, one of the basic principles of PITs is to promote team process capabilities. The team process is valued as highly in this environment as the product because it helps develop the skills and principles employees need in order to thrive in a high-performing organization. PITs are often the first place where employees are exposed to the participative leadership environment that is not directly related to their day-to-day activities.

When employees begin their employment in Campbell County, they attend an in-house leadership development program that orients them to high performance and the use of the parallel organization to ensure that resources are tapped from all levels and areas of the organization. When PITs are working on Performance Improvement Plans and Timelines (described next) and other planning issues, they collaborate as equals with managers, elected officials, and staff members from other departments to address common challenges and accomplish their objectives. The PIT structure allows employees to share their ideas, weigh the possibilities, and make decisions in the best interest of the county. The internal cooperation fostered by the PITs has helped Campbell County sustain a highly productive, fiscally sound organization for more than a decade. Examples of the improvements created by the PITs include

- development of a full curriculum for front-line supervisor training
- improved signage to better direct citizens within the county complex
- enhanced communication with the public, employees, and other stakeholders through changes to publication formats and the implementation of more web-based information
- development and implementation of a variety of citizen survey methods

PLANNING: PRIORITY INITIATIVES

To enable a grounded and comprehensive long-term planning process, employees and elected officials collaborate on the future direction of the county. Each year, employees and their respective department heads develop major projects that they believe to be most beneficial to citizens and the organization to be carried out over a three- to ten-year period. Detailed Performance Improvement Plans and Time-lines (PIPTs) are created for each project or process, identifying the overall benefit to citizens or the organization, key staff responsibilities, direct and indirect staff time involved, employee hours anticipated for completion, anticipated budget requests for the project or process, and a detailed time frame for implementation. Written objectives are submitted during the budget process for the approval of the Board of Supervisors and subsequent funding allocations. This system gives employees valuable insight and buy-in to the planning and budgeting process and also brings employees and administrators together with a common goal of solving issues cooperatively.

Projects are divided into four categories: Ongoing (occur every year and a general part of the overall operation), Priority 1 (upcoming fiscal year), Priority 2 (two years away), and Future (three to ten years away). Each project is accompanied by an electronic PIPT. The Board of Supervisors then allocates the needed resources to the projects they approve through the budgeting process. Each year, priorities are evaluated and moved up to the next tier (e.g., Priority 2 moves up to Priority 1; Future priorities slated for implementation move up to Priority 2). This process was originally handled manually but is now computerized and managed through the county's online PIPT tracking system.

Campbell County's employee-driven organizational planning model has proven to be a highly valuable, efficient, and sustainable program for effective problem solving, budgeting, and long-term planning for the locality. Table 5.3 shows the schedule used by the county to develop its annual priorities and initiatives.

Campbell County Annual Priorities and Initiatives Planning Schedule	
October	Board holds annual planning retreat with staff.
November	Staff provides input on priorities and initiatives and verifies that all priority items have corresponding Performance Improvement Objectives that are current.
December	Staff drafts proposed priorities and initiatives.
January	Board reviews and adopts priorities and initiatives.
February	Staff develops Capital Improvement Plan (CIP) to support the priorities and initiatives along with corresponding Performance Improvement Objectives.
March	Staff develops operating budget to support priorities and initiatives along with corresponding Performance Improvement Objectives.
May	Board adopts budget.
June	Employee Coaching Appraisals and Work Plan reviews for prior fiscal year are completed to provide input for annual merit increases.
July	Staff updates Performance Improvement Objectives and timetables to match the Board-adopted budget and to transfer to staff to accomplish the adopted priorities and initiatives for the coming fiscal year. Work plans at individual and team level are completed to let employees know what is expected from everyone in the upcoming fiscal year.

TABLE 5.3

This mechanism ensures that all employees have an active role in making the major decisions that affect the locality's long-term direction. Everyone involved has a comprehensive view of future plans and their individual and departmental responsibilities. By linking a democratic organizational model to its long-term planning system, Campbell County enables employees to express ideas to initiate change, while citizens benefit from employee ingenuity and commitment in helping departments and the county as a whole attain desired goals using more efficient business practices.

Many innovative changes have been made to internal processes with a shift of leadership responsibility to all employees throughout the organization. Employees feel valued, better ideas have emerged by drawing on the collective expertise of staff, and long-term planning is approached as a collaborative effort among employees, managers, and elected officials. The system has been sustainable and produced a more positive work culture in the county. The long-term investment in this culture has accomplished the following:

- enhanced interdepartmental cooperation
- streamlined processes developed by employees who serve citizens daily
- resources refocused on important tasks and services from less critical and urgent, but not important issues
- increased buy-in from employees in all areas of service
- provided open and honest feedback from teams seeking to improve the overall organization
- an effective planning and budgeting tool that defines long-term goals and funding allocations
- improved personal and organizational teamwork and bonding arising from common goals

This significant effort has come with relatively small direct costs, primarily in staff development and the staff time used to coordinate the PIT and SLT process. The county uses an external consultant who provides development for staff members on leadership and high performance and also sends Senior Leadership Team members to the LEAD program at the University of Virginia to gain an understanding of the HPO Model.

The county's parallel team structure seems to work well for a variety of reasons:

- Teams are goal directed and focused through a document that clarifies the team's mission, issues to consider, and possible assignments.
- Teams have enormous flexibility in working on the change areas to which they have been assigned but also have a clear purpose, especially in the planning process.
- Each team has support from a team leader who convenes and facilitates its meetings and a mentor from the Senior Leadership Team to provide support and alignment with operations and other change efforts in the organization.
- Employees from all over the organization are offered an opportunity to serve on PITs and thus to participate in the work of leadership.
- To maximize team service opportunities, employee team terms are limited to two years. This length of participation is typically sufficient to document specific, rewarding achievements while providing healthful employee turnover on the teams.

- Leadership work is an expectation, but individuals are afforded choices regarding participation and the teams on which they would like to serve.
- Leadership work on PITs is part of the job: Employees serve on teams during regular work hours and are recognized for the efforts in their individual work plans.
- Specific processes are used to integrate the work of PITs, including the use of PIPTs and the systematic nature of the planning process (e.g., priority definition, role definition, calendar, linkage to individual work plans).
- The Senior Leadership Team evaluates PIT outputs and performance on a regular basis through an established review schedule.
- The use of leadership team mentors ensures that there is a coordinating function for all team efforts and makes it possible to address individual team needs or problems quickly.
- The parallel structure is relatively low cost with high benefits.
- Development to enable successful participation in PITs (leadership, high-performance principles, overview of the planning process, team skills) is provided annually, and all employees are required to attend upon employment; refreshers are also provided.
- The parallel structure is adapted to meet the changing needs of the organization, including improvements in coordination and the number, type, and focus of the teams.

PRINCIPLES IN ACTION

Let's review each of Laurrell's five principles briefly to understand how he used them to initiate and maintain the organizational change to improve performance:

1. **Embrace Change.** Laurrell began by talking with his direct staff and others about the compelling need for the county to shift the way in which it does business. He foresaw that the traditional technical approach to services would not stand up well against the forces of advancing technology, citizen demands, and constrained resources. He conveyed that the county staff could not successfully meet these challenges without improving its ability to do adaptive thinking. He was developing, in ADKAR[8] terms (explained later), awareness of the environment and the need for change. He shared his view of the three environments they collectively face in a simple three-circle Venn diagram, then

developed and taught his synthesizing principles of how to approach the coming transition.

He utilized the local university workshop to engage the staff in more pragmatic discussions and give them an opportunity to address their concerns. He was intuitively dealing with the Desire aspect of the ADKAR model as he engaged his Senior Management Team in the concepts of the quality movement.

After attending SEI and seeing the relationship between his principles and the HPO Model, Laurrell saw a natural way to strengthen the county's work of leadership by introducing the idea of a Senior Leadership Team to his SMT. He helped them to understand how they could work differently and also began to send the team members to the LEAD program to broaden their awareness of how business needed to continue to shift. This reinforced the commitment to the PITs as well as the long-term devotion of senior staff time to leadership work.

2. **Achieve Alignment.** From the beginning of this work, Laurrell ensured the change efforts were aligned directly to the direction of the county. The extensive visioning work followed by citizen-involved comprehensive planning efforts and subsequent iterations help focus the staff's work on the community's top priorities. Today, the online Performance Improvement Plan and Timeline tracking system provides a clear link between input from employees and departments regarding their recommendations on county priorities and the planning process that involves the elected body. This automated version of priority management makes it easier to share information across responsible departments and parties and to track progress.

   Alignment is continually ensured through the county's annual planning process. The planning process to identify and accomplish important goals is so ingrained in the organization that there is no question whether the board's annual planning session will be held. All parties see what is gained from the session. Priority management is directly linked to resources, and there is clear communication regarding priority initiatives among different levels of the organization and among staff members and the elected body.

3. **Develop Your People Assets.** One of the first tasks of the Senior Leadership Team was to prepare the rest of the workforce to take a more active role in organizational leadership. To develop fundamental awareness, over a

three-month period, a two-day leadership development program addressing high-performance concepts was provided for every employee in the organization. Opening the workshop each time, Laurrell talked about the environment in which the county was operating and the need for change and adaptability, then shared the five principles for high-performing local government. The leadership development program is now offered annually, and new employees are scheduled for it as early as possible so that they understand their role in Campbell County's success.

In addition to providing an orientation to high performance, the classes give participants an opportunity to identify issues that they think should be addressed to improve organizational performance. Later, these issues are prioritized by the Senior Leadership Team to determine where improvements should be made.

Other strategies to expose staff members to common development opportunities emerged, training needs were identified, and resources were allocated to deliver programs to address them. A series of "lunch bunch" meetings was held, often focusing on the personal skills area that Laurrell believed to be important. A local employee assistance and training agency used by the county was brought in to take advantage of the high-quality, "just in time" training modules that it offered. It has continued to be valuable in providing high-performance skills training, along with serving as a source of performance coaching and intervention.

The county has implemented other learning strategies since its inception. A comprehensive customer service project resulted in the development of Service Excellence Principles and a training program that is provided for every employee. A front-line training program was developed by a team to meet the specific needs of supervisors, especially knowledge and skills that would enhance their role in managing policy, developing employees, and working with natural teams. Employee orientation has been expanded to ensure that employees understand the entire operation of the county versus the typical information regarding policies and benefits.

4. **Adapt Organizational Structures.** Fluid structural adaptation to a matrix decision-making model is most clearly seen with the long-standing PITs, the shift to a Senior Leadership Team, the institutionalization of the annual priority initiatives planning process, and the ongoing employee orientation and

development programs. This allows for consistent and reliable decision making at the most appropriate point.

Many opportunities exist for adaptation in organizational structures—people, functions, and processes. Especially challenging is working with individuals, particularly those at the top of the organization, to find the place where they can contribute the most. Laurrell has demonstrated a willingness to try a variety of managerial placements to give managers new experiences or a change of scenery and to give the organization a chance to work through a particular dynamic. He seems to have a sixth sense about when a department's employees "need a break" before dealing with a new director. Furthermore, he has not been afraid to experiment with dual directors to achieve the right mix of top management, on either a temporary or permanent basis. Lastly, he's been firm in assisting those who do not have a propensity for the work of leadership to leave the organization with grace and dignity.

5. **Support Experimentation and Renewal.** The PITs are a primary way that Campbell County lives out this principle. Not only do they provide an ongoing avenue for experimentation and creative ideas, they also seed the organization with people who understand that learning and growth are important and valued. As the PITs shift in emphasis over the years, they focus on areas of renewal and change that cover new ground. The regularity of the process helps the organization be attentive to the next window of opportunity for renewal and improvement.

We know that high performance is correlated with a positive work culture that can enable, empower, engage, and energize. Yet a successful mechanism for doing this eludes many local governments. Often we hear about "getting more done with less" or becoming "more efficient and effective" without a clear mechanism to make it safe for employees to question what, why, or how things are being done. Campbell County employees are effectively enabled by a strong organizational culture that emphasizes getting things done in a planned and structured way while looking for new ways to do things. There is a strong sense of evolution and growth within the culture.

Laurrell advocates fostering a learning environment that provides for change and adaptability. He talks about shifting from a traditional "contracting" concept to one of "agreement" as a way to positively shape expectations and involvement—based on achieving the intent of the shared objectives rather than meeting the letter of the contract. This culture has its foundation in the county's organizational values. Those values, captured in both core values and operating principles and seen in Table 5.4, were initially identified in the county's 1999 visioning process and have been expanded over time. Employees shaped the county's values from the beginning and are continuously exposed to them in employee orientation, leadership development, and "on the wall."

The Values and Operating Principles for Success for Our Organization and County		
CORE VALUES These are the five concepts that are common in our organization: Cooperation, Dedication, Quality of Life, Trustworthiness, Family/Community		
OPERATING PRINCIPLES		
• **Honesty, openness, and integrity** in all our efforts to serve the county. • **Sharing of information** to keep the citizens of our community informed • **Civility and consciously motivated organizational behavior** that is ethical and serves the higher good. We will constantly serve the higher good of the individual, the organization, the communities, and the county. • **Value**—we constantly strive to bring the greatest value to our citizens for their tax dollars.	• **Learning/competence**—we are constantly enhancing the capabilities and competencies of our public servants, our employees. • **Cooperation**—we are cooperative (and maintain partnerships) within and without. We cooperate for the higher good with those around us, with the Commonwealth, with neighboring counties and communities. We strive for cooperative, win-win situations within, between board members, county leadership, management, employees, citizens, business and industry, and other related organizations.	• **Serving**—unrelenting dedication to serve our communities and our county. • **Dedication** to effective and democratic local government and to effective and efficient service to our constituents. • **Intellectual honesty**—we create a culture that is open, honest, and direct. People are flexible and capable of change. There is no game playing or self-interest.

TABLE 5.4

These values and operating principles create the expectation that employees will work in a learning environment, where they can speak honestly and openly and contribute to the improvement of the organization. This is exactly the culture that supports the effective functioning of the PITs. These teams provide a place for experimentation and learning while giving employees an opportunity to address issues that can make a positive difference in the organization.

Not all plans succeed, of course. Innovation and positive change are possible only through hard work and the opportunity that permits a fair share of failure, even from PITs. The organization has shown a remarkable ability to change the course of a strategy when it proves to be ineffective. For example, a highly structured plan to address HPO elements and change levers in the Senior Leadership Team with a follow-up discussion in each departmental management team proved unwieldy. By the next year, the SLT had changed direction and sought a different way to reinforce dialogue on high performance within the departments.

In summary, Campbell County has had the benefit of a well-articulated philosophy regarding how change can be successfully managed. Beginning the process with his five principles for high-performing local government, Laurrell has worked collectively with organizational members to shape leadership at all levels, create an effective parallel structure to address improvement and long-term planning, and ensure that the organization fosters adaptation, learning, and high performance. The success of this locality suggests that local government managers who take the time to reflect upon and commit to a personal philosophy and strategy for change, and pursue it in concert with the collective organization, will see the highest performance.

When an organization creates a parallel organization to become higher performing, it begins a series of changes that it hopes will be widespread and long-lived. Thus, one of its principal challenges is also creating the capability for managing change over the long term. David Laurrell knew intuitively what research has been validating. Change management is an essential part of moving to higher performance. When organizations introduce changes to improve performance—whether they are systems, processes, technology, or behaviors—they impact individuals who are frequently required to modify what they work on, how they work, and/or their personal behaviors. Change management provides the structure, intent, and tools for encouraging and supporting individuals through their own personal changes as they become proficient with the new requirements.

A growing body of data[8] shows a direct correlation between change management effectiveness and the likelihood that a project or initiative delivers the intended outcomes. That correlation rests on this fact: Organizational results are delivered when individuals make their own changes successfully. A perfectly designed process that no one follows does not deliver value to the organization. A perfectly designed technology solution that no one uses does not deliver outcomes or objectives to the organization. The "people side" of change is what drives benefits for the organization when it takes on a change effort.

Regardless of the nature, shape, and size of any change, they all are attempts to move the organization from a current state, through a transition state, to a future state (see Figure 5.16). The effort aims for a future state that is better than the current state and enables the organization to achieve its vision and enhance performance.

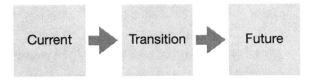

FIGURE 5.16 Organizational States of Change

UNDERSTANDING CHANGE MANAGEMENT: THE "PEOPLE SIDE" OF CHANGE

When thinking about how to help this individual or organizational transition process, it is useful to borrow from the concepts of the Change Management Learning Center and its sponsor, Prosci Research, an independent research company in the field of change management. Their most recent benchmarking study on successful projects, based on surveying 822 participant organizations in sixty-three countries, finds that the number one obstacle to success for major change projects is employee resistance and the ineffective management of the people side of change.[10]

Many organizations use the concept of project management[11] to implement change in their organizations, but Prosci's research indicates that most don't integrate well the people side of change into the change management process. What is required is shown in Figure 5.17.

Unfortunately, all too often the integration of these two processes fails to occur. As a result, frequently the change effort being attempted is far along in its planning, design, and development before everyone realizes they're about to go to the implementation stage without a plan for dealing with the people side (see Figure 5.18).

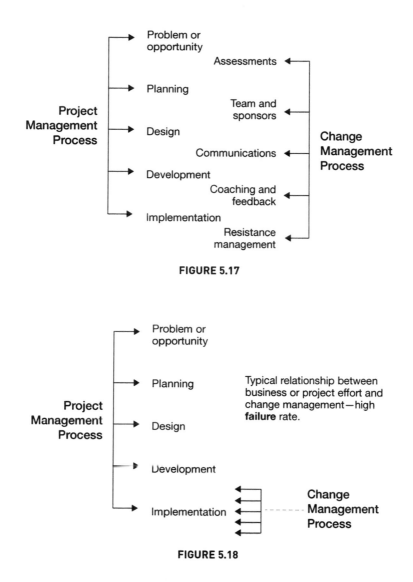

FIGURE 5.17

FIGURE 5.18

Fortunately, there are tools associated with the change management process, just as there are with project management. Prosci defines three phases in the change management process, each with its own set of tools:

Phase 1: Preparing for change involves defining the change management strategy, preparing the change management team, and developing the sponsorship model.

Phase 2: Managing change involves developing change management plans, taking action, and implementing plans.

Phase 3: Reinforcing change involves collecting and analyzing feedback, diagnosing gaps, managing resistance, implementing corrective actions, and celebrating successes.

One of the most useful tools for assessing where to focus in preparing people for change is described in Jeffery Hiatt's book *ADKAR: A Model for Change in Business, Government, and Our Community.*[12] Fundamentally, effective management of the people dimension of change requires managing five key goals that form the basis of the ADKAR model:

- **Awareness** of the need to change
- **Desire** to participate and support the change
- **Knowledge** of how to change (and what the change looks like)
- **Ability** to implement the change on a day-to-day basis
- **Reinforcement** to keep the change in place

We can assess an individual's readiness for change using these concepts. For example, a person's knowledge of how to make the change has little impact if she doesn't understand why she is asked to change, thinks that it will lead to a bad outcome, or is determined to undermine it. We can also assess where we might need to focus our efforts to move organizational change along. For example, if we have done a good job of explaining, from a business point of view, why a change needs to be made in the organization (awareness) but have not dealt with the perceived loss of power of some individuals (desire) then increasing the "pitch" of why we need to make the change will not help. We need resistance management tools instead. (More information on change management and available tools is available at www.change-management.com.)

Laurrell focused on awareness when he framed the work in Campbell County in terms of his five principles. He took the time with his Senior Leadership Team and others in the organization to set the framework for why change was necessary and the way people in the organization needed to respond to it if the county was to achieve its vision. Only after the context was set was he able to move through the remaining stages—which continue through today—in managing the transition to the desired future state.

SUPPORTING CHANGE MANAGEMENT ACTIVITIES: YOU MAY NEED SOME HELP

Senior managers, especially those with technical backgrounds, often need help with the organizational development/change management process. At about the 300-person level, an organization begins needing one or more part- or full-time change professionals on staff—people with organizational development, change management, business analytical thinking, project management, and team-development skills.

Experienced change agents can staff the leadership team's efforts and deliver "just-in-time" training, change-team facilitation, and encouragement/reinforcement/coordination as well as build a network of part-time change agents dispersed throughout the organization. They can also play a "sensing function," pulling together information from all parts of the organization that touch the whole organization or a microbusinesses within it (e.g., support staff from HR, IT, finance/budget/procurement, facilities, legal, or EEO). Based on this information, a picture of the organization or the microbusiness begins to emerge that can suggest (in consultation with the managers and members of the microbusiness) which specific interventions may be useful to significantly improve the organization or the unit's performance. Finally, they can integrate with any outside contract support secured to help with the change process; this will continue to increase the in-house staff's skills and may alert you to problems with the contractors.

Bellevue Development Services (see Chapter 1), Sarasota County (see Chapter 4), and the Fairfax Public Works Environmental Services (this chapter) all have such staff to support the improvement work described in their stories. In the following case study, two change agents describe their experience, this time in the federal government sector.

CASE STUDY

Change Agents in NAVAIR[13]

—Joan Goppelt and Keith W. Ray on their experience when employed in NAVAIR

The Naval Air Systems Command (NAVAIR) undertook a journey toward higher performance beginning in 2000. NAVAIR is responsible for acquiring and maintaining Navy and Marine aircraft and associated systems. The employees at NAVAIR do a variety of technical work, including research, product development, contractor oversight, product testing, troubleshooting of deployed products, pilot training, and operations of land, air, and sea-based test facilities. The employees come from a wide range of professions, including engineers, scientists, technicians, military officers, enlisted personnel, and support staff. This case study will focus on the Systems Engineering Department, which took the lead for using the HPO Model and built an internal support capacity.

In 1999, an Activity Based Costing (ABC) and Business Process Reengineering (BPR) study concluded that a primary area for cost saving and efficiencies was in the software engineering function. Brad, newly appointed to the Senior Executive Service, was charged with implementing the recommendations from the software engineering section of the BPR. Brad brought the Commonwealth Centers for High-Performance Organizations (CCHPO) to NAVAIR to act as improvement consultants and change partners and began a series of three-day HPO seminars.

Brad placed on his staff a group of change agents from other ongoing improvement efforts, which included: software process improvement via the Software Engineering Institute Capability Maturity Model/Integrated (CMM/CMMI), knowledge management, learning organization, and rapid response team inspections for programs in trouble. The HPO Model provided an overarching framework upon which to tie together these ongoing efforts. In addition, use of the seven key diagnostic questions provided a structure for systematically approaching organizational performance improvement. As a result of the first few seminars, Brad challenged his group of change agents to "pick what is good and do something with this HPO stuff." From there, the internal change support team for HPO began.

FORMING INTERNAL CHANGE SUPPORT TEAM

At the beginning, there were three full-time change agents tasked with "doing something with the HPO stuff." These three, which included the authors of this case study, and a few other part-time staff, convened to apply the seven Key Diagnostic Questions (KDQs) of the HPO Model to the change agent team. The strategy was to learn the process by using it first with our own team. This would accelerate our learning as well as provide insight to potential stumbling points within the context of the NAVAIR organization. For example, we chose to organize around the Likert System 4 principles with a fully networked and self-directed team. Doing so caused confusion when interacting with other parts of the organization that expected there to be a single lead.

To begin with, the initial set of change agents had a set of characteristics that we would consider requisite for doing this type of work within NAVAIR. Each had a proven record of leading and managing successful projects—either within NAVAIR or in the commercial sector; this provided credibility when working with other project managers and technical subject matter experts. Each of us had an interest in organizational dynamics and systems thinking. We had each independently been studying and learning about organizations and the systems within them, so there was a natural tendency for each of us to connect to the concepts within the HPO Model. Finally, we had credibility with the senior managers we supported. We were viewed as bringing in new ideas and providing advice on sticky organizational issues.

We worked closely with our CCHPO partners to identify key competencies we would need to have in order to support use of the HPO Model within the organization. We developed a model for building capacity that included knowledge and areas of expertise. Two of us chose to learn to teach the three-day HPO seminar. Teaching and fielding class questions helped us get a deeper understanding of the application of the material in situations that participants encountered in their actual work situations. It also made our group visible to those who attended the HPO seminars. We could easily step up after seminars to offer our support in their subsequent activities.

As a group, we accelerated our learning by constantly reflecting and debriefing after every seminar or event, such as facilitating a leadership team. This constant experience and reflection enabled us to adjust and hone our support skills. In the first years, we often co-taught and co-facilitated with our CCHPO partners. Having one or more people to reflect with provided a valuable learning process.

DEVELOPING PRODUCTS AND SERVICES

We developed a suite of services that we could market and sell to our internal clients. These products and services were derived from our mission to increase performance in the software and systems engineering teams by supporting the use and expansion of the HPO Model. The initial services included leadership team facilitation, Vision to

Performance workshops, Values to Work Culture workshops, and a larger contiguous five-day TeamWay workshop that included individual development, team development, and organizational development concepts. We experimented with adjusting these services to the size of the team being served.

In general, these services were well utilized by teams in NAVAIR; however, if the manager was only requesting our services because Brad (as the department head) said they must, then we had limited influence and, ultimately, little long-term success with the team. As we learned, when we had "prisoners"—people who felt forced to attend—we made less progress than when we had willing managers who were genuinely on board with improving their teams' performance.

Initially, we also planned to have more front-line managers be part of the instructor and facilitator staff for the TeamWay workshops. This approach was not successful because the managers seemed unwilling to place themselves directly in the role of change agent.

We also staffed targeted organizational change efforts, such as the implementation of a standard set of performance metrics across programs. The approach, at the time, was to require performance measures across the diverse set of eleven product teams within the Systems Engineering Department. This effort was met with significant resistance; in hindsight, we likely did not appreciate the complexities of what we were attempting. Brad was supportive, but each project team lead had sufficient influence to stave off the attempts to develop measures of performance. Interestingly, today, many of the teams collaborate and work across their boundaries despite the lack of explicit accountability for each other's performance.

While the internal support group received direct funding, we also decided to use a fee-for-service business model in order to remain viable during budget ups and downs. With the NAVAIR organization, if project managers volunteer to pay for a service that is optional for their project, it is deemed to be a valuable service. We targeted the intact project teams (e.g., F-14 aircraft team) and functional areas (e.g., financial management) for delivering products and services. We negotiated outcomes, drafted informal contracts, and arranged for internal payment of our services. We were able to report our metrics in a balanced scorecard format. This was in alignment with answering the "How would you know?" question in the HPO Model.

ADAPTATION

In our first three years, we tried many things and learned a great deal about what worked and what didn't work within the NAVAIR organization. It was through this constant trial-and-error that we were able to adapt the use of the HPO Model to the NAVAIR setting. We developed expertise in recognizing when a manager was definitively ready to work on performance improvement. We became more adept at applying effort in areas where we would gain the most leverage. In other words, as internal change agents, we learned how to say "no" when a manager was approaching us for what we felt was the wrong reason. We continually evolved the concepts we were teaching and facilitating and engaged in regular dialogue with our CCHPO partners about what we were learning.

After about eight years, Brad retired, and another senior executive took over the department. The energy and vision from the top waned for both improvement efforts in general and the use of an internal support capacity. The HPO Model concepts remained a foundation of our work with teams, but we did not have an active senior executive voice to take the efforts to another level. We adapted our products and services to remain viable and useful. This ability to adapt is a key ingredient in sustainment of any type of internal support capacity for organizational development.

WHAT WE LEARNED

Our journey in developing an internal change team was full of twists, turns, and dead ends. However, the journey also had high points and grand vistas from where we could see what we had accomplished and a vision of the future. There is much that makes sense to us now that at the time was a mystery. With perfect retrospective vision, we offer a few key points that summarize what we learned.

1. **Have Autonomy with Purpose.** We were essentially given free rein to do what we thought was best, within the boundaries of improving performance for the organization. This autonomy to do the right thing without a preconceived direction had two lasting effects. First, we were highly motivated to develop creative solutions to the organization's persistent problems. We could innovate and try things out, and if they did not work, we could quickly abandon them for another idea. If the ideas worked, we were just as motivated to keep them going. Having a purpose shared within the team and with our sponsor, Brad, allowed us to maneuver the complexities of organizational life while also staying coordinated and moving in the same direction.

   Second, autonomy to do the right thing allowed us to feel responsible and accountable for results. We were not implementing someone else's ideas that we were unsure about or that were unclear to us. We knew what we were doing, why we were doing it, and what to expect. We wanted our ideas to work, and we could learn from our mistakes.

2. **Fit in the Culture and Context.** Because we each had several years of experience in the organization, we understood its culture and complexities. This was both an asset and a liability. As an asset, we could quickly understand what might work and what might not. For example, we knew that the predominant culture of the organization was a technocracy (while another organization might value formal education or hierarchical position). We knew that having technical backgrounds would bring us some degree of legitimacy and trust even though we were working in an area in which our technical experience was of little use. But being in the culture for so long can also produce filters and blind spots. We needed to be extra careful of these, and we often relied on our external consulting partners to point them out.

    When we chose our business model—fee-for-service—we knew that it was risky yet critical for the group's survival. From past experiences, we knew that administrative budgets and positions were often the first to go in difficult financial times. We also knew that in the organization's internal economy, what the program managers decided to pay for directly became a valuable service. This motivated us to ensure that we were responsive to our internal customers and made it easy for us to show our value to senior managers.

3. **Use the HPO Model on Self.** One important step we took was to use the HPO Model to help define and form the team. Our initial purpose was two-fold: to learn the model and to decide what we were, what we would do, and how we would do it. We quickly proved the adage "Tell me, and I'll forget. Show me, and I'll remember. Let me do it, and I'll understand." Performing all the steps in the HPO Model allowed us to understand both its subtleties and how to adapt the process to our culture.

    Collectively working through all key diagnostic questions gave us clarity of purpose and vision that would have been difficult if one person had developed the idea and tried to sell it to the others. We were able to stay coordinated much more easily because of how we jointly made sense of our team's purpose and operations.

    One added benefit was that we could quickly counter the "That will never work here" argument. When people imagine using such a model, they often cannot see their way through the fog of complexity that is organizational life.

A common excuse: "The model is nice but does not apply to our organization." Whenever this objection was raised, we could say that we had proof that it works and argue, with integrity, that we understood which parts work well and which parts are difficult.

4. **Always Learn and Adapt.** Though we each had experience in organizational change, we knew we had much to learn and we needed to learn fast. Putting learning as a central focus of our group allowed us to expand our vision beyond what had been done in the past. Learning became a value and a practice that sustained us through confusing, difficult moments and allowed us to innovate much faster. We were consciously mirroring what we believed the entire organization needed as well—to learn about social systems and change. One manager remarked to our team, "You guys bring us new ideas that we would have never known about."

    Focusing on learning allowed us to adapt what we were doing and how we were doing it. Organizations are constantly in flux and adapting to a changing environment, new managers, and intentional change. Our organization was no different. We needed to respond just as quickly and to occasionally even be able to predict what was about to happen. Taking a learning stance helped us be prepared to change our products and services in response to shifts in vision and needs of the rest of the organization.

5. **Lead, but Not Too Fast.** As we tried to become an innovative learning group, we were attempting to play a role in leading the organization toward its vision. Occasionally, we got too far out ahead and our group became a "them" to the rest of the organization. For example, by quickly adopting the System 4 leadership philosophy and "leaderless" team structure, we looked too odd and different to the rest. We wanted to become an example, but by moving too far and too fast, we were foreigners who spoke a strange tongue in our own land. We adapted by creating translating structures such as individual client points of contacts (project leads) and better ways of talking about what System 4 actually was—in the organization's language.

6. **Be Passionate.** Finally, we learned the importance of having a passion for our work. Developing an internal change group is filled with difficult moments, and they will need intrinsic self-motivation. By definition, the change group is not doing the core work of the organization and therefore will not be valued

as much as those who are. In addition, organizational change is a slow process that reveals its successes in subtle ways. Passion for the work kept us going when we felt undervalued and underappreciated. We constantly reminded ourselves of our purpose and the answers to the question "Why be high performing?"

People who work in local government face many immediate substantive challenges; some play active roles with their councils and boards, and others increasingly engage with their residential and business communities, have a wide range of technical knowledge about the services being delivered, and assure that a continuously competent and engaged workforce is committed to achieving the community's goals. As individuals progress through these responsibilities, many tend to focus their personal attention on the earlier ones.

Often neglected is that last area: engaging, growing, and developing the workforce. Frequently, this is a less immediately pressing area, in which people have less personal experience, and which is more difficult to explain to a probing council or board. Yet an investment in support of this area, like professional change agents, often repays quickly and repeatedly as the workforce improves and service delivery becomes more efficient and effective. Strategic plans often lay out longer-term community goals and then identify the actions and resources to achieve them. Organizations need to think the same way about laying out the goals for the workforce's capabilities and the actions and resources that will enable the workforce to achieve the community goals. Providing the staff support to carry out that strategic change management plan is a vital component.

1   See Covey, Stephen, *The Seven Habits of Highly Effective People*, Simon and Schuster, Anniversary Edition 2013. Covey calls the cells in his matrix *Quadrants* and uses the terms *urgent vs. not-urgent* and *important vs. not-important* to describe the two axes of his matrix; the cells in the HPO analytical lens (Figure 5.1) intentionally follow the numbering in Covey's matrix to emphasize the parallel nature of the two constructs (Covey's to examine the individual level and HPO's to examine the organizational level).
2   Katzenbach, Jon R., and Douglas K. Smith, 1993. *The Wisdom of Teams*. Boston, MA: Harvard Business School Press.
3   Lencioni, Patrick. 2002. *The Five Dysfunctions of a Team*, San Francisco, CA: Jossey-Bass, p 195ff.
4   Michelle Poche Flaherty is currently President of City on a Hill Consulting.
5   Craig Gerhart is currently the president of Gerhart Enterprises.

6 *Potomac News*, February 4, 2007.

7 A. Tyler St.Clair is a Principal Associate with Commonwealth Centers for High-Performance Organizations, Inc. and a team member with the University of Virginia's Senior Executive Institute who has assisted with Campbell County's high-performance development efforts, and R. David Laurrell is the retired county administrator in Campbell County, Virginia.

8 Hiatt, Jeffrey M, *ADKAR: A Model for Change in Business, Government, and our Community*, Prosci Learning Center Publications, 2006.

9 *Best Practices in Change Management*, Prosci Learning Center Publications, 2014.

10 Chanage Management Learning Center, *Prosci's Change Management Program: Certification Course*, (Loveland, CO: Prosci Research, 2006), p. 5.

11 See: Project Management Institute. *A Guide to the Project Management Body of Knowledge* (PMBOK Guide) Fifth Edition (2013).

12 Jeffrey Hiatt is the President of Prosci and the founder of the Change Management Learning Center.

13 Joan Goppelt and Keith W. Ray are principals in Act Too Consulting.

CONCLUSION

Perhaps now it is a bit easier to see why we fear that many local governments will fall back into old patterns and become complacent in their new status quo. Improving performance over time requires that we be relentless in (1) developing and sustaining the culture to work together in effective teams everywhere in the organization, (2) assessing how we fare on the key factors that matter most in performance, and (3) using the change levers to act on what we have diagnosed. This is not easy to sustain, and many are overcome by the daily challenges that distract them from the longer-term difficult work of performance improvement. So many believe that leadership is required primarily at the top of an organization and that they must do the heavy lifting themselves. And, frankly, in a lot of places, that lifting never gets done because those senior managers focus on more immediate crises and priorities.

The evidence is pretty clear that broader engagement of the workforce can provide that extra lift to make a substantial performance difference. In the preceding chapters we have outlined a different view of how a much larger number of talented people in our organizations can contribute in far greater ways than are normally seen in local governments. This reconceptualization of roles is usually welcomed by staff whose capabilities have been ignored and whose opportunities for growth have been shortchanged. True, to believe it, they have to experience that when managers say leadership should be exercised at all levels, they demonstrate it by putting the words into practice. But when employees see it, they often jump fully in—they become engaged. And while the model we have outlined may seem to be complex, individuals at all levels grasp the concepts and apply them in their work.

We have seen through our case studies that compelling visions of "what we are after together" and "what we can become" energize people to create the direction, perform the work, measure their progress and evaluate their efforts. Clarity of purpose pulled together police and fire paramedics in Montgomery, united development services in Bellevue, energized workers in Lynchburg, and refocused the fire protection plans reviewers in Prince William County.

Common values alive in the workplace provide a work culture that encourages people to pull together, support each other, and bring forward their best ideas and efforts. In Prince William County, a redefinition of how they needed to collaborate to redefine their stakeholders, objectives, and work processes led to speedy building permits, and in Lynchburg, a revaluing of people's abilities led to significant improvements in operations and outcomes.

Assuring that what we do is appropriate for the customer resulted in the Prince William County reviewers' total redesign of their method of operation, enabling good plan submissions and reducing their review process to a fraction of the previous time. It also helped the city of Round Rock tailor its programs to the desires of its citizens.

Work teams, where members not only use their skills in actual service delivery but also take time to focus on their vision and mission, their customers, and how they produce, operate, and bring together their full range of talents, become a powerful force that results in expansion of their impact in service to their communities.

Many local governments have efforts underway to improve performance examples of good things going on consistent with some of the concepts in this book. Often, though, their efforts are episodic, opportunistic, or reactive to the needs that arise or are based on a good idea that somebody brings back from a conference. They may start a process in one part of the organization, and a different process in another. Efforts are rarely integrated, and undertaking a significant cultural change to support improvement in performance is even more rare. So, the authors are often asked how to become more systematic and focused on higher performance.

The first step is to really understand that the problem is systemic, complex, and deeply rooted in our historic approaches. We hope that the concepts in this book, coupled with the local government examples, lay out the basic issues and approaches. Within their own context, people need to grapple straightforwardly with their own legacy and determine that they want to do something about it Then, as we have seen in the case studies, those people need to share these concepts more widely within their organization. Sometimes managers share this awareness themselves or enlist others to help. Alternatively, they send colleagues to a course or bring in an HPO seminar to build a network of support within the jurisdiction. If they feel they have a reasonable understanding of the concepts and breadth of the work, some organizations may embark straightaway on the steps below.

Once the determination to begin a more systematic approach is made, a natural course is to form a senior leadership team at a level appropriate for cross-organizational leadership work. These teams often begin substantively by tackling the work at the top of the Vision to Performance and Values to Work Culture cycles.

Simultaneously it is critical to develop a trusting, collaborative culture on the senior leadership team focused on the whole organization reaching its collective goals. This is in contrast to the individual department managers seeing their goals as their primary or, sometimes, only concern. They must develop a consultative/participative leadership philosophy in practice among the members. We have found that when the person in charge runs the leadership team meetings, little cultural improvement occurs. This is not because she is uncommitted or not skilled, but because it is very difficult under these circumstances to shift the perspective from the belief that hierarchical rules remain in effect. The higher in the organizational hierarchy these teams are, the more they need a facilitator from outside the group. Teams frequently need some help, whether from internal or external sources, on getting such a team chartered, its culture formed, and its roadmap or workplan established.

Based on this start, an early and vital next step is the development of an organizational consultative/participative leadership philosophy that is widely promulgated throughout the organization. This requires an inclusive process on what *our* philosophy should be. Imagine the impact of autocratically declaring that from now on we will not be autocratic, but consultative and/or participative! This significant change needs to get off to a good start. Along with the new leadership philosophy there need to be examples of the behaviors we seek. This hard, multi-year work involves the team taking the required steps that will align systems and processes—as well as the personal behavior changes—to the new leadership philosophy. These steps must be incorporated in the roadmap or workplan that will guide the team's agenda.

Another early step is to confront the concepts we have discussed in the Networked Talent Model. Are we ready to commit to the goal that leadership is expected at all levels of the organization? If we agree, then we must begin to integrate these concepts in our systems—particularly the human resources systems and processes. Once we determine that we want everyone to be leaders at all levels, then we must create the mechanism—the opportunity—for that to happen, or it will become a slogan, not a reality. The workforce needs to be able to step away from their technical duties for an appropriate period of time to do their work of leadership. Instituting a parallel organization throughout all levels, over time, enables an organization to engage its workforce and see significant improvement. This requires departments, microbusinesses, and units to form teams to focus their leadership work on achieving our common vision and living our collective values within their scope of responsibilities.

In general, two things hold most localities back in their quest for higher performance: (1) the failure to adopt and bring to life the appropriate leadership philosophy; and (2) the inability of people in the workforce to realize the goal of performing their leadership work because there are no teams with time set aside to accomplish it.

One can imagine how significant the changes would be if leadership were spread throughout the organization, compared to the traditional hierarchical approaches most organizations still use. To make this transition will require a lot of learning, skill development, and support to people as they change their outlook, roles, and responsibilities. This may require a reprioritization of resources both human and financial. Organizations will need to gauge and plan for the development of internal capacity to assist the senior leadership team and others as they modify both what they work on and how they work together.

Many local governments have developed visions that have been distributed or posted on the walls but have little practical impact on how people do their work every day. To create higher performance requires creating a vision that is compelling, getting clear about the outcomes, assuring that we have the right programs to deliver those outcomes, executing those programs, and then measuring their consequences. Organizations often focus early energies on the first several of these steps as their vision to performance work. They sometimes do strategic planning exercises or work through a vision to performance process to jumpstart the subsequent work. While some localities do this work themselves, it can also be the subject of a retreat or a several-day team meeting, often with an outside facilitator.

All this has to occur within the reality of continuing to deliver daily services and dealing with the latest emergencies. To make that happen, higher-level managers have to begin to shift their personal workload—relying more on others to handle important daily matters while they spend more time on their work of leadership. Likewise, middle managers have to shift the perspective of their roles. They will have to pick up additional responsibilities that their managers delegate to them and take on larger leadership roles in developing their workforce's capabilities to assume more autonomy and responsibility for leadership work. This, in turn, requires middle managers to delegate more technical work to the people at the front lines of the organization. This cascading effect can be scary and threatening at first, but solid teams can create supportive environments to make the journey easier. It will indeed take time, though—that's why we will need to be relentless in our continuing pursuit of our goals but also be patient, especially when we fall off course and may be tempted to just let it go.

As you begin your process of considering what is right for you, take a look at the Appendix in this book. The Appendix provides an Organizational Assessment that you may find helpful. If you and your colleagues go through the questions, you should find the areas where you could most profitably start your work.

We wish you a successful journey, as we believe that the future of our communities rests on your organizations becoming even higher performing. It is a worthy cause. Please let us know if we can be of any assistance.

Acknowlegments

··

There are a great many people who have helped shape this book and to whom we owe much gratitude.

First of all, are those with whom we have worked or taught. They have contributed not only their commitment to create more effective organizations, but have also shared willingly their viewpoints and experiences. They freely granted us access to their organizations as "learning laboratories" and helped us reflect, refine, and redesign our approach over time; they helped us find and incorporate leading practices for performance improvement into our consulting practices and into this book.

We are indebted academically to our friends and colleagues Robert Matson, Allen Hard, and others at both the U.S. Office of Personnel's Federal Executive Institute and the University of Virginia's Weldon Cooper Center for Public Service who saw the need for the *High-Performance Organizations Diagnostic/Change Model* and contributed significantly to its early development. Vision and Values play a large part in this book, due in no small part to their passion for public service.

We owe heart-felt thanks to our three Principal Associates, Kay Hudson, A. Tyler St.Clair, and Tom Ward, who helped shape this book and create case studies that bring alive the theoretical concepts herein. And of course, the book would not be what it is without the commitment and diligent work of the authors of the case studies throughout the book. While many are named herein, there are also those who contributed but preferred to remain anonymous. We thank them all.

On a very personal level, we owe a great deal to the support and patience of our spouses, life-partners, and families. They endure our obsessive, peripatetic lifestyles and give us counsel and comfort when we return.

We also must recognize the early editorial assistance guidance from Katy Lindenmuth. In the publication process we were generously aided by the many on staff of the Greenleaf Book Group and River Grove Books. In particular Amber Hales and Sheila Parr handheld us through the editorial and art design stages of preparation. We appreciate their contributions.

Notwithstanding the generous assistance we received, if there are any misstatements or errors herein, we accept them as ours.

APPENDIX

Included in this section are a number of items which may be of use as you further pursue building your High-Performance Organization.

INDEX

4. **Performance Expectations**
   a. Rockville, MD, Performance Expectations
5. **Customer Service**
   a. Rockville, MD, Customer Service Standards
6. **Articles**
   a. David Laurrell article
7. **Assessments**
   a. Profile of Organizational Characteristics Survey
   b. CCHPO Organizational Assessment for gauging the state of your organization
   c. CCHPO Leadership Philosophy Questionnaire (LPQ)
8. **Roadmap to Higher Performance**

---

1. **Vision and Values**
   a. **Fairfax County, VA, Department of Public Works and Environmental Services**

GUIDING PRINCIPLES

The Vision, Mission, Values, and Leadership Philosophy—the guiding principles are important leadership functions in developing and creating a work culture for a successful, high-performing organization.

These principles guide both the strategic direction of the organization and shape day-to-day decisions about what the organization does and how it does it. They focus the energy of the organization on a common goal. People with a stake in the organization must be actively engaged in the development of the guiding principles. They must see themselves in the guiding principles, and they must feel that they are theirs and that these principles are something they can embrace.

Successful organizations begins with the end in mind. Consequently, DPWES has developed

- A **vision** that is intended to provide a direction for the organization. It is also intended to motivate and inspire the workforce toward becoming a higher-performing organization.

- A **mission** statement that describes the purpose of organization and what it does.
- A **leadership philosophy and values** which describe the beliefs of the organization and how we will treat each other and our customers.

The guiding principles are extremely important in changing the direction and culture of an organization. Consequently, the most important work of leadership is to ensure that all members of the organization embrace these principles.

Our Vision

We, the members of the Department of Public Works and Environmental Services, share a commitment to enhance the community, protect the environment, and provide for the health, safety, and welfare of those who live, work, and visit in Fairfax County.

We look with pride at what we accomplish each day and strive for excellence in public service by partnering with the community and our customers to ensure continuous improvement of our performance.

Our Mission

The mission of the Department of Public Works and Environmental Services is to enhance the quality of life and protect the public interest by establishing sound environmental policies, enforcing codes, and constructing, operating and maintaining the County's infrastructure. We provide effective and efficient public service in the areas of land development, capital facilities, stormwater, wastewater, solid waste, and facilities management.

Our Leadership Philosophy

- We believe in and support the desire and motivation of all of us to excel.
- We ensure teamwork and a collaborative environment.
- We foster innovation and the creative talents and knowledge of all to produce excellent service.
- We take pride in and celebrate our service excellence through recognition of those who exemplify it.
- We accept responsibility and hold ourselves accountable for our actions.

Our Values

We, the members of the Department of Public Works and Environmental Services, in our quest to provide the highest level of public service, embrace these values to guide our daily actions.

Integrity is demonstrating consistent adherence to the principles of honesty, fairness, sincerity, and openness.

Respect for People is valuing diverse contributions and demonstrating fairness, compassion, appreciation and understanding toward everyone.

Trust is assuring those individual obligations and responsibilities are fulfilled and relying upon others to do the same.

Open Communication is listening and sharing information in all directions to create common understanding.

Initiative is taking action and creating opportunities to prevent or resolve problems and get the job done consistent with organizational goals and values.

Teamwork is collaborating with colleagues, customers, and organizations to achieve the best results.

Personal Growth is fostering and seeking continuous personal and professional self-improvement.

---

b. Prince William County, VA, County Executive Communiques on Values

County Executive's Corner May 16

In recent months, I have used this column as an opportunity to discuss the County's vision of working together to make our community the best. Doing the right thing for the customer and the community every time is our contribution to that vision. Over the next few months, I hope to use the "County Executive's Corner" to share my thoughts about the organizational values, known as the RICTER scale, we are embracing. RICTER stands for Respect, Integrity, Creativity, Teamwork, Excellence, and Responsibility. These values are important tools to aid us as we serve our customers and Prince William County.

We began the journey to make our community the best some time ago. We are making real strides to achieve the goals that the community has set for us through our County's Strategic Plan. To continue our progress toward these goals, we need two different sets of tools: hard, technical skills and softer, more intangible assets. The County is pretty experienced at the hard attributes, such as strategic planning, goal setting, measurement, and analysis. We have only recently begun to focus on the softer attributes, such as our vision, our values, and our leadership philosophy. The hard skills are essential to our success. The soft skills are what tap our passion for our jobs, our services, and our community. It is here where we can make the trip from good to great, from competent to outstanding, from successful to the best. It is also where we, as employees, make the difference. All of us need to believe, support, and be excited about the County's vision and core values. They provide the guidance about how we use the flexibility and empowerment I believe employees need to serve our customers. In a world where you can order a car off the Internet or watch the military advance in times of war through the eyes of an embedded reporter, it is obvious that we are in an era where time is instant. Customers have come to expect immediate service that is tailored to their personal situation.

As we work on our soft skills together, I ask that each of you spend some time learning our vision and our values. You may have already seen our values video starring a number of County employees sharing what our values mean to the community tells us the time is now. I look forward to sharing my thoughts about each of our specific values in upcoming issues of "Communique."

August 8

Over the past several months, I have written about what it means for our organization to have adopted Vision and Values Statements. Our Vision describes our desire to be the best, do the right thing, and provide employees with tools and opportunities. Our Values describe the behaviors we strive for as we interact with our customers and with each other. This article is the first in a series of articles that will talk about each of our Values—the definition of each and then an example of employees just like you and me who have demonstrated that particular Value through their actions and the work they perform. I think by the time we get to the end of the RICTER "scale," you will see that Prince William County is an organization where employees are embracing our Values and truly living them each and every day.

RESPECT—The definition of Respect on our RICTER Scale is as follows: We believe all people have value and we show consideration for all persons with whom we have contact—our customers and fellow employees. To demonstrate how we are living the value of Respect, I want to share two examples. One example demonstrates respect for our external customers—our citizens. The other demonstrates respect for our internal customers—our fellow County employees.

All of us have used the services of the Library system—checking out books, attending a program, or getting our research questions answered. We know that the Library shows great respect for its many customers—but what about the customers that don't necessarily need Library services? That question is at the heart of this story. Library staff at the Potomac Library found a couple of papers in a book that had been returned. The papers were disturbing; the writer talked about feeling that life was not worth living and the desire to end it. Rather than ignore the issue—after all, it was not a Library issue—the Library staff researched and found that the book had been checked out to a sixteen-year-year-old. The Library then contacted Social Services, thinking it would be their job to provide assistance. It was not, but Social Services staff did not stop there. They contacted Community Services—whose job it is to help our citizens with these types of problems. Although the correct staff person was on the road, she had left her cell phone number behind. Once she was given the information, she set up a counseling session for the teen and the parents for that very evening. By not considering whose job it was, by showing respect and valuing all persons with whom they have contact, Library, Social Services, and Community Services staff helped a citizen in real need.

None of us ever want to face the prospect of being laid off from work—but sometimes it happens. It has happened here in Prince William when revenues go down but, fortunately, we have a policy to try to help employees faced with the prospect of being laid off. Not too long ago, the County's Employment Manager with Human Resources was asked to help relocate an employee scheduled to be laid off on July 1. Seeing the person's qualifications, she contacted the Finance Department to explain that the about-to-be-laid-off employee was interested in applying for a vacancy in their department. However, Finance informed the HR staff that Finance's hiring manager was out on extended sick leave and they could not interview for the vacancy without their participation. The HR manager explained to Finance that this was the only available opportunity that existed for this employee and unless we moved right away to consider them, they were going to lose their job on July 1. Finance sprang into action—within 48 hours, they had put together an interview panel, interviewed the employee, and had the paperwork to hire this person to HR. By acting quickly and acting together, we were able to demonstrate to the employee in danger of losing a job how our Value of Respect truly works.

There are ways each of us can show our Value of Respect. It is not always the big things. It can be as simple as pronouncing a customer's or employee's name correctly, being on time for meetings, returning phone calls in a timely manner, or asking a citizen in one of our buildings if they need assistance. Much of it is thinking about how we ourselves like to be treated.

As you read these articles over the next few weeks, I invite you to share with us your experiences of employees demonstrating a particular Value in the work they perform. I think that you will soon see that examples are found—it is choosing which example to share that will be the hard part.

August 22

As we continue on our journey throughout the organization to find examples of employees demonstrating our Values and living them each and every day, I am struck by how many things we are doing right. In a society where we tend to hear only about the negative, it is a true testament to the people of this organization that there are so many examples of employees doing the right thing that it is hard to choose which example to use as they pertain to our RICTER Values.

INTEGRITY—The definition of Integrity on our RICTER scale is as follows: We have the courage to consistently do what is right, honest, and fair each and every time. We do what we say we will do—we honor our commitments.

I personally wrestled with this notion of INTEGRITY not too long ago when two teenage sisters from our At-Risk Youth program were in need.

Victims of sexual abuse, they could no longer stay with their parents. Foster care was an option, but it is known that kids generally do better when they can stay in the community with family. In this instance, an aunt and uncle indicated a willingness to take the sisters into their home. However, the aunt and uncle's house had only two bedrooms and was not large enough to accomodate the two sisters.

The caseworker creatively arranged for the County to grant funds to the couple for a bedroom and bathroom addition to their home. This would only be slightly more expensive than foster care placement and offered the advantage of keeping the girls with family. The proposed arrangement eventually came to the attention of executive management staff. It created a reaction. So many questions were asked that a memo was drafted to the involved agencies strongly suggesting that insufficient review of this approach occurred and that this shouldn't happen again

The next morning, I looked at the draft memo and was confronted by our stated Vision and Values. The memo—with its "why didn't someone bring this to my attention" tone, its "what if something goes wrong" attitude, and its "what were you thinking" approach—just didn't fit our Vision of providing employees with the opportunity to do the right thing for the customer. It didn't embody our Value of Integrity which is doing what is right, honest, and fair each and every time. In a situation where employees were finding creative solutions, accepting responsibility to improve things for our community, and striving for excellence in serving our customers, I was saying, "Why wasn't I informed?" and "Why wasn't this decision made by 'higher' management?" If INTEGRITY means doing what we say we'll do, how can I encourage acceptance of our Values while ignoring the very essence of the Values when confronted with a situation that goes against the traditional "business as usual" mentality?

The memo was torn up. Instead, I talked with staff about how we could serve these customers while protecting the interests of the community. Faced with this challenge, staff found a housing program built on the concept of a forgivable loan. The aunt and uncle agreed to this solution and it was put in place, which served the customer and the community right away. The opportunity to live out our Vision through our Values survived. More important, two sisters survived a difficult experience and both are doing extremely well in their new home.

Through this experience, it became quickly evident to me that INTEG-RITY is not always an easy concept. At times, it goes against what we are trained to think and do. It causes you to step back and ask yourself if something is the right, honest, and fair thing to do. The answer is not always easy to accept, but if we are to be the type of organization that has INTEGRITY for its customers, its employees, and its community, then we need to be an organization that has the courage to take risks and embrace our Values.

September 5

CREATIVITY— The definition of Creativity on our RICTER scale is as follows: We find better ways to do things. We are innovative in achieving excellence.

One of the things I enjoy most about my job is being able to recognize employees who excel at their job. Whether it is recognizing someone for their great customer service or it is recognizing someone for their innovative ideas, it is really fun and rewarding to be able to tell someone "Good job" and "I appreciate all that you do." That is one of the reasons why I look forward each year to the County Executive's Awards. These awards are given to employees whose exemplary performance sets a standard of excellence for the County government and demonstrate that leadership can originate from any level within the organization. It allows employees to recognize fellow employees for a job well done, and it allows me the opportunity to commend these employees for their excellence.

Every year, my office receives many nominations for the County Executive's Awards. Every year, it is difficult to choose only a few recipients, and every year, the nominations reflect employees that are living our Vision through our Values. This year was no exception. All of the nominations spoke to employees excelling in their jobs as they mirrored the Values in their daily routines. Creativity is a value featured in many nominations. One such example is the Fire and Rescue employee who took it upon himself to research and develop a new procedure for his department and the County. In June 2002, Matt Russell was hired as a Fire and Rescue Technician. Upon completion of recruit school, he was assigned to a station and was asked to learn the location and operation of all the dry hydrants in his station's area. It was during this time that Matt realized and identified inconsistencies with the process of installing dry hydrants and the performance of the system. Matt brought these inconsistencies to the attention of his immediate supervisor and was told that these issues stemmed from a lack of policy and procedures for identifying, installing, and operating the dry hydrant systems.

Instead of accepting this as is, Matt took the initiative to develop a draft policy and procedures for the system. He formed working relationships with several departments and outside agencies, including the County's sign shop, Public Works' plan review division, and the Virginia Department of Transportation. In April, he presented the draft policy of the program to the Fire and Rescue Association and they adopted the program during their meeting. Not bad for a probationary employee. (We have since let Matt off probation.)

Matt, his supervisors, and those he worked with showed Creativity with their superior response to this issue. They were innovative; they found a better way of doing things; and they achieved excellence. Their hard work and dedication has created a system that will allow us to better serve our community.

Creativity is all around us. It is in the front-line employee who helps an irate customer with their personal property tax; it is in the case worker who finds a way to get medication for a client that desperately needs it; and it is in the librarian who finds a way to make reading fun for children.

To be an organization that does the right thing then we will have to be an organization that is innovative in finding better ways to do things. That is how we will achieve excellence.

September 19

TEAMWORK—The definition of Teamwork on our RICTER scale is as follows: We support and encourage others as we work together to achieve our Vision. We value everyone's contribution and strengths.

In these past issues of Communique, I have talked about the importance of stellar customer service for the community, as well as employees; about how fun it is to reward employees for a job well done and how it is imperative for employees to believe in and live the Values of our organization in their daily routines. The following examples of Teamwork that I'm going to share with you exemplify and reinforce all three of those things.

The first example comes from September's Employee of the Month award. Sgt. Bill Anzenberger of the Crime Prevention Unit of the Police Department and Tim McCormick of the Office of Information and Technology are commended for their successful efforts in streamlining the monthly distribution of crime statistics to the Watch Coordinators of the Neighborhood Watch program. The Crime Prevention Unit (CPU), which generates a summary of certain criminal activity by area and distributes it to the various Neighborhood Watch Coordinators, is a monthly process that was time consuming and costly. These gentlemen created a way to make the process easier.

The new process is far more streamlined and cost efficient. The data is now directly accessible by the CPU staff; summaries are easily extracted for use by staff and electronically distributed to the Watch Coordinators; and in turn, the Watch Coordinators can make secondary dissemination to members of the Neighborhood Watch.

Feedback from the Watch has been very positive. This process has reduced staff hours, postage, and stationary costs. It is estimated that it will save the Police Department well over $15,000 annually. Moreover, it has resulted in a far faster delivery of the information to the citizens.

This is an excellent example of Teamwork improving a service to our community partners, this time to improve safety in our neighborhoods, which is an outcome measure for the public safety strategic goal. Bill and Tim's innovative thinking demonstrates the concept of small team Teamwork (Police and OIT working together) to support larger team Teamwork (Neighborhood Watch) to achieve a strategic goal. It demonstrates the correlation of our Value of Teamwork to our goal of working with the community regarding the strategic plan to improve neighborhood safety, which is one of the ways we define in our Vision a community that is the best.

Another great example of Teamwork is the FISH! training that the MAGIC librarians brought to our employees. FISH!, based on the successful Fish Philosophy of Seattle's Pike Place Market, promotes having fun at work while improving productivity and customer service. This team of librarians worked hard to bring this innovative training to our team of employees. A proposal of funds had to be written to allow for the purchase of the video, training materials, and refreshments. That proposal then had to be presented to the Friends of Chinn Park, which agreed to fund the project.

The team also had to facilitate the FISH! workshops, which demanded preparation, set up, travel time, and presenting. During the workshops, they led discussions with participants regarding ways of applying the FISH! philosophy to each employee's own work. These principles—Play, Be There, Make

Their Day, and Choose Your Attitude—are complements to all facets of our RICTER Values.

Through all of this, the team encouraged thoughtful discussion of how to "be there" for our customers and coworkers, while setting an example of this concept themselves. The training is so successful that this team of librarians has been asked to take their show on the road and present the FISH! training to several different departments.

The librarians who brought us FISH! received a County Executive's Award this year. Not because it is a different and new program to the County, although it is. But because it exemplifies our coworkers supporting and encouraging us to be better at what we do. Because it demonstrates that we can choose to have fun while providing exemplary customer service to all of our clients. And it proves that by working together, we will find success in achieving our goal to make our community the best.

October 3

EXCELLENCE—The definition of Excellence on our RICTER scale is as follows: We set high standards for ourselves and exceed expectations for the quality of our services and the interactions with our customers.

There are several examples of Excellence occurring throughout all levels of the organization. This is evident through the many awards and recognitions County agencies have received over the past few months, some of which are listed below.

- Public Safety Communications was granted status as a nationally-accredited public safety communications agency. Only 18 other jurisdictions in the nation have this distinction.
- The Police Department was recently reaccredited by the Commission on Accreditation for Law Enforcement Agencies, Inc. (CALEA)
- The County ranked number one in utilizing information technology to deliver high quality service to its customers and citizens based on a population category of 250,000 to 499,999.
- Two County programs received NACo Achievement Awards: the Safety Orientation Program and the Commercial Motor Vehicle Operators Safety Program.

- The Department of Economic Development was honored as a "Top Economic Development Group" in North America by two different organizations, and received several awards for securing the Eli Lilly and Company deal.
- For the 22nd consecutive year, the County received the Certificate of Achievement for Excellence in Financial Reporting.
- For the 17th consecutive year, we received the Distinguished Budget Presentation Award.

These awards do not include the recognition our co-workers have received. Their hard work has not gone unnoticed by us or by their peers. In previous issues of Communique, I have talked about the County Executive's Awards, in which I am extremely proud to recognize our co-workers for a job well done. In March, the New York Fire Department Counseling Service Unit and National Fallen Firefighters Foundation recognized the County for invaluable service following the September 11 terrorist attacks. In August, Fire and Rescue Chief Mary Beth Michos was named Fire Chief of the Year by PRIMEDIA's *Fire Chief* magazine.

It is an honor to be recognized by others and is a validation of the work we do. It is also proof that as an organization, and as employees, we can continually exceed standards and expectations. A recent example of that is the response our County had to Hurricane Isabel.

Two weeks ago, Prince William County employees were busy planning for the effects Hurricane Isabel could bring to our community. On Thursday morning, September 18, we opened the County's Emergency Operations Center (EOC). Although we had closed the County that day, essential employees from different agencies reported to the EOC, were out in the field, or doing their everyday jobs efficiently and effectively throughout the storm. Representatives from the Office of Executive Management, Communications, Fire and Rescue, Police, Public Safety Communications, OIT, Social Services, Public Works, Finance, the Health Department, and several other agencies worked diligently to serve our customers; many worked overnight. Employees stayed throughout the storm and into the aftermath to help any way they could. Representatives were here until we closed the EOC, which was not until Saturday afternoon.

As a result of this hard work, the effects of the storm were not nearly as severe as they could have been. Granted, we were fortunate that the storm moved west of the County, but our employees worked together to serve our community and certainly exceeded expectations for quality of their services and their interactions with our customers. For their Excellence, I thank them

It's been said "Good, better, best; never let it rest till your good is better and your better is best." As we continue to excel, we will continue to gain strides to our goal of being the best.

October 17

RESPONSIBILITY—The definition of Responsibility on our RICTER scale is as follows: We seize the opportunity to do the right thing in carrying out our commitments and obligations.

Responsibility is often something that we know we should do, but sometimes shy away from doing because it takes too much time, too much effort, and/or too much investment. The benefit, though, of taking that extra step to carry out our commitments far outweighs any inconveniences that we may experience. By taking Responsibility, we can better serve our customers—internally and externally. This is exemplified in the October Employee of the Month.

Tess Shannon, a receptionist at the McCoart Building and a new employee, was working at the front desk at McCoart when a citizen called with a problem: she had mistakenly placed her Service McCoart Building. The citizen told Tess that the water bill needed to be paid that day, or her water service would be cut off.

Realizing that the box in front of McCoart was for tax payments, Tess called the Finance Office where she was referred to the County's mailroom. A mailroom employee opened the box and gave the envelope with the water payment to Tess. She called the citizen, told her she had the water payment and would leave it at the front desk for the citizen to pick up. However, the citizen said she worked in the District of Columbia and would not be able to pick up the envelope before the next day. At this point, on own initiative, Tess offered to take the bill to the Service Authority when she got off work. She not only took the water payment to the Service Authority, but walked inside and handed it to a clerk there to ensure it was received and the citizen's water would not be cut off.

"It's always good to see a fellow employee do something for someone with-out being asked," wrote Nancy Copeland, who nominated Tess. "She took responsibility for something . . . simply as a kindness from one human being to another."

Taking Responsibility for something ultimately boils down to doing the right thing for the customer. Tess's story is a great example of that.

Over the past six issues of Communique, I have talked about the definition of each of our Values and given an example of our co-workers demonstrat-ing the Values on a daily basis. As I've said before, it is great to talk about the Vision and Values, but we have to live them. It is by living these Values that we will be an organization that works together to make our community the best, that does the right thing for the customer and community each and every time, and that provides support and opportunities for our co-workers to achieve our Vision. I hope that through these articles I have demonstrated that our Values are at work, and I do believe that we are well on our way to being the kind of organization that moves our community closer to being the best. This is an evolving process. I challenge each of you to take Responsibility for our Values and embrace them as you work toward achieving our Vision.

---

2. Charters
  a. Fairfax County, VA, Department of Public Works and
     Environmental Services

LEADERSHIP COUNCIL CHARTER
Purpose
The Department of Public Works and Environmental services' Leadership Council is a participative leadership team that leads DPWES in cross-organi-zational issues that have significant, long-term impact. The Leadership Coun-cil creates mechanisms that allow the Department's Lines of Business to be integrated, thereby accomplishing the Department's Vision as a whole.

Function
The Leadership Council is responsible for developing the Department's Vision, Mission, and Values and ensures that all strategic initiatives endorsed

are in concert with these established parameters. The Leadership Council is responsible for continually assessing the elements that comprise the Vision, Mission, and Values to ensure that these guiding principles keep current with the need for continuous improvement and renewal of the organization. Types of strategic initiatives that are addressed by the Leadership Council include

- Leadership Philosophy
- Individual Behavioral Values
- Operating Systems Values
- Management/Supervisory Development
- Employee Motivation, Empowerment, and Development
- Internal Communications
- Strategic Goals and Direction
- Broad Policy Development
- Performance Measurement
- Financial Management
- External Relations
- Information Technology Development and Direction
- Organizational Structure

Relationships with other DPWES Teams

The Leadership Council is a parallel organization in that it operates outside the hierarchy of the Department's organizational structure and does not have decision making authority over the Department's activities and operations. Informally, the Leadership Council communicates with any hierarchical or parallel body within the Department as needed. The Leadership Council implements its recommendations through the Department's hierarchical structure. The Council's official association with the Department's hierarchical structure is through the Department Director, a member of the Leadership Council and the head of the hierarchical structure. The Director is responsible for assigning the implementation of the Council's recommendations to the appropriate hierarchical body, such as the Senior Management Team, Management Council, Line of Business Core Teams, Human Resources Departmental Team, or a specific organizational unit. The Leadership Council also serves as a resource for other departmental teams in their leadership work.

Composition

All Departmental Lines of Business, including the Business Planning and Support function, are represented on the Leadership Council. Members are appointed on a long-term basis to facilitate stability and continuity of the Council. The Leadership Council, in the Department's current organizational Structure, is comprised of the Department Director; the Strategic Initiatives Manager; two representatives from each Office area, of which one is the Office Director; and a representative from the Stormwater Management Line of Business. After the migration of the Line of Business Core teams, the composition of the Leadership Council will be reevaluated.

Method of Operation

The Leadership Council operates in a participative manner, whereby each member has equal standing. Members are expected to become stewards of the Department as a whole and to rise above individual roles within the Lines of Business to link together to address cross-organizational issues. All endorsements are made through consensus, whereby all members must be in agreement.

Conduct of the Leadership Council Members

Each member is expected to be an active participant by committing to attend meetings, communicating the Council's activities to members of the Line of Business not included in the Leadership Council with the proper discretion, and demonstrating candor, openness, and honesty. For endorsements made by consensus of the members, each member is expected to be an advocate of the outcome. Members are to respect the process and one another by respecting all ideas expressed, abiding by the established ground rules, being thoroughly prepared for each meeting, staying within the agreed upon agenda, maintaining the confidentiality agreed upon, and sharing equally in the responsibility to reach consensus successfully.

Administrative Procedures

Meetings are held all day, generally off-site, on the second and fourth Wednesday of each month. At the end of discussion of each topic, items needing follow-up will be assigned with expected time frames to complete. At the end of each meeting, the results of the meeting will be summarized, the agenda will be set for the next meeting, and the responsibility of the logistics for the meeting will be assigned. Meetings will be facilitated and recorded by individuals who are agreed upon by the members.

SENIOR MANAGEMENT TEAM CHARTER
Purpose
The Department of Public Works and Environmental Services Senior Management Team is a consultative group to the Department Director operative within the hierarchy whose goal is to achieve consensus and positive support of decisions related to significant immediate departmental issues that affect the Lines of Business. The Department Director has final authority, but has chosen to manage the Department in a consultative, collaborative manner via the Senior Management Team.

Functions
The Department of Public Works and Environmental Services Senior Management Team is responsible for developing and implementing programs and policies in cooperation with the Line of Business Core Teams or other teams which include, but may not be limited to the following:

- Develop programs and policies that implement the strategies such as
    - Delegation of authority and accountability systems
    - Training programs and policies
    - Safety programs and policies
    - A communication plan
    - A resource plan
    - A customer service program

- Monitor progress of tactical operational plans such as
    - Data on task accomplishment including resource utilization
    - Timely start and end date

- Monitor performance of Lines of Business such as
    - Performance measures
    - Efficiency and effectiveness of Lines of Business operations
    - Customer service satisfaction

- Compliance
- Continuous improvement plan

- Respond to appropriate issues from the Department Director, Line of Business Core Teams, and Senior Management Team members such as
  - Budget submittals
  - Recruiting efforts
  - Performance evaluation process

- Respond to short-term immediate departmental issues such as
  - Lines of Business operational issues
  - Interdepartmental coordination issues
  - Unexpected events

Composition

The Senior Management Team membership is identical to the Leadership Council membership. It is comprised of the Department Director; the Strategic Initiatives Manager; two representatives from each Office area, of which one is the Office Director; and a representative from the Stormwater Management Line of Business. The members are appointed on a long-term basis to facilitate stability and continuity of the team. The composition of the team will be reevaluated after migration of the Line of Business Core Teams.

Relationships with other DPWES Teams

The Senior Management Team is a consultative group to the Department Director, which operates within the hierarchy of the Department's organizational structure. The SMT is a parallel team with the Leadership Council, and therefore, will receive requests from the Leadership Council via the Department Director to consider implementation of recommendations within the Department's hierarchical structure. The SMT has a hierarchical relationship through the Department Director to the Management Council, Line of Business Core teams, and other departmental teams.

Method of Operation

The Senior Management Team operates within the hierarchy as a consultative group to the Department Director. Although consensus is not mandated, all efforts are made to come to consensus on issues. Members are expected to provide positive support of all decisions made after full discussion, consultation, and deliberation.

Conduct of the Senior Management Team Members

Each member is expected to be an active participant by committing to attend meetings; communicating, with proper discretion, the SMT's activities to members of the Lines of Business not included on the SMT; and demonstrating candor, openness, and honesty. Each member is expected to be an advocate of all decisions made in the SMT. Members will respect the process and one another by considering all ideas expressed, abiding by the established ground rules, being thoroughly prepared for each meeting, staying within the adopted agenda, maintaining the confidentiality agreed upon, and sharing relevant information necessary to make logical, sound decisions.

Administrative Procedures

The Senior Management Team is chaired by the Department Director. Meetings are held every Monday afternoon for half a workday or at other times at the Director's discretion. At the end of each meeting, results of the meeting will be summarized, the agenda for the Management Council meeting will be set, and a facilitator for the Management Council Meeting will be designated based upon the alphabetical rotation of the team member's last name. The Strategic Initiatives Manager is the designated record keeper for the team.

Guidelines for Team Liaisons

The purpose of this document is to provide guidelines for team liaisons. In order to further the work of leadership within the department, Leadership Groups such as the DPWES Leadership Council (LC) or a specific Line of Business, charter teams within the parallel organization perform specific tasks or provide expertise on technical matters. As part of the chartering process of the team, a liaison may be designated who is a member of the Chartering Group to coordinate with the newly formed team. Typically, the liaison will not serve as a member of the team, and therefore they need not attend every meeting but must fulfill the responsibilities outlined below. There may be circumstances where it is appropriate for the liaison to be a team member.

Responsibilities

Team composition—The liaison will develop the initial composition of team members and forward it to the chartering group/individual for approval. When considering potential nominees, the affected entities should consider the qualifications specified in the charter and strive to achieve a balanced and diverse team. All nominees should be capable of representing the broader organizational perspective. Once the team has been established, the liaison will serve more of a "checks and balances" role to ensure that the membership of the team continues to meet the intent of the charter and will so advise the team in this capacity.

Facilitation—The liaison will secure another person as a facilitator for the first and subsequent team meetings and review their mutual roles in the team process.

Organization—The liaison in coordination with the facilitator is responsible for organizing the first team meeting and communicating with all team members the time and place for the meetings. The liaison and/or facilitator should set the agenda for the first meeting including topics such as the review of the charter, team deliverables and associated timelines, the meaning of consensus, the role of the hierarchy and the liaison, and future meeting schedules. Some team training should be accomplished in the initial stages of the development of the team. The team training should be coordinated by the liaison and the facilitator based upon their analysis of the needs of the team and the duration of the team's charter.

Communication—The liaison is responsible for clarifying the intent of the Chartering Group's assignment and conveying background information when needed. The liaison will provide informal updates to the Chartering Group on the progress of the team on at least a quarterly basis. The progress report may communicate actions of the team or discuss barriers and constraints that the team is facing. The liaison is responsible for informing the Chartering Group if the team is not meeting their goals and objectives or designated time frames.

Conflict Resolution—The liaison may be involved in issues where the team process has languished and/or failed:

- In situations where the team has failed to reach consensus on significant issues, after thorough deliberation, the team may request the liaison to bring the issue to the Chartering Group for further discussion and decision by consensus. Where consensus cannot be reached in that forum, the Chartering Group can either redefine the issue for the team's further consideration or send the issue to the hierarchy for action.

- In situations where a team member is not performing in accordance with the charter and the team itself has tried to resolve the issue with that member but has been unsuccessful, the facilitator in cooperation with the liaison has the responsibility to meet with the team member and try to come to resolution. The liaison and/or the facilitator are responsible for informing and collaborating with the hierarchy to resolve issues when a team member is not performing appropriately.

Debriefing—The liaison will ensure that at the end of the assignment a process is accomplished to analyze how the team functioned and what, if anything, could be done differently to improve the process in the future.

Liaison Skills

The liaison should have the following skills, knowledge, experience and other attributes:

- The ability and willingness to work in a team environment
- Good understanding and support of the DPWES guiding principles
- Good knowledge of the team they are supporting and general knowledge of other business areas in DPWES
- General communication and skills

Liaison Tenure

The selection of the liaison is done on a voluntary basis from members of the Chartering Group. The liaison assignments should be rotated periodically not to exceed three years.

Conduct of the Liaison

The conduct of the liaison will reflect the DPWES values. Each liaison will be aware of the team's deliberations and promote the carrying out of team assignments where appropriate. The liaison will respect the team process and all members of the team by considering all ideas expressed, abiding by the established ground rules, and maintaining the confidentiality agreed upon.

The liaison should be cognizant of his or her presence within the team as being viewed as a leadership "heirarchical figure," particularly in the early developmental stages of the team's establishment and deliberation. At this stage, the team may commonly look to the liaison, as a hierarchical adviser, to provide the answers or suggest solutions. While some dialogue pertaining to the Chartering Group's intent and any relevant background can be helpful, any "steering" may be detrimental to the parallel nature and intent of the team and should be avoided.

COUNTY PROVIDED APPAREL TEAM CHARTER

Team Purpose

The DPWES Leadership Council (LC) has identified a need for a department-wide policy on apparel or uniform provided by the County. The County Provided Apparel Team (CPAT) will investigate this issue and, if need be, formulate a policy on use of apparel or uniform for approval by the LC. The proposed policy is not intended to get into such details as design and color of uniforms. Rather, it should provide general framework or guidelines that would be helpful for citizens and customers in identifying County employees and facilitate the latter's work performance and improve their morale.

Team Responsibilities

- Evaluate current practices and policies in all business areas regarding the use of apparel or uniform excluding shoes. Also, survey other public and private organizations.
- Solicit input from the DPWES employees regarding any changes to the current policies and practices that would benefit employees and improve their work performance. This should be done in a manner that would ensure participation/representation of vast majority of field staff.
- Formulate new guidelines on use of uniforms providing flexibility and eliminating discrepancies among various LOBs.
- Solicit feedback on the recommended policy from the employees.
- Submit recommended policy to the LC for feedback by June 27, 2002.
- Incorporate LC comments and obtain LC's approval.
- Submit final draft policy to the DPWES Director for implementation.

Team Member Skills

The following skills, knowledge, experience, and other attributes should be considered in selecting and developing members of the CPAT:

- The ability and willingness to work in a team environment
- Good understanding and support of the DPWES guiding principles
- Good knowledge of the team member's own business area and general knowledge of other business areas in DPWES
- General communication and team facilitation skills

Team Membership

Taking into consideration needed skills, diversity, and organizational representation, the members will be nominated by the business areas and approved by the LC. The CPAT members will serve on the team until its task is completed. The LC liaison will work with business areas to develop the initial team membership based on the considerations listed above.

Method of Operation

The CPAT will operate as a parallel organization with each member having an equal standing. The team members will make every effort to reach consensus, whereby all members will agree with or agree to fully support the team's recommendation for each decision or action. Those matters where consensus cannot be reached will be referred back to the LC. The issues discussed by the CPAT will be documented with a summary of the discussion and the alternative solutions or actions, including the explanation of opposing views if consensus is not reached.

All team members will share the responsibility to inform, collaborate, and consult with all core teams. All team decisions and actions must be supportable and sustainable in the organization's hierarchy for implementation. The LC's liaison will assist in obtaining the LC's support for the team's recommendations. The LC liaison will also work with the team to establish his or her role on the team, to ensure meeting facilitation that will best meet the team's needs, and to debrief the team at the completion of this initiative.

Conduct of the Members

The conduct of team members will reflect the DPWES values. Each member will actively participate in the team's deliberations and in carrying out team assignments. Members will respect the team process and one another by considering all ideas expressed, abiding by the established ground rules, being thoroughly prepared for each meeting, maintaining the confidentiality agreed upon, and sharing equally in the responsibility to reach consensus successfully.

Meeting Schedule

The CPAT will meet biweekly or more frequently as necessary, beginning in March 2002, and will determine its own meeting schedule as needed to meet the goals outlined in this Charter.

---

3. Job Descriptions
    a. Job Descriptions for fighter/medic and police officer from Montgomery, OH.

CITY OF MONTGOMERY
POSITION DESCRIPTION

Position Title: Firefighter/Paramedic   **FLSA Status:** Non-Exempt
Reports to: Fire Chief   **Civil Service Status:** Classified

General Function

Is responsible to the Fire Chief and acting company officer for responding to fire calls, participates in fire suppression activities and responds to, and participates in, requests for emergency medical care, hazardous materials incidents, and other calls for assistance to the public within the scope of the department. Work involves responsibility for specialized duties under emergency conditions, which involve personal hazard. Is committed to the mission, vision, and values of the City through ethical conduct, community stewardship, individual initiative, and responsive service. Demonstrates leadership, management, and technical skills through effective collaboration, using team resources, progressive decision making, and personal responsibility.

Competencies

Leadership

Exhibits behavior consistent with the mission, vision, and values of the City of Montgomery.

Furthers the mission, vision, and values of the City through excellent customer service, creative problem solving, decision making, and stewardship of City resources.

Engages in and supports the long-term direction of the department through progressive strategic planning and departmental goal setting that is responsive to the needs of the community.

Contributes to a learning/thinking/renewing department through customer feedback and continuous improvement.

Provides teaching, mentoring, and motivation to other employees within the organization through the sharing of knowledge, skills, and information; is proactive in performing and improving his/her own work and suggests and participates in projects and activities to improve the function of the entire organization.

Demonstrates emotional intelligence in day-to-day work, decision making, and problem solving.

Initiates and suggests actions to improve departmental and City operations, employee performance, morale, and work methods.

Demonstrates a commitment to provide and require excellent customer service through cooperative team and individual efforts.

Communication

Provides suggestions, advice, and support to supervisor, department head, other City employees, employee teams, and the City's customers.

Communicates the City's mission, vision, and values through words and actions.

Communicates effectively, both orally and in writing, with the supervisor, department head, City employees, employee teams, and the City's customers.

Works cooperatively with all City employees toward the common goal of providing high-quality services.

Exhibits excellent interpersonal and human relationship skills.

Management

Participates in development and mentoring of staff to achieve a cohesive work unit consistent with the City's mission, vision, and values.

Is accountable for the delivery of quality services and work product as a part of the overall departmental and City-wide strategic direction, goals, and objectives.

Contributes to a superior work culture through participation in training and mentoring to develop leadership, management, and technical skills in all employees.

Assists fellow employees with developing and implementing programs and objectives to improve departmental and City-wide efficiency.

Effectively manages multiple assignments and priorities to ensure the fulfillment of projects, tasks, and responsibilities.

Assists in the preparation of, and adherence to, operational and capital budgets and exhibits good stewardship of the organization's resources.

Carries out suggested procedures to assure the highest standards of risk management, employee safety, and risk avoidance.

Technical Tasks

Performs all functions of a Firefighter/Paramedic; responds to all critical incidents.

In the absence of an officer, assumes authority of the fire department operations.

Maintains authority for shift personnel; assigns personnel responsibilities for all shift employees.

Maintains and inspects equipment, vehicles, buildings, and facilities as needed or directed.

Assists company officer(s) in special projects as required or as directed.

Performs fire prevention and public education activities.

Enforces provisions contained in the Ohio Fire Code and the City of Montgomery ordinances and laws.

Attends fire and EMS drills and training.

Performs all job duties in compliance with the established rules and regulations of the Fire Department and the City of Montgomery.

Trains departmental employees.

Demonstrates accountability and responsibility for completion of work assignments in the absence of a department supervisor; provides responsive and timely feedback to supervisory staff on status and progress of work activities.

Promotes safe work practices and ensures compliance with City safety policies.

Assists in the development of operating procedures, policies, rules, and regulations.

Evaluates the purchase of City equipment; orders department supplies and equipment.

Prepares letters, reports, purchase requisitions, legal notices, memos, and other written documents.

Attends meetings, seminars, conferences, and other related events.

Maintains individual knowledge and skills to be able to carry out all duties of department personnel.

Reviews and investigates complaints and requests for service(s).

Maintains professional certifications and training through attendance at related trainings and conferences and membership in professional organizations and other professional affiliations.

Handles other responsibilities and duties as assigned or needed.

Equipment Used

Operates all fire suppression and EMS equipment as well as other mechanical equipment as required; uses ladders, fire extinguishers, bars, hooks, lines, and other related fire suppression, hazardous materials, and emergency medical equipment in hazardous conditions and inclement weather. Uses automobile, computer, copier, fax machine, calculator, paging equipment, two-way radios, and telephones in an office setting or while deployed. Uses personal protective equipment per normal standards under national firefighting and EMS-recognized organizations.

Location of Work and Physical Requirements of Position

Must be able to safely and effectively operate a motor vehicle under normal and emergency conditions; must be able to move an incapacitated individual and physically subdue and restrain an individual when conditions require; demonstrate physical strength and dexterity in the use of hands and feet; work requires extensive walking, standing, and running on varying types of terrain and irregular surfaces; must be able to move/transport oneself from one work site to another; must be able to perform frequent heavy lifting, dragging, and pushing; requires climbing, working from heights, balancing, stooping, kneeling, crouching, crawling, reaching, fingering, grasping, feeling, and repetitive motions; vocal communication is required for expressing or exchanging ideas by means of the spoken word, and conveying detailed or important instructions to others accurately, loudly, or quickly; hearing is required to perceive information at normal spoken word levels; visual acuity is required for preparing and analyzing written or computer data, visual inspection involving small defects and/or small parts, use of measuring devices and medical equipment, operation of motor vehicles or equipment, determining the accuracy and thoroughness of work, and observing general surroundings and activities; requires working in adverse weather; requires ability to work flexible shift hours (to include nights and weekends); and to be able to deal with stressful and sometimes life threatening conditions in a calm and professional manner; must be able to work in off-site locations, including residential structures. Work is performed primarily in the Montgomery Safety Center, throughout the physical environs of the City, and wherever mutual aid necessitates a response.

Minimum Requirements for the Position

High School diploma or GED; must possess Ohio EMT-Paramedic certifica tion, Ohio Firefighter II certification; Ohio Fire Safety Inspector certification preferred. Ability to interact effectively with the public, agencies, and staff at all levels; knowledge of training and experience in fire, emergency medical service, and hazardous materials incidents operations. Must pass a medical exam and be free of medical conditions that would preclude one from successfully performing said functions or would pose a direct threat to the health or safety of oneself or others; must pass Civil Service exam; knowledge of current office equipment and procedures including computer data entry and retrieval; ability to coordinate, train, and direct personnel resources; ability to maintain effective working relationships; ability to communicate effectively orally and in writing; must possess a valid driver's license from state of residency.

CITY OF MONTGOMERY
POSITION DESCRIPTION

Position Title: Police Patrol Officer   **FLSA Status:** Non-Exempt
Reports to: Police Sergeant   **Civil Service Status:** Classified

General Function

Is responsible to Police Sergeant for performance of the City's law enforcement function including crime prevention, police patrol, security of property, and public education. Is committed to the mission, vision, and values of the City through ethical conduct, community stewardship, individual initiative, and responsive service. Demonstrates leadership, management, and technical skills through effective collaboration, using team resources, progressive decision making, and personal responsibility.

Competencies

Leadership

Exhibits behavior consistent with the mission, vision, and values of the City of Montgomery.

Furthers the mission, vision, and values of the City through excellent customer service, creative problem solving, decision making, and stewardship of City resources.

Engages in and supports the long-term direction of the department through progressive strategic planning and departmental goal setting that is responsive to the needs of the community.

Contributes to a learning/thinking/renewing department through customer feedback and continuous improvement.

Provides teaching, mentoring, and motivation to other employees within the organization through the sharing of knowledge, skills, and information; is proactive in performing and improving his/her own work and suggests and participates in projects and activities to improve the function of the entire organization.

Demonstrates emotional intelligence in day-to-day work, decision making, and problem solving.

Initiates and suggests actions to improve departmental and City operations, employee performance, morale, and work methods.

Demonstrates a commitment to provide and require excellent customer service through cooperative team and individual efforts.

Communication

Provides suggestions, advice, and support to supervisor, department head, other City employees, employee teams, and the City's customers.

Communicates the City's mission, vision, and values through words and actions.

Communicates effectively, both orally and in writing, with the supervisor, department head, City employees, employee teams, and the City's customers.

Works cooperatively with all City employees toward the common goal of providing high-quality services.

Exhibits excellent interpersonal and human relationship skills.

Management

Participates in development and mentoring of staff to achieve a cohesive work unit consistent with the City's mission, vision, and values.

Is accountable for the delivery of quality services and work product as a part of the overall departmental and City-wide strategic direction, goals, and objectives.

Contributes to a superior work culture through participation in training and mentoring to develop leadership, management, and technical skills in all employees.

Assists fellow employees with developing and implementing programs and objectives to improve departmental and City-wide efficiency.

Effectively manages multiple assignments and priorities to ensure the fulfillment of projects, tasks, and responsibilities.

Assists in the preparation of, and adherence to, operational and capital budgets and exhibits good stewardship of the organization's resources.

Suggests and carries out procedures to assure the highest standards of risk management, employee safety, and risk avoidance.

Technical Tasks

Enforces provisions of the Ohio Revised Code and the City of Montgomery ordinances and laws.

Investigates criminal offenses and internal investigations.

Responds to emergency and non-emergency incidents as directed.

Performs all job duties in compliance with the established rules and regulations of the Police Department and the City of Montgomery.

Demonstrates proficiency with all department issued firearms and less-lethal weapons.

Provides testimony in court and other legal proceedings.

Assists injured persons, notifies families of injury.

Assists stranded motorists.

Performs crime prevention and other public education activities.

Demonstrates accountability and responsibility for completion of work assignments in the absence of a department supervisor; provides responsive and timely feedback to supervisory staff on status and progress of work activities.

Promotes safe work practices and ensures compliance with City safety policies.

Assists in the maintenance of vehicles, buildings, equipment, tools, and property.

Assists in the development of operating procedures, policies, rules, and regulations.

Evaluates the purchase of City equipment; orders department supplies and equipment.

Prepares letters, reports, purchase requisitions, legal notices, memos, and other written documents.

Trains departmental employees.

Attends meetings, seminars, conferences, and other related events.

Maintains individual knowledge and skills to be able to carry out all duties of position.

Reviews and investigates complaints and requests for service(s).

Maintains professional certifications and training through attendance at related trainings and conferences and membership in professional organizations and other professional affiliations.

Assists other police, fire, and EMS departments as well as other City, county, state, and federal agencies.

Handles other responsibilities and duties as assigned or needed.

Equipment Used

Uses automobile, two-way radio, copiers, telephones, fax machines, calculator, paging equipment, computers, mobile data terminals/computers, radar/laser units, a variety of firearms (i.e., handgun, shotgun, and patrol rifle), batons, chemical agents, and other less-lethal weapons, handcuffs, and traffic light controls. May use personal protective equipment such as helmet, face mask, gas mask, body armor, and pads.

Location of Work and Physical Requirements of Position

Must be able to safely and effectively operate a motor vehicle under normal and emergency conditions; must be able to physically subdue and restrain an individual; demonstrate physical strength and dexterity in the use of hands and feet; must be able to sit for extended periods of time; work requires extensive walking, standing, running on varying types of terrain and irregular surfaces; must be able to move/transport oneself from one work site to another; must be able to perform frequent heavy lifting and pushing; requires climbing, balancing, stooping, kneeling, crouching, crawling, reaching, fingering, grasping, feeling, and repetitive motions; vocal communication is required for expressing or exchanging ideas by means of the spoken word, and conveying detailed or important instructions to others accurately, loudly, or quickly; hearing is required to perceive information at normal spoken word levels; visual acuity is required for preparing and analyzing written or computer data, visual inspection involving small defects and/or small parts, use of measuring devices, operation of motor vehicles or equipment, determining the accuracy and thoroughness of work, and observing general surroundings and activities; requires working in adverse weather; requires ability to work flexible shift hours (to include nights and weekends); and to be able to deal with stressful and sometimes life threatening conditions in a calm and professional manner; must be able to work in off-site locations, including residential structures. Work is performed primarily in the Montgomery Safety Center, throughout the physical environs of the City, and wherever mutual aid necessitates a response.

Minimum Requirements for the Position

High School diploma or GED; Associate's or Bachelor's Degree in Criminal Justice, State of Ohio Peace Officer Training Certificate, and three years prior experience as a police officer preferred. Ability to interact effectively with the public, agencies, and staff at all levels. Thorough knowledge of police methods, criminal law. Must pass a medical exam and be free of medical conditions that would preclude one from successfully performing said functions or would pose a direct threat to the health or safety of oneself or others; must pass Civil Service exam; must have knowledge of current office equipment and procedures including computer data entry and retrieval; demonstrated leadership skills and abilities; ability to maintain effective working relationships; ability to communicate effectively orally and in writing; must possess a valid driver's license from state of residency.

---

b. Job Descriptions in Rockville, MD

CITY OF ROCKVILLE, MD
JOB DESCRIPTIONS

Elements of the networked talent model are incorporated into every employee's job description. In addition to the job-specific duties of any given position, each job description includes standard language regarding "Expectations of All City Employees" that describes how employees at all levels of the organization are expected to exercise leadership, management, and teamwork responsibilities as well as task/technical competence.

Expectations of All Rockville City Employees

Leadership

- Learn and demonstrate an understanding of City, department, division, and team goals.
- Demonstrate the Rockville Way by contributing to a positive work culture.
- Serve and meet the needs of customers during routine or emergency situations.

Management

- Ability to assess his/her work performance or the work performance of the team.
- Plan and organize his/her own work, time, and resources, and if applicable, that of subordinates.
- Contribute to the development of others and/or the working unit or overall organization.

Task/Technical

- Produce desired work outcomes including quality, quantity, and timeliness.

Teamwork

- Ability and willingness to work as part of a team, to demonstrate team skills, and to perform a fair share of team responsibilities.
- Communicate effectively with peers, supervisors, subordinates, and people to whom service is provided.
- Understand and value differences in employees and value input from others.
- Consistently report to work on time and prepare work assignments on schedule.
- Consistently display a positive behavior with regard to work, willingly accept constructive criticism, and be respectful of others.

---

4. Performance Expectations

CITY OF ROCKVILLE, MD
PERFORMANCE EXPECTATIONS

Non-Supervisory Administrative Employees

Leadership

1. Rockville Way Values

   Demonstrates a positive attitude, ethical action, and related behavior consistent with the Rockville Way values.

2. Customer Service

Serves and meets the needs of customers, including the public and fellow employees.

3. Development

Continuously strives to learn and improve.

Management

4. Managing Work

Effectively plans and organizes work, time, and other resources.

5. Innovation

Contributes to a work culture of continuous improvement—of others, of the work team, and/or of the organization.

Teamwork

6. Collaboration

Demonstrates collaborative interpersonal skills and a positive attitude toward teamwork.

7. Communication

Communicates effectively with other employees and customers.

8. Bridging Differences

Understands and values differences.

Task/Technical

9. Quality

Produces high-quality work.

10. Quantity

Demonstrates initiative and produces an appropriate quantity of work on time.

11. Knowledge, Skills, Abilities

Demonstrates the knowledge, skills, and abilities required to accomplish assigned job duties.

Supervisors

Leadership

1. Vision and Goals

   Promotes a shared understanding of the team's mission and goals, and their alignment to the broader vision for the whole department and the organization.

2. Rockville Way Values

   Leads by example in demonstrating a positive attitude, ethical action, and related behavior to model and promote the Rockville Way values.

3. Customer Service

   Serves and meets the needs of customers, including the public and fellow employees.

4. Development

   Continuously strives to learn and improve.

Management

5. Managing Work

   Effectively plans and organizes the team's work, time, and other resources.

6. Managing People

   Assesses and manages the performance of team members.

7. Innovation

   Promotes a team culture of innovation and continuous improvement.

Teamwork

8. Collaboration

   Models collaborative interpersonal skills and promotes teamwork.

9. Communication

   Models effective communication with team members, other employees, and customers.

10. Bridging Differences

    Sets the tone for the team by consistently valuing and understanding differences.

Task/Technical

11. Quality and Quantity

    Demonstrates initiative and produces an appropriate quantity of high-quality work on time.

12. Knowledge, Skills, Abilities

    Demonstrates the knowledge, skills, and abilities required to accomplish assigned job duties.

Managers

Leadership

1. Vision and Goals

   Inspires a shared commitment to the team's mission and goals, and ensures their alignment to the broader vision for the department and the organization.

2. Rockville Way Values

   Leads by example in demonstrating a positive attitude, ethical action, and related behavior to model and promote the Rockville Way values.

3. Customer Service

   Promotes a culture of exceptional customer service for all customers, including the public and fellow employees.

4. Recognition

   Recognizes contributions by showing appreciation for individual and group excellence.

5. Development

   Continuously strives to learn and improve.

Management

6. Managing Work

   Effectively plans and organizes the team's work, time, and other resources.

7. Managing People

   Assesses and manages the performance of team members.

8. Innovation

   Promotes a team culture of innovation and continuous improvement.

9. Developing Others

   Contributes to the development of others.

Teamwork

10. Collaboration

    Models collaborative interpersonal skills and promotes teamwork.

11. Communication

    Models effective communication with team members, other employees, and customers.

12. Bridging Differences

    Sets the tone for the team by consistently valuing and understanding differences.

Task/Technical

13. Quality and Quantity

    Demonstrates initiative and produces an appropriate quantity of high-quality work on time.

14. Knowledge, Skills, Abilities

    Demonstrates the knowledge, skills, and abilities required to accomplish assigned job duties.

---

5. **Customer Service**

CITY OF ROCKVILLE, MD
CUSTOMER SERVICE STANDARDS

Preamble

"Customer Service is the reason for our existence as a city government. Our customers have the right to respect, safety, appropriate assistance, honesty, and competency, regardless of age, ancestry, color, creed, disability, marital status, national origin, presence of children, race, gender, or sexual orientation."

Standards Covering All Customer Interactions

"Customers have a right to expect and staff will . . ."

- Be courteous, respectful, honest and professional.

- Listen to their request/question, ask for clarification if necessary, and provide complete, knowledgeable, accurate, precise information regarding their inquiry.
- Make a reasonable effort to provide information about the City and, as appropriate, other outside agencies related to their department's/division's function.

Telephone/Voicemail

"Customers have a right to expect and staff will . . ."

- Answer telephones promptly (within three rings) whenever possible.
- Answer calls in a courteous manner (with a smile).
- Make sure that a person, not voicemail, answers the main number at each answering station during business hours.
- Listen and understand the nature of requests before transferring a call; inform callers to whom they are being transferred; and provide callers with the telephone number and division of the person to whom they are being transferred. If a call comes during interdepartmental coverage, staff will explain that they are covering for a different division and offer to take a message or transfer the call to voicemail.
- Before transferring a call, provide the caller with the option to go to voicemail or leave a message.
- Acknowledge their voicemail messages within 24 hours on regular business days.
- Keep outgoing voicemail messages current and change voicemail messages at answering stations on days that the City is closed.
- Provide at least one optional telephone number to call in voicemail messages.
- Answer and return calls in the order received. Callers may be given the option to be put on hold or called back.
- Provide periodic updates to a caller who is on hold for an extended period of time.
- Answer all incoming telephone calls from external sources with a consistent greeting such as "City of Rockville, [name], may I help you?"
- Leave a full name, department, telephone number, and the best time to reach you when leaving a message.

Meetings and Open Houses

"Customers have a right to expect and staff will . . ."

- Provide reasonable advance notice of meetings.
- Make sure that meeting notifications contain accurate information (date, time, place, point of contact, telephone number, and directions).
- Advise the public of any schedule changes or cancellations prior to the meeting.
- As much as possible, make available and distribute agendas in advance of meetings.
- Start and end meetings on time.
- Conduct meetings in an organized, efficient (proper equipment and handouts), and professional manner.
- Provide security at meetings involving sensitive issues as determined by the department head and/or facilitator.
- Remove meeting notices after a meeting has completed.

Public Amenities

"Customers have a right to expect and staff will . . ."

- Provide properly maintained facilities, which are sanitary, completely operational, fully stocked and supplied, accessible, adequate to need, and compliant with ADA (Americans with Disabilities Act) standards.
- Respond appropriately and timely to problems identified at a facility.
- Post and observe hours of regular operation.

Money/Currency Exchange

"Customers have a right to expect and staff will . . ."

- Provide user-friendly bills/statements.
- Ensure that bills and permits may be paid via cash, check, or credit card.
- Make sure that the City is prepared to handle the daily monetary exchanges.
- Provide accurate financial transactions.
- Provide a receipt or verification of transaction, if requested.

Written Correspondence
(Includes Letters, Memoranda, Emails & Faxes)
"Customers have a right to expect and staff will . . ."

- Provide written correspondence that is formatted to City standards.
- Make sure that information provided in response to inquiries is complete, accurate, and precise.
- Respond in a timely manner to a customer's request, or send an interim communication explaining the delay. A timely response for email is within 24 hours on a regular business day and for letters is within five business days.
- Use a complete email signature block including: the staff person's name, title, department, City of Rockville, address, telephone number, fax number and email address.
- Use blind carbon copies when sending emails to a large group of people.
- Use legible Fax cover sheets, to include name, telephone number, and department of the sender and the name and fax number of the receiver.

In Person
"Customers have a right to expect and staff will . . ."

- Respond with a timely, courteous acknowledgement, such as eye contact or a positive indication that the staff person knows they are there, especially if the staff person is on the telephone or with another customer.
- In the event there is a person at a counter and the phone rings, excuse themself, answer the telephone, ask the caller if they prefer to be put on hold or have their call returned, and continue to help the customer.
- Ensure staffing for each main informational counter during business hours or, if staff is unavailable, provide signage referring them to the appropriate department.
- Inform, via parking lot signs, sign-in logs on each floor and at front counters, of the need for visitors to sign-in their car to avoid a ticket when visiting City Hall.

In Person Contacts with Field Personnel

"Customers have a right to expect and staff will . . ."

- Attempt to answer a question when approached by a resident in the field, if it pertains to the employee's duties, or if the employee knows the answer.
- If a question pertains to an area outside of the employee's scope of duties or department, the employee will explain it is outside of the scope of their duties, and will provide the resident with a helpful numbers to call card. This will provide the resident with the correct information they need to contact the department that can answer their question.
- If the employee cannot answer the question and it is related to their duties, staff will offer the option to the resident of contacting a supervisor, so that the supervisor can speak to the resident either by a mobile phone at the site, or by coming to meet the resident in person.
- If employees are speaking with a resident who wants to make an inquiry to the Gude Maintenance facility, they should make sure to let the customer know that the Gude offices and phone lines at the facility are answered from 7 a.m. to 3 p.m. All crews (refuse, parks, utilities) work a 7 a.m. to 3 p.m. schedule in the fall and winter. In the summer employees should let residents know that while the Gude office hours are the same, refuse and parks crews work on a 6 a.m. to 2 p.m. schedule, and the utilities division works a 7 a.m. to 3 p.m. schedule.

---

6. Articles

EMBRACE CHANGE

David Laurrell

Changing the way we have always done things, along with making the corresponding cultural changes, must occur to foster high performance. The transformation from a hierarchy to an organic, adaptive environment is likely to be long and painful. The metaphor of a caterpillar transforming into a butterfly comes to mind. The experience is an intensely unpleasant one for the caterpillar. In the process, it goes blind, its legs fall off, and its body is literally torn apart to allow beautiful wings to emerge.

To add to the difficulties of instituting change, citizens and staff members fall into patterns of dependency that place impossible burdens on those at the top to pull the next rabbit out of the hat. And if the magic fails, we collectively do away with the leaders. Rarely do we blame ourselves for our unsuitable expectations. This is nowhere truer than in the context of government. The democratic process often reflects the fact that the collective leaders have failed to see their role in the process, have developed unsuitable expectations through a variety of factors (some of their own doing and some of our doing), and have proceeded, albeit not too speedily at times, to expel the offenders and replace them with "better" leaders.

When thinking about cultural change that requires participation, we need to appreciate the differences between technical and adaptive situations. Technical situations can be addressed because the necessary knowledge about them already has been absorbed and reduced to a set of accepted organizational procedures that guide what should be done and who should do it. Conversely, for many problems, particularly during times of rapid change, no adequate response has yet been developed. Adaptation must take place; habits, attitudes, and values must change; and organizational roles, norms, and procedures have to be relearned. If you think in terms of the historic command-and-control leaders, and their personality attributes, you will see that they are not trained or inclined to invent new norms or role structures, but to direct, defend, and maintain order within the established routines.

Achieve Alignment

Three separate environments run concurrently within the local government setting: the Democratic Process (citizens), the Political Arena (governing bodies), and Operations and Service Delivery (organizations.) For high performance to exist, there must be a shared vision among the three. If we envision the three to be represented by circles, then high performance can only exist in the area where all three circles overlap. If there is no shared vision and thus no overlap, then high performance is impossible. Maximum performance is possible when all three circles exactly overlap and have the appearance of being one. A coordinated dynamic needs to be maintained so that there is continual alignment among efforts and any chaos that is caused does not become uncontrolled. If one element is changed, then the others need to change as well so that the overlap can continue to exist and the process can keep its effectiveness.

Develop Your People Assets

Energize your organization by developing needed skills in all of your members. First, the organizational environment, individuals, and groups must have the traits and attributes necessary to effect the incorporation of high performance into the organizational culture. Second, flexibility must exist at both the personal and organizational levels to adapt to the needs of the situation. Gaining the ability to recognize and anticipate the needs of the situation and provide organizational members with the skills to adapt is necessary to achieve effectiveness in the 21st century.

Individual skill flexibility will play an important role in organizational effectiveness. Everyone within the organization must possess a skill set that includes leadership, management, technical, and personal skills (within the context of the individual's responsibilities). This model shifts responsibility from an external to an internal control perspective. Basic to this notion is the assumption that every organizational member has the attributes that can help identify the needs of the situation and help make the changes necessary to adapt to the emerging circumstances. Tomorrow's high-performing organizations will be those that can help employees develop and exercise these personal attributes.

Individual customer service providers, for example, will have to recognize the need to provide leadership among their peers by taking the initiative to make changes that bring about better ways to provide customer service. They can no longer wait for other organizational groups to figure out that what they are doing is not in the best interest of citizens, the organization, or themselves. The adapting takes place on the front lines and the organization must be willing and able to provide support.

Another example would be organizational members who are needed to shift assignments. High performance requires that they possess the ability to reassess their situations and to apply the appropriate techniques where the needs are clearly different, as they are in administrative operations as opposed to emergency response. This ability to reassess the case and to apply different skills is no less critical for the high-performing manager as for the front-line emergency responder.

Many organizations overlook a fundamental priority to become more adaptive, and that priority is personal balance within organizational members. In a metamorphosis as tough as from the caterpillar to butterfly, humans need to be helped to accomplish personal change and find balance from within. Individual health and balance are the foundations for any effective cultural change process and the prerequisites for acquiring effective technical, management, and leadership skills.

Author and novelist Rumer Godden's model[2] suggests that we all have "four rooms" within us that reflect our emotional, spiritual, physical, and mental (intellectual) selves. Simply speaking, individual balance occurs when we visit all four rooms and "exercise" within them so that their sizes develop equally. When this occurs, we attain a personal balance and can achieve a purposeful centeredness. The model further suggests that we all have preferences to "exercise" in one room more than others and therefore fall out of balance. How many of us know someone who has exercised their mental capabilities and the size of this room overpowers others? Or someone who is exercised emotionally, spiritually, or physically but sacrifices his or her intellectual time and becomes unbalanced? Unfortunately, in our society, we tend to take these capacities for granted and do not think to develop them systematically in the service of self-understanding and wisdom, particularly in our workplaces. We act as if, magically, our work is somehow disassociated from our intellectual, emotional, spiritual, and physical selves.

Adapt Your Organizational Structures

Enable your jurisdiction to accomplish great things by restructuring it and allowing staff members to be more creative and entrepreneurial. As individuals within the environment acquire new skill sets, structural adaptations should occur to remove roadblocks and to allow functioning at the next level. As organizations become more oriented toward service flexibility and cost-effectiveness, the use of networks will increase, staffing is likely to decrease or remain stable, and mid-level managers will become less critical to fulfill objectives. Employees and the organization must be positioned to deal with the inherent flexibility that will be needed to achieve this outcome. It should be apparent that placing more decision making at the appropriate points, in conjunction with structural changes, creates a need for our organizational vision, values, and goals to be clearly articulated and reinforced consistently. There is also a need for decision making that is based on an identified, principled foundation.

Support Experimentation and Renewal

An organization must understand and commit itself to the concept of fostering a learning environment that enables change and adaptability to occur. It must continuously look at what is being done, why it is being done, and how it is being done, while seeking ways to pool resources at every opportunity—whether they are internal or external, or public/public or public/private partnerships. Look for new ways to provide services despite imaginary boundaries and parochial interests, and then implement those opportunities when they present better ways to carry out your purpose. Clearly define what the "right" things are that should be done. "Doing more with less" should mean focusing resources on doing the right things right.

To start off any successful effort to develop a learning organization and to initiate continuous renewal, it is absolutely imperative that high levels of trust exist within the organization. Trust is a lubricant for human relations. Without it, the mechanisms of interaction are damaged and will grind to a stop. Because of this, our reliance on the commitments of coworkers, management, and others must be an organizational value and instilled in the culture. Developing trust through open, honest, and direct communications is a seriously underrated value in many organizations yet is crucial to achieving high performance. To develop effective relationships, managers must change their perspectives on how they manage implicit and explicit contracts in interpersonal relationships. People often look at contracts as a means of ensuring compliance instead of ensuring that everyone knows what is going on and what is expected of them. When a contract is broken, we have traditionally begun punitive action for compliance. But we need to shift our frame of reference to a positive posture, instill trust, and use our contracts as agreements, expecting that involvement will be based on achieving the intent of the objectives, instead of meeting the letter of the contract. One approach calls for restrictive behavior and holds people back, while the other opens positive opportunities to move forward.

If we allow the individuals who are directly involved in the provision of a service to be directly responsible for the expected organizational performance, we will find trust, responsibility, accountability, and ultimately the highest levels of empowerment. These assets will in turn result in effective service delivery and high performance.

7. Assessments

a. "Profile of Organizational Characteristics" Survey

INSTRUCTIONS FOR PROFILE OF ORGANIZA-
TIONAL CHARACTERISTICS SURVEY

This survey instrument is intended to assess where you think your unit or organization is on a series of dimensions that have been shown to be important in determining organizational performance. It is critical that you respond honestly about where you see your unit or organization—"grading high" or "low" doesn't help when we are trying to see where we are. Please **DO NOT** identify yourself on the instrument; your answers will be merged with those of other respondents before presentation to preserve confidentiality.

You need to place **THREE** marks on each scale. The first will be an *"O"* to indicate *where you think your ORGANIZATION is right now* on the scale; the second mark will be a *"U"* to indicate *where you think your UNIT is right now* on the scale; and an *"L" where you would like any organization you are a part of to be – your ideal organization.*

Example:

			Item No.
1. How much confidence and trust is shown in subordinates?	Virtually none ⌊ ⌊ ⌊ ⌊ *O* ⌊ Some ⌊ Substantial amount *U L* ⌊ A great deal ⌊ ⌊		1

COMMENTS AND EXPLANATIONS: *If you wish to explain any of your answers (e.g., you feel that none of the choices represents your thoughts or your answer needs qualification, etc. please write the item number below and write any comments you have).*

PROFILE OF ORGANIZATIONAL CHARACTERISTICS

Organization or Unit to be Assessed:

_____

Item No.

1. How much confidence and trust is shown in subordinates?	Virtually none	Some	Substantial amount	A great deal	1
2. How free do they feel to talk to superiors about their job?	Not Very Free	Somewhat free	Quite Free	Very free	2
3. How often are subordinates' ideas sought and used constructively?	Seldom	Sometimes	Often	Very frequently	3
4. Is predominant use made of 1 fear, 2 threats, 3 punishment, 4 rewards, 5 involvement?	1, 2, 3, occasionally 4	4, some 3	4, some 3 and 5	5, 4, based on group	4
5. Where is responsibility felt for achieving organization's goals?	Mostly at the top	Top and middle	Fairly general	At all levels	5
6. How much cooperative teamwork exists?	Very little	Relatively little	Moderate Amount	Great deal	6
7. What is the usual direction of information flow?	Downward	Mostly downward	Down and up	Down, up, and sideways	7
8. How is downward communication accepted?	With suspicion	Possibly with suspicion	With caution	With a receptive mind	8
9. How accurate is upward communication?	Usually inaccurate	Often inaccurate	Often accurate	Almost always accurate	9
10. How well do superiors know problems faced by subordinates?	Not very well	Somewhat	Rather well	Very well	10
11. At what level are decisions made?	Mostly at the top	Policy at top, some delegation	Broad policy at top, more delegation	Throughout but well integrated	11
12. Are subordinates involved in decisions related to their work?	Almost never	Occasionally consulted	Generally consulted	Fully involved	12
13. What does the decision-making process contribute to motivation?	Not very much	Relatively little	Some contribution	Substantial contribution	13
14. How are organizational goals established?	Orders issued	Orders, some comments invited	After discussion, by orders	By group action (except in crises)	14
15. How much covert resistance to goals is present?	Strong resistance	Moderate resistance	Some resistance at times	Little or none	15
16. How concentrated are review and control functions?	Very highly at top	Quite highly at top	Moderate delegation to lower levels	Widely shared	16
17. Is there an informal organization resisting the formal one?	Yes	Usually	Sometimes	No—same goals As formal	17
18. What are the cost, productivity, and other control data used for?	Policing, punishment	Reward and punishment	Reward, some self-guidance	Self-guidance, problem solving	18

SOURCE: *Adapted from Appendix II in* The Human Organization: Its Management and Values *by Rensis Likert (McGraw-Hill, Inc.)*

> **b. CCHPO Organizational Assessment for gauging the state of your organization**

INTRODUCTION TO THE HPO ORGANIZATIONAL SELF-ASSESSMENT

Prior to the start of any performance improvement effort, it is helpful, perhaps critical, to get an accurate understanding of current performance. A well-designed, systems-based, organizational self-assessment provides raters with a way to look at their organization's performance, to draw conclusions, and to create a development plan to address the issues. Obviously, accurate self-assessment requires introspection and realistic self-perception. Multi rater assessment from a variety of members from different functions and levels of the organization will be more valid and will present a more well-rounded, less biased view.

The value of self-assessment lies in its ability to help the raters take responsibility for the results and for the subsequent development of improvement plans. Moreover, recent studies of neuroscience and leadership indicate that self-assessment runs a reduced risk of creating a "threat" response in individuals. Since the rater is an active participant in evaluating performance and is not at the mercy of a supervisor, consultant, or other evaluator, there is a greater chance that the results of the assessment process will be accepted as valid and allow the rater to internalize the need for change and improvement.

The HPO Organizational Self-Assessment is built upon CCHPO's *High Performance Organizations Diagnostic/Change Model* and is, therefore, a systems approach to evaluation. This means that any weakness found in the system will likely inhibit the performance of the entire system. Like the human body, all parts must be functioning well in order to ensure the health, performance, and longevity of the organization.

Overview of the Assessment

The HPO Organizational Self-Assessment is in two parts: the first section, with thirty scales, is primarily a "capability maturity model," This type of approach was first developed and deployed at the Carnegie-Mellon University and became the basis for the creation of their Software Engineering Institute.

We have taken the "maturity model" concept from that approach and applied it to assessing overall organizational performance. The term *maturity* relates to the degree of formality, stability, and resulting optimization of processes: from ad hoc practices, to formally defined steps, to managed result metrics, to active optimization of the processes—the responses on the assessment are reflective of the organization's ability to deliver excellent and improving results on a consistent basis. The further to the "right" on these scales an organization is, the greater its ability to deliver according to the characteristics and leading practices of high-performing organizations.

The second section of the Assessment is focused on the team that the respondent identifies as his/her "primary team." There are eleven questions modified from Russ Linden's *Working Across Boundaries: Making Collaboration Work in Government and Nonprofit Organizations* (2002); they assess the degree to which the team has the basics for collaborative problem-solving/decision-making. The last set of six questions is derived from Patrick Lencioni's *Five Dysfunctions of a Team* (2002). Lencioni's approach says that to build a high-performing team, it is necessary to build **TRUST** among team members, so that an environment is created where honest and constructive **CONFLICT** can occur, so that authentic **COMMITMENT** to shared team objectives exists, so that team members can hold each other **ACCOUNTABLE** for their commitments, so that the team produces the **RESULTS** it seeks.

Each of the questions/scales of the Assessment taps into one or more of the principles contained in the HPO Diagnostic/Change Model. For an Interpretation Guide linking the results to steps that may be taken by the organization to improve its performance, email solutions@highperformanceorg.com

HPO ORGANIZATIONAL SELF-ASSESSMENT

Directions: Decide what 'organization' will mean for you in this self-assessment (e.g., the overall organization as a whole, an Office, a Division, a business area or cross-cutting them, etc.); write that organization's name here: _____; it should be several levels above you unless you are the head of the overall organization; questions near the end will focus on your own team.

1 <u>Performance</u> <u>of</u> <u>the</u> <u>organization</u> (defined as quality products/services, administrative and work process efficiency, delivery of customer value, and sound financial performance over the last year) has been objectively measured and demonstrated to be:

1	2	3	4	0
Degrading	Flat	Improving	Improving and better than our external benchmark	Don't Know or Can't Tell (lack capacity to determine)

2 We have a fully developed and deployed <u>performance</u> <u>measurement</u> <u>and</u> <u>management</u> <u>system</u> where all levels can trend data, monitor performance, identify issues, and take corrective action.

1	2	3	4	0
We don't have such a system	In some units	In most units	Throughout the organization	Don't Know

3 We have <u>Leadership</u> <u>Teams</u> *at every level* of our organization whose <u>primary</u> <u>focus</u> is on strategic, longer-term issues, nesting unit strategic work to high level objectives, and ensuring that tactical initiatives are successfully supporting the achievement of strategic goals.

1	2	3	4	0
We don't have Leadership Teams at any level	Only at the top and/or only in a few units	At the top and in many units	Throughout the organization at every level	Don't Know

4 Our Leadership Teams <u>spend</u> <u>enough</u> <u>time</u> (at least 5 to 10% of each individual's total work time; maybe more if a manager) on strategic, longer-term issues to ensure we are ready for the future; these teams are disciplined about working on these items.

1	2	3	4	0
We don't have Leadership Teams at any level	Although we have some Leadership Teams, they rarely focus on the right issues, they lack the discipline to accomplish what they should, or they spend insufficient time on the issues	Most of our Leadership Teams are mostly focused on the right issues and generally spend the right amount of time working on them, but we could still improve	Our Leadership Teams are disciplined about working on the right issues and they spend just the right amount of time to ensure the strategic work is accomplished	Don't Know

5 The <u>networking/team</u> <u>skills</u> (facilitation, group decision-making, managing personality differences, coaching, delivering feedback, interpersonal communications, etc.) of our Leadership Teams are:

1	2	3	4	0
Poor	Adequate	Good	Exemplary	Don't Know

6   We have an <u>overall</u> <u>strategic</u> <u>plan</u> that articulates our goals and objectives and defines the direction we need to go and the capacity we need to build; each unit/business area has a similar plan that nests within the overall plan.

1	2	3	4	0
We don't have a strategic plan	We have a strategic plan that articulates our strategies, goals, and objectives	Our strategic plan is a 'living document' -- the goals, objectives, and tactical actions are measured and monitored for corrective action	Same as 3 plus: the goals and objectives form the basis for 'nested' plans in our units, having engaged the entire workforce	Don't Know

7   To what extent do employees <u>at</u> <u>every</u> <u>level</u> understand the overall organization's '<u>business</u> <u>model/</u> <u>strategy</u>' (i.e., how we will efficiently and effectively produce our goods and services to meet the wants, needs, and expectations of our customers and other stakeholders) and how the business model/strategy of their unit or business area contributes to the overall organization's performance?

1	2	3	4	0
Most don't understand our organization's overall business model/strategy or that of their unit/business area	Many don't understand our organization's overall business model/strategy but more are familiar with that of their unit/business area	Many understand our organization's overall business model/strategy and that of their unit/business area, some may not see how they 'nest' together	Most all understand our organization's overall business model/strategy, that of their unit/business area, and how they 'nest' together	Don't Know

8   To what extent do we assess the <u>*effectiveness*</u> of our performance relative to our business partners (both inside and outside the organization), beneficiaries (those who directly use our goods and services), food chain (those who give us policy direction and resources), competition, others?

1	2	3	4	0
We don't assess our business/stakeholder environment	We do limited or infrequent assessment	We have a systematic approach to assessment and frequently use the results	We have a disciplined approach which results in strategies to improve our effectiveness and customer value	Don't Know

9   To what extent do we effectively <u>involve</u> <u>these</u> <u>customers/stakeholders</u> appropriately in establishing their wants, needs, and expectations and determining the appropriate level of goods and services we deliver?

1	2	3	4	0
Not very well	To a moderate degree, not consistently	To a substantial degree, but with some variation across the units/ business areas	To a very high degree across all levels of the organization	Don't Know

10 To what extent are we confident that we are delivering the <u>*appropriate*</u> <u>goods</u> <u>and</u> <u>services</u> to our customers/stakeholders at the <u>*appropriate*</u> <u>*level*</u> of <u>features</u> -- i.e., we are neither 'gold plating' (excessive design, features, complexity) nor failing to meet our stakeholders' basic wants, needs, and expectations?

1	2	3	4	0
There is a low level of confidence that we are delivering the appropriate goods and services at the appropriate level to our customers/stakeholders.	There is a moderate level of confidence that we are delivering the appropriate goods and services at the appropriate level to our customers/stakeholders.	There is a substantial level of confidence that we are delivering the appropriate goods and services at the appropriate level to our customers/stakeholders.	There is a high level of confidence that we are delivering the appropriate goods and services at the appropriate level to our customers/stakeholders.	Don't Know

11 Thinking specifically about the efficiency of our administrative/business systems (e.g., procurement, contracting, financial management, IT, HR, facilities and maintenance, legal, safety, etc.), what percentage of the total effort expended in the organization is taken up with 'non-value added' work related to these systems (e.g., excessive sign offs and approvals, unnecessary waiting for responses, having to redo a request because the requirements were unclear, failure to comply with requirements the first time, excessive requirements that go way beyond what's necessary given the risk involved, little risk assessment employed in setting the requirements, etc.)?

1	2	3	4	0
Over 30 % is wasted effort	16 to 30 % is wasted effort	6 to 15 % is wasted effort	0 to 5 % is wasted effort	Don't Know

12 Thinking specifically about the efficiency of our technical work processes, what percentage of the total effort expended in the organization is taken up with 'non-value added' work related to these production processes (e.g., lack of a world-class production processes, excessive wait times between steps, having to redo a process step because of an error in execution, failure to comply with specifications the first time, etc.)?

1	2	3	4	0
Over 30 % is wasted effort	16 to 30 % is wasted effort	6 to 15 % is wasted effort	0 to 5 % is wasted effort	Don't Know

13 To what extent is the structure of our organization optimized to efficiently and effectively achieve the vision, values, goals, and objectives of the organization (e.g., is 'turf' a problem, how about 'stovepiping' or 'silos', do we have effective mechanisms to handle cross-cutting initiatives, are roles and responsibilities clear, do support units integrate smoothly with line units)?

1	2	3	4	0
Our structure is poor	Our structure is adequate	Our structure is good	Our structure is exemplary	Don't Know

14 How realistic are the expectations for what people can achieve within this organization?

1	2	3	4	0
Either too much is expected to be done in an unrealistic amount of time OR too little is expected of people	The expectations are largely unrealistic and demanding OR largely too undemanding	For the most part, the expectations are realistic	The expectations are realistic and fully appropriate	Don't Know

15 The extent to which we have (and have implemented) an organizational leadership philosophy and statement of shared values that describe the values, beliefs, desired behaviors, and work culture for our organization is:

1	2	3	4	0
We don't have one	Written and published, but not implemented	Communicated through discussion and understood and followed by most people	Translated into observable behaviors; used for performance feedback and coaching and as part of our assessment and development processes	Don't Know

1. Exploitative Autocratic ('master/serf'):	2. Benevolent Autocratic ('parent-child'):	3. Consultative Adult-Adult:	4. Participative Adult-Adult:	0. Mixed or Absent:
people are seen as basically lazy and avoid responsibility thus requiring close, constant supervision and control; you motivate them by applying strong negative sanctions when they don't perform; managers/ supervisors keep tight control of the decision-making process; 'it's my way or the highway,' work needs to be broken into small pieces and closely supervised; manager is controller; can feel abusive/disrespectful; workforce is likely to be disengaged	people can be fairly productive if properly managed, but they require direction and supervision; people can be fairly productive if properly managed, and are provided with the appropriate external motivators ('carrots and sticks'); managers try to promote a feeling of openness but maintain control of the decision-making process; managers take care of things so first line workers don't have to 'worry about them'; the workforce is seen as somewhat technically competent, but requires frequent supervision and direction; may feel condescending/belittling; workforce may be somewhat disengaged	most people want to do a good job and can be productive; at times the manager/ team leader needs to help focus their efforts; people are generally self-motivated when presented with interesting, challenging work, personal development, and participation in decisions that affect them; managers/ supervisors seek the opinions and views of others, but can also be decisive when needed: 'if we can't agree, I'll use your valuable input and decide -- and I'll explain my reasoning,' work is seen as complex, involving networks of people working together to reach collaboratively established goals. management's role is to create a consultative work culture; workforce is mostly engaged	people have an inherent desire to achieve and make a positive contribution and will deliver beyond expectations in an engaging, supportive, and mutually beneficial environment, especially when presented with interesting, challenging work, personal development, and participation in decisions that affect them—members of the workforce understand the principles of collaborative action and effectively share the decision-making process; work is seen as complex, involving networks of people working together to reach collaboratively established goals: plus teams are responsible for task/technical, managerial, and leadership functions; workforce is highly engaged	We don't seem to have a strong or consistent belief about the nature of people or work; it seems to be OK for managers/ supervisors to adopt any of these styles or to 'just be absent'

16 Thinking about the <u>behavior of managers/supervisors overall</u> in this organization, what percentage of managers/supervisors do you think fall in each of the categories described above:

%s must total 100%

1. Exploitative Autocratic ('master/serf'):	2. Benevolent Autocratic ('parent-child'):	3. Consultative Adult-Adult:	4. Participative Adult-Adult	0. Mixed or Absent:
_____%	_____%	_____%	_____%	_____%

17 Based on the way our <u>administrative/business systems</u> treat us overall (e.g., the HR, IT, Purchasing, Finance, Facilities, Legal, etc.), the <u>statement that best describes</u> the organization's beliefs about people and work is:

1	2	3	4	0
Use the descriptions above, substituting 'administrative/ business systems' for 'managers'	Use the descriptions above, substituting 'administrative/ business systems' for 'managers'	Use the descriptions above, substituting 'administrative/ business systems' for 'managers'	Use the descriptions above, substituting 'administrative/ business systems' for 'managers'	Use the descriptions above, substituting 'administrative/ business systems' for 'managers'

18 Based on the way our <u>technical work processes</u> treat us overall (e.g., how we do our work, production processes, technical support services like engineering, laboratory tests, etc.), the <u>statement that best describes</u> the organization's beliefs about people and work is:

1	2	3	4	0
Use the descriptions above, substituting 'technical work processes' for 'managers'	Use the descriptions above, substituting 'technical work processes' for 'managers'	Use the descriptions above, substituting 'technical work processes' for 'managers'	Use the descriptions above, substituting 'technical work processes' for 'managers'	Use the descriptions above, substituting 'technical work processes' for 'managers'

19 How strong is the <u>climate of trust, teamwork, and mutual commitment</u> between the first level of the organization and senior management?

1	2	3	4	0
Very weak	Somewhat weak	Somewhat strong	Very strong	Don't Know

20 The extent to which our Human Resource (HR) systems require individuals to <u>demonstrate leadership, management, and team skills</u>, in addition to technical skills, for identification of development opportunities, promotion, rewards, and retention?

1	2	3	4	0
Not at all	Slight extent	Considerable extent	Completely	Don't know

21 The extent to which our current set of managers, supervisors, and team leaders, as a whole, have the required <u>knowledge of the technical area</u> for which they are responsible be successful?

1	2	3	4	0
Not at all	Slight extent	Considerable extent	Completely	Don't know

22 The extent to which our current set of managers, supervisors, and team leaders, as a whole, have the required <u>leadership, managerial, and people/team skills</u> to be successful in our organization?

1	2	3	4	0
Not at all	Slight extent	Considerable extent	Completely	Don't know

23 The extent to which we have <u>aligned our Human Resource (HR) systems</u> (beginning with the interview and hiring process, through our development, assessment, and retention systems) with our Values, Vision, Mission, and Strategic Plan?

1	2	3	4	0
Not at all	Slight extent	Considerable extent	Completely	Don't Know

24 We use <u>ORGANIZATIONAL assessment instruments</u> (e.g., USOPM's Federal Employee Viewpoint Survey, CCHPO's *Performance Diagnostic Questionnaire*, CCL's Keys Instrument, or locally designed work culture surveys) as well as interviews, focus groups, benchmarking/best practices studies, etc. to assess the overall 'health' of the organization.

1	2	3	4	0
No such assessments are used	Only when they are imposed on us from above; we may do something occasionally to see if we're making progress on an effort	We do regular assessments in a variety of forms and use them to prioritize our improvement efforts	We do regular assessment in a variety of forms and communicate the results to the entire workforce to focus and prioritize all of our efforts	Don't Know

25 We use <u>INDIVIDUAL</u> <u>assessment</u> <u>tools</u> to provide members of the team with competency and values/ behaviors based feedback (e.g., CCHPO's *Leadership Philosophy Questionnaire*, OPM's Leadership 360, CCL's Benchmarks 360, Lominger's VOICES, or something of our own design).

1	2	3	4	0
No assessment tools are used	When they are a part of the larger organization's development policy or in special cases to gather data for potential personnel actions	When they are a part of the larger organization's development policy or on a voluntary basis for those who want feedback and coaching	On a regular basis to form the basis for feedback, coaching, and developmental assignments	Don't Know

26 Describe the <u>process</u> <u>improvement</u> <u>efforts</u> in the organization in recent years (e.g., Lean, Six Sigma, Theory of Constraints, etc.). Is everyone skilled in the tools of process improvement and engaged at their level in significantly reducing the waste in our administrative and work systems and processes, while improving our overall efficiency, effectiveness, and productivity?

1	2	3	4	0
No, little, and/or ineffective effort	Mixed efforts and results; less than expected	Mixed results; toward the positive	We have significantly improved our performance	Don't Know

27 We have highly trained and effective <u>internal</u> <u>change</u> <u>agents</u> / <u>organizational</u> development <u>professionals</u> to support the organization at every level.

1	2	3	4	0
None are available	Less than one for every 1,000 people in the organization	One for every 300-1,000 people in the organization	More than one for every 300 people in the organization	Don't Know

28 How much <u>negative</u> <u>energy</u> (destructive competition, protecting turf, hording resources or information, etc.) is there within the organization?

1	2	3	4	0
A great deal of negative energy across the organization	Quite a bit of negative energy across the organization	Some negative energy across the organization	Virtually non-existent	Don't Know

29 How much <u>cynicism</u> is there in this organization concerning efforts to improve organizational performance?

1	2	3	4	0
There is a great deal of cynicism within the organization	There is some commitment to improving performance, but there is also much cynicism within the organization	For the most part, there is commitment to improving performance, with only pockets of cynicism	There is a strong sense of mission and a high level of commitment to improving the performance of the organization, with little or no cynicism	Don't Know

30 The percentage of the workforce that is 'fully engaged' in the organization (note: fully engaged employees work with passion, feel a profound connection to the organization, drive organizational innovation, and move the whole organization forward) is:

1	2	3	4	0
Less than 20%	20-49%	50-66%	67% or more	Don't Know

For the following questions, rate the Leadership Team THAT YOU CONSIDER TO BE YOUR PRIMARY TEAM (write name of team/unit here:) according to the following scale:

| 1 = Never | 2 = Rarely | 3 = Sometimes | 4 = Often | 5 = Usually | 6 = Always |

31 The members of the team have a shared interest, which they can't achieve on their own.

    1   2   3   4   5   6

32 There are champions for cross-cutting projects and organizational structures.

    1   2   3   4   5   6

33 An open, credible process exists to bring the various parts of the organization together as a team.

    1   2   3   4   5   6

34 Clear roles and responsibilities have been established within the team, across the organizational units represented by members of the team, and within cross-cutting projects.

    1   2   3   4   5   6

35 There are adequate resources for these projects.

    1   2   3   4   5   6

36 The members of the team want to work together and are willing to contribute something to the effort.

    1   2   3   4   5   6

37 The appropriate people are at the table.

    1   2   3   4   5   6

38 There is transparency among members of the team; no behind the scenes decision making.

    1   2   3   4   5   6

39 We share accurate, timely information, both when requested and when others on the team need to know, even if not requested.

    1   2   3   4   5   6

40 We feel a connection for being part of something larger than ourselves and our own units.

    1   2   3   4   5   6

41 We think systematically and can easily see the connections to the larger purpose.

    1   2   3   4   5   6

42 We have successfully created an environment where openness and vulnerability about our individual strengths, weaknesses, mistakes, and need for help are the norm. Team members have confidence that their peers' intentions are positive and that there is, therefore, no need to be protective or careful around other members of the group.

    1   2   3   4   5   6

43 We have successfully created an environment where passionate and open discussion around important and difficult topics is the norm. We engage in unfiltered conflict around ideas and issues in order to identify the best possible solution for the team and the organization. Because the heated debate is focused on ideas and issues rather than personal attacks, we emerge with no residual feelings or collateral damage.

    1   2   3   4   5   6

| 1 = Never | 2 = Rarely | 3 = Sometimes | 4 = Often | 5 = Usually | 6 = Always |

44 We have successfully created an environment with clear direction and priorities; we commit to common objectives and take advantage of opportunities faster than others. We learn from mistakes and move forward without hesitation.

     1   2   3   4   5   6

45 We have successfully created an environment where team members are willing to call their peers on performance or behaviors that might hurt the team, even when this causes interpersonal discomfort. We have difficult conversations, rather than avoiding them.

     1   2   3   4   5   6

46 We have successfully created an environment where we relentlessly focus on our results; we value collective outcomes more than individual recognition, personal ego and power, or attainment of personal status/career development. We have developed effective performance measurement systems to aid in our outcome focus.

     1   2   3   4   5   6

47 All the members of our Leadership Team see this team as their 'primary team;' we are able to represent our unit while maintaining our focus of success on the organization as a whole (i.e., 'stewardship of the whole' is the norm on the team).

     1   2   3   4   5   6

48 If this were your organization, would you run it this way? What would you keep doing or do more of and what would you stop doing? Be as specific as possible; attach additional pages if necessary.

COMMENTS/NOTES:

Note: Questions 32-42 are from Russell M. Linden, *Working Across Boundaries: Making Collaboration Work in Government and Nonprofit Organizations* (Jossey-Bass: 1994; questions used with author's permission). Questions 43-48 are adapted from Patrick Lencioni, *The Five Dysfunctions of a Team* (Jossey-Bass; 2002).

c. CCHPO Leadership Philosophy Questionnaire (LPQ)

LEADERSHIP PHILOSOPHY QUESTIONNAIRE (LPQ) DESCRIPTION

The LPQ is a 360-degree feedback instrument designed to assess an organization relative to the standards of a *High-Performance Organization* (HPO). Specifically, a Likert-type scale approach is used to evaluate the implicit leadership philosophies of individual team leaders/managers in four areas: Nature of People, Motivation, Distribution of Knowledge and Creativity, and Nature of Work. An HPO model incorporates performance efficiency and a positive work climate. Using both qualitative and quantitative questions, performance and team cohesiveness are simultaneously investigated. Descriptions of Rensis Likert's leadership styles (exploitive autocratic, benevolent autocratic, consultative, participative, and passive) are used to obtain quantitative ratings, teach the HPO values, and condition respondents toward textual commentary on the specifics of the performance of the manager being evaluated. As part of the teaching process, the LPQ uses language consistent with HPO values. The LPQ was designed specifically to meet the need for an instrument with updated language, i.e., language consistent with participative (System 4) leadership values.

Structure of the LPQ

The LPQ consists of four sections:

1. Assumptions About the Nature of People and Their Attitudes Toward Work
2. Assumptions About How People Choose to Be Motivated
3. Assumptions About the Distribution of Knowledge and Creativity and the Resulting Way Decisions Are Made
4. Assumptions About the Nature of Work

Each of these four sections contains five performance questions, each dealing with a specific subarea of the overall topic for that section. For example, in the section on *Motivation*, question B4 asks *"How well does this team leader/ manager motivate co-workers to higher levels of efficiency and productivity?"*

The question is followed by five descriptions, each of which fits one of Likert's five management systems, from System 1, Autocratic (*"Motivates in a manipulative fashion using threats, punishment, and intimidation."*) to System 4, Democratic (*"Has great skill in . . . {helping to} create a motivating environment."*), plus System 0 (*"Abdicates the responsibility . . ."*). As the respondent completes the ratings for each of these five specific questions two performance questions call for textual response with the question *"How could this team leader/manager improve in the area of motivating co-workers?"* and the question *"How does this team leader/manager excel in the area of motivating co-workers?"*

Following the performance ratings and textual commentary in each section, there are three questions on which inferred beliefs are rated. In the *Motivation* section, for example, the first of these three questions (question B6) asks *"On the basis of this team leader's behaviors that you have just rated, which of the following beliefs about motivation would you infer to be closest to hers/his?"* The second asks, *"Which of the following beliefs do you think this team leader would endorse as his/her own?"* The third asks, *"Which of the following beliefs would you choose as ideal?"* Following these three belief inference questions, the final question is textual: *"Please comment on this manager's apparent beliefs in the Motivation area."*

This pattern is repeated for all four sections of the LPQ. At the end of the four sections two additional textual response questions are given:

1. "Describe the three most important specific ways this person could improve her (his) leadership effectiveness—things this person should stop doing, do differently, or start doing."
2. "If you were to identify the two or three most important ways this person demonstrates effective leadership, what would they be?"

Features and Benefits of the LPQ

Textual feedback is particularly valuable. It is usually much more targeted, unique, and specific than the quantitative rating scale feedback. However, the combination of quantitative and textual is more valuable than either alone. The strength of quantitative ratings is that they provide a basis for comparison. They also condition the rater to give more carefully thought-out textual feedback. That is, after reading five alternative kinds of behavior on each of the five questions, the rater has a basis for comparison in giving detailed textual feedback to the manager.

Quantitative data provides a different kind of precision. It provides a context of comparison both of the manager with himself/herself and also to other managers. The "within manager" comparisons are important. When areas of either strength or weakness are identified on which raters seem to have consensus, it helps the manager to focus in order to amplify strengths and remedy weaknesses. Also, quantitative comparisons in successive years are helpful in demonstrating progress. "Between manager" comparisons can also be helpful. Of course specific results of individual managers are confidential, but each manager can see his or her own standing relative to all other managers, with their identities hidden, giving at least some idea of relative standing in specific areas.

The LPQ has many uses within an organization. It can be used to provide orientation, to help answer the question "Where are we as an organization?" It provides senior management with a global assessment of leadership philosophy of those who help to lead the organization. It also provides the individual team leader/manager with targeted feedback and individual insight for creating an action plan to become a better leader. It can be used as a method of performance evaluation, and to monitor continuous improvement. One of the most important functions of LPQ profiling is to teach the HPO values. In this sense, the wording of the individual items of the LPQ sections is very important. As managers continue to be profiled with the instrument they become very familiar with descriptions of the five Likert systems in each specific area of rating, with the clear implication of what is valued by the organization and where they need to improve. A sample section of the LPQ appears below.

The LPQ is available from the Commonwealth Centers for High-Performance Organizations—solutions@highperformanceorg.com. Section A of the LPQ is illustrated on the following page.

---

1 Excerpted from an article entitled *Why Strive for High Performance?* originally published in *PM* magazine in 2002.

THE LEADERSHIP PHILOSOPHY QUESTIONNAIRE (LPQ)

LPQ Section A. The Nature of People

Five Performance Ratings

a1. Overall how does this person relate to others in the organization?	System 0. Generally passive and unassertive. "do whatever you want."	System 1. For the most part is judgmental and critical of others and sees them as in need of constant supervision. "I'm the boss, so do what I tell you or else."	System 2. Is congenial toward others but can be somewhat paternalistic.	System 3. Takes a basically positive view of others and treats them as adults. Provides firm direction for the team and for individuals when needed.
a2. How willing is this person to share control for the sake of higher performance?	System 0. Abdicates the responsibility for control and organization.	System 1. Dominates and openly maintains control at all costs.	System 2. Congenial, but uses subtle methods to keep control.	System 3. Seems to understand that higher performance is the result of shared control and decision making. Usually shares control.
a3. How good is this person at fostering autonomy and personal growth?	System 0. Provides no evidence of understanding the value of fostering individual development.	System 1. Unconcerned with the development of others--sees them as merely the means to accomplish work.	System 2. Encourages others to an extent--especially in the technical area-- but holds tight reins and considers employee performance as a reflection on himself.	System 3. Teaches others, builds them up, and strengthens them in their skills and confidence so they can help make the organization better.
a4. With respect to personal development and continuous learning, this person:	System 0. Does little to help others in their learning and development.	System 1. Uses demands, peer pressure, and manipulation to get others to perform and improve.	System 2. Tells others what they need to do to progress in their work, but does little to facilitate.	System 3. Tries to encourage others in their learning and development.
a5. How well does this person evidence trust and confidence in others?	System 0. Has a low level of engagement with others within the organization.	System 1. Shows little trust and confidence in others and makes all important decisions unilaterally.	System 2. Congenial and shows some trust in others but uses bargaining and maneuvering to subtly control.	System 3. Evidences trust in allowing others to take risks and help with decision making.

Two Textual Comments

a9. How could this person improve in the areas of honoring ownership of work, treatment of others and empowering others?

a10. How does this person excel in the areas of honoring ownership of work, treatment of others and empowering others?

Three Philosophy Ratings

a6. On the basis of this person's behaviors that you have just rated, which of the following beliefs about the nature of people and their attitude towards work would you infer to be closest to his?	System 0. Doesn't seem to have strong or consistent beliefs about the nature of people.	System 1. "People are basically lazy and avoid responsibility thus requiring close, constant supervision and controls."	System 2. "People can be fairly productive if properly managed, but they require direction and supervision."	System 3. "Most people want to do a good job and can be productive. At times, the team leader/manager needs to help focus their efforts."
a7. Which of the following beliefs do you think this person would endorse as his own?	System 0. Would not claim to have strong or consistent beliefs about the nature of people.	System 1. "People are basically lazy and avoid responsibility thus requiring close, constant supervision and controls."	System 2. "People can be fairly productive if properly managed, but they require direction and supervision."	System 3. "Most people want to do a good job and can be productive. At times, the team leader/manager needs to help focus their efforts."
a8. Which of the following beliefs would you choose as ideal for this organization?	System 0. There is no need for strong or consistent beliefs about the nature of people.	System 1. "People are basically lazy and avoid responsibility thus requiring close, constant supervision and controls."	System 2. "People can be fairly productive if properly managed, but they require direction and supervision."	System 3. "Most people want to do a good job and can be productive. At times, the team leader/manager needs to help focus their efforts."

One Textual Comment

a11. Please comment on this manager's apparent beliefs in the "Nature of People" area.

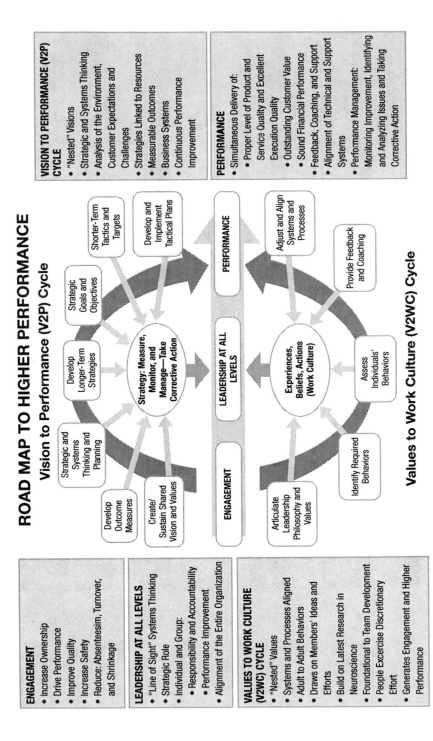

ROAD MAP TO HIGHER PERFORMANCE

Vision to Performance (V2P) Cycle

Values to Work Culture (V2WC) Cycle

Diagram labels (V2P Cycle, upper portion):
- Strategic and Systems Thinking and Planning
- Develop Longer-Term Strategies
- Strategic Goals and Objectives
- Shorter-Term Tactics and Targets
- Develop and Implement Tactical Plans
- Develop Outcome Measures
- Create/Sustain Shared Vision and Values
- Strategy: Measure, Monitor, and Manage—Take Corrective Action
- PERFORMANCE

Center band:
- PERFORMANCE
- LEADERSHIP AT ALL LEVELS
- ENGAGEMENT

Diagram labels (V2WC Cycle, lower portion):
- Adjust and Align Systems and Processes
- Provide Feedback and Coaching
- Experiences, Beliefs, Actions (Work Culture)
- Assess Individuals' Behaviors
- Articulate Leadership Philosophy and Values
- Identify Required Behaviors

ENGAGEMENT
- Increase Ownership
- Drive Performance
- Improve Quality
- Increase Safety
- Reduce: Absenteeism, Turnover, and Shrinkage

LEADERSHIP AT ALL LEVELS
- "Line of Sight" Systems Thinking
- Strategic Role
- Individual and Group:
- Responsibility and Accountability
- Performance Improvement
- Alignment of the Entire Organization

VALUES TO WORK CULTURE (V2WC) CYCLE
- "Nested" Values
- Systems and Processes Aligned
- Adult to Adult Behaviors
- Draws on Members' Ideas and Efforts
- Build on Latest Research in Neuroscience
- Foundational to Team Development
- People Excercise Discretionary Effort
- Generates Engagement and Higher Performance

VISION TO PERFORMANCE (V2P) CYCLE
- "Nested" Visions
- Strategic and Systems Thinking
- Analysis of the Environment, Customer Expectations and Challenges
- Strategies Linked to Resources
- Measurable Outcomes
- Business Systems
- Continuous Performance Improvement

PERFORMANCE
- Simultaneous Delivery of:
- Proper Level of Product and Service Quality and Excellent Execution Quality
- Outstanding Customer Value
- Sound Financial Performance
- Feedback, Coaching, and Support
- Alignment of Technical and Support Systems
- Performance Management: Monitoring Improvement, Identifying and Analyzing Issues and Taking Corrective Action

INDEX

About the Authors

. . . .

The primary authors are principals of the Commonwealth Centers for High-Performance Organizations (CCHPO) Network.Collectively, the CCHPO Network of organizational development/change management professionals has extensive experience in assisting local, state, and federal governments, non-profits, and the private sector improve their organizational performance. Areas of consulting emphasis are large-scale organizational improvement, development of high-performance executive leadership teams, employee engagement, organizational diagnosis and work culture surveys, integration of the continuous learning and improvement philosophy into organizational work cultures, design and implementation of product quality, service quality and project/program management programs, executive coaching, and delivery of executive development programs. CCHPO is a Strategic Partner of ICMA (International City/County Management Association)—the *HPO Diagnostic/Change Model*® and performance improvement materials have been designated by ICMA as a Leading Practice in Local Government. All of the Network professionals are certified in a variety of development instruments including Lominger's Leadership Architect Suite and Prosci's Change Management process.

JOHN PICKERING, PH.D., is Founder and President of the Commonwealth Center for High-Performance Organizations, Inc. Pickering is the primary author of the *HPO Diagnostic/Change Model, the Building High-Performance Organizations* (HPO) seminar, and the implementation-focused HPO Organizational Improvement Process. Pickering was Deputy Director, Dean of the Faculty, and a Senior Faculty Member at the Federal Executive Institute (FEI). He has been an adjunct in the University of Virginia's Senior Executive Institute. He has worked in the Federal Department of Housing and Urban Development (HUD) and has held teaching positions at the University of Memphis, Florida State University, Lamar University (Texas), and the University of Southern Mississippi. He was Associate Director of the Institute of Governmental Studies and Research (a Master of Public Administration degree program) at the University of Memphis.

GERALD BROKAW is a designer and facilitator for a variety of custom HPO *Vision to Performance, Values to Work Culture,* and *Continuous Learning and Improvement Process* workshops; for CCHPO's Project Management Curriculum; and for the HPO *Organizational Diagnostic/Change Model* and change process. He has also been an adjunct faculty member at the U.S. Office of Personnel Management's Federal Executive Institute for senior federal executives and the Naval Sea Systems Command Project Management College, and has been a guest lecturer for the Federal Quality Institute, Naval Medical Quality Institute, and the University of Maine. Brokaw was Managing Associate in Coopers & Lybrand's Organizational Change Management Group (now IBM consulting) and was the Executive Director of the Management Technology Corporation. In these capacities he led major improvement initiatives for divisions of General Electric, General Motors, International Paper, Continental Telephone, Honeywell, and the Department of the Navy as well as a variety of other Fortune 100 and public sector organizations.

PHILIP HARNDEN, PH.D., is a primary presenter and facilitator of the *Building High-Performance Organizations* (HPO) seminar and designer and facilitator of various CCHPO workshops. Additionally, he has developed 360-degree feedback and other culture survey instruments related to performance improvement. He has also been an adjunct faculty member at the U.S. Office of Personnel Management's Federal Executive Institute and for the Executive MBA Program at Rensselaer Polytechnic Institute (RPI). Harnden spent twenty-three years in increasingly responsible positions with the Knolls Atomic Power Laboratory (KAPL), which operates, under contract with the

Department of Energy, a government-owned laboratory dedicated to designing Navy nuclear reactors and training Navy personnel to operate the reactors. As a KAPL Nuclear Plant Manager, He was responsible for the safe operation and maintenance of a nuclear-powered training prototype, with three hundred operators, qualifying eight hundred students per year. For his last five years at KAPL, he functioned as an internal change agent, assisting the senior staff with an extensive organizational improvement effort.

TONY GARDNER, M.A., is Director of Leadership Development at the University of Virginia's Weldon Cooper Center for Public Service—the residential programs presented, including the Senior Executive Institute, are focused on senior executives in local government. He is a primary presenter and facilitator of the *Building High-Performance Organizations* (HPO) seminar at the university and for individual local governments. He also assists them with the HPO *Organizational Diagnostic/Change Model's* change process. Gardner served the last ten years of his twenty-six year career in Arlington County, Virginia as County Manager. In this role, he led an organization-wide change effort to improve the county's performance and introduced a number of economic development and redevelopment initiatives, in addition to managing the operations of this full-service jurisdiction. Twice during his tenure in Arlington County, the county received the John F. Kennedy School of Government "Innovations in American Government" award. He has been designated as a *Credentialed Manager* by the International City/County Management Association (ICMA).